MW00824037

I WOULDN'T
SAY IT IF IT
WASN'T TRUE

A MEMOIR OF
LIFE, MUSIC, AND
THE DREAM SYNDICATE

STEVE WYNN

JAW
BONE

I WOULDN'T SAY IT IF IT WASN'T TRUE
A MEMOIR OF LIFE, MUSIC,
AND THE DREAM SYNDICATE
STEVE WYNN

A Jawbone book
First edition 2024
Published in the UK and the USA by
Jawbone Press
Office G1
141–157 Acre Lane
London SW2 5UA
England
www.jawbonepress.com

ISBN 978-1-916829-06-0

Printed by Short Run Press, Exeter

1 2 3 4 5 28 27 26 25 24

CONTENTS

INTRODUCTION
SUDDEN DEATH OVERTIME

I gave up being a musician and playing in bands sometime in 1973, right around the time I reached the peak of my pre-adolescent career, playing onstage to a packed auditorium at Emerson Junior High with my band Sudden Death Overtime. We played a version of 'Jumping Jack Flash' with me strumming like Keith Richards on my blonde Telecaster while our barely pubescent lead singer, Tom Finn, wowed the pre-teen girls in his gold velvet jumpsuit, open to his navel, exposing his hairless chest. The hulking, long-haired Kris Kimball flanked Tom on the other side of the stage and resembled a twelve-year-old version of Neil Young slashing against my rhythm on a Gibson knockoff. They were the bad boys while our drummer, Andy Kaplan, was, like me, more of a nerdy 'good kid' who qualified for the band more with dedicated practice and a love of music than with any kind of attitude or coolness. I don't remember the bass player.

We had started out about a year before as Purple Passion, named for a short-lived soda pop. We even learned to play the jingle from the soft drink's commercial. I'm sure I could still play it today if I tried. We played mostly covers—some Stones, a Beatles song or two, and my own personal fast-strumming showcase, 'Pinball Wizard' by The Who. I had begun writing songs at the age of nine, so we snuck in a few of those as well, with lyrics written by my close friend Paul Engel, until one of us found a Rod McKuen poetry book and realized that Paul had stolen all his lyrics, word for word, from that same book. It was my last collaboration with another songwriter for a long time.

Kris and I had already been strumming guitars together in his bedroom for a couple of years before the band got together, starting around when we were ten. He loved Neil Young. In my memory, he actually looked like Neil Young—the picture I conjure is of an adult about the same age as Neil would have been at that point. Of course, this isn't possible, but he was a few months older than me and seemed like a grownup. We mostly jammed on endless versions of 'Down By The River' and 'Cowgirl In The Sand.' Kris took all the leads. I learned to be a patient and dutiful rhythm guitarist at a young age.

Tom and Kris smoked weed. So did the cool rock chicks who hung out with us at the pizza parlor in Westwood Village. Smitten by the bell-bottomed sirens, I knew that if I smoked weed as well, it might improve my chances of making out with one of them, but I just couldn't bring myself to do it—I was too much of a goody-goody. All my rebellion came in the form of music, with posters of Alice Cooper hanging (literally—it was the macabre gallows inner sleeve of the *Killer* album) on my wall alongside Hendrix, Townshend, Rod Stewart, and baseball great Hank Aaron.

Purple Passion gave way to Sudden Death, which got expanded to Sudden Death Overtime. We practiced at the Bel Air home of Andy and his brother Steve, who played piano and was easily the best musician in our gang. He was able to transcribe chord progressions from our favorite albums, and I can still see his handwriting on my inner-sleeve lyric sheet for *Ziggy Stardust*. I should also point out that their mother was dating my father for a while around that time, further cementing our connection as bandmates—or at least adding to the time we could spend together and the rides I could get over to their house, where we were allowed to practice at full volume in the living room. Divorced parents tend to be the most tolerant.

We played our only full gig on the school's playground, not far from where I had once given Michael Jackson change for a quarter. It was only a couple of years after that initial burst of rapid-fire Jackson 5 hit singles, and right about the time he had gone solo with the alluring but less successful 'Got To Be There.' In other words, he was on the verge of being a has-been at the age of twelve, and his parents put him in public school for a semester, maybe to give him a sense of grounding, maybe to save a few bucks. Based on my one encounter with him, this apparently wasn't the best idea, since moments after giving him a couple of dimes and a nickel, he ended up being chased by screaming girls across the concrete field, just past the spot where we had gigged only weeks earlier. I wonder if he saw our set.

That was the end of my first go-around as a performing musician. I had started getting more and more into baseball and sports. I wasn't an athlete. I had never played Little League and had done all I could to avoid taking part in competitive sports, insecure as I was about my abilities to hit or catch a ball. But I quickly developed a knack for journalism and sportswriting. The thrill of being good at something and being recognized for my talent was enough to steer me away from any notion of being a rock star.

This was 1973. There wasn't an indie-music scene; the clubs were only seen as stepping stones to playing sports arenas. You were a star or you were a nobody, and the odds were far better for me to be local sportswriting legend Jim Murray than crash-and-burn rock icon Jim Morrison.

I kept the Telecaster, but it stayed in the closet for the next five years. I was done. I quit. I wasn't looking back.

PART ONE
I DREAMED LAST NIGHT I WAS BORN A THOUSAND YEARS AGO

1.1

AN ONLY CHILD IN LOS ANGELES IN THE SIXTIES

There were definite advantages to growing up as the only child of a single, working mom in the Pico / La Cienega district of Los Angeles during the 1960s.

First and foremost, I had a lot of autonomy. I was allowed to walk around the block on my own from the age of six, and a couple of years later I was covering even more ground, both on foot and on my bike, exploring the Miracle Mile section of Wilshire Boulevard and a couple of the record stores in the area. This kind of freedom and self-determination planted a love of travel and exploration that I still feel when I arrive in a new city on tour and set off walking randomly with the expectation of surprise and discovery. Few things bring me more happiness than feeling like I know a city and can navigate the streets both in real time and from memory after returning home.

Second, I had plenty of time on my own. I was alone with my thoughts and not hampered or hindered by the distraction of other people. I had friends, of course, but my most reliable and constant companions were the radio and the few records in our house. 1966 was a good time to be getting a first taste of music, and I was a voracious, obsessed listener and fanboy.

Being alone as much as I was meant that my imagination could run wild. I invented everything from imaginary friends to imagined movies and books and eventually songs. I lived largely inside my own head, and that was a breeding ground for creative ideas and rumination. This need to create my own world, coupled with my love of music, made songwriting a natural choice.

We didn't have a lot of money. My mother worked a day job as a secretary, and she would often go on dates in the evening, making a point to eat only half of her meal and take the rest home in a doggie bag, which was my lunch at school the next day. While other kids were eating their peanut butter and jelly sandwiches, I was unwrapping a piece of filet mignon from a tin-foil swan accompanied by tiny potatoes. Sounds good now, but at the time I tried to trade my lunch for someone else's, rarely getting any takers.

The most monumental by-product of one of my mother's dates was the time she brought home a new beau for me to meet. This wasn't something she did often, so I should have known that it was serious, if that was indeed something that would have occurred to me at the time. His name was David, and I guess she had told him that I liked The Beatles because he showed up at the apartment with a copy of *Sgt. Pepper's Lonely Hearts Club Band*, which had just come out that week. He instantly won me over. They married two years later.

You'd think that hearing a groundbreaking album at the age of seven would have been a first spark, an awakening, an early start in the life of a music obsessive. But I was already full in—hook, line, and sinker. How did this happen? There wasn't much family history beyond having family members who enjoyed music as an accompaniment to life. My grandfather, Matthew Weinzweig (the name was anglicized and shortened to Wynn in the early 1920s), wrote a few songs when he was young, but he gave it up after that.

Maybe I was just lucky to be born at the right time. 1964 was a year of upheaval, musically, politically, culturally, and sexually. For me, it was the year I searched beyond the handful of Elvis, Jack Jones, and cocktail-jazz albums in our home and discovered The Beatles through the unlikely source of the band's cartoon show. My earliest musical memory is a segment when cartoon George is holding cartoon Ringo by a thread of his jacket while he perilously dangles from the Statue Of Liberty while the band sings 'Hold Me Tight.' I felt the panic, empathy, and blood-rushing exhilaration in that very moment—a combo that still fuels much of my favorite music as both a fan and as a musician.

It was easy to be a music fan in those days, even at the age of four. All you needed was a transistor radio and a few TV shows. There was the Beatles cartoon show, and then, a year or two later, the Monkees TV show. Cartoon characters, both animated and physical, put a face to the exciting music I was discovering. And The Beatles' own evolution allowed me to progress from *Meet The Beatles* to *Revolver*, developing a sense of real-time musical adventure that captured my imagination. Multiplication tables and spelling quizzes somehow seemed a lot less fascinating than the weird, inexplicable sounds on 'Tomorrow Never Knows.'

It was a weekly event to go to the neighbors' house across the street at 8pm and watch *The Monkees* with the kids, who were just a little older than me. I don't remember their names, but I do remember sitting in their living room, watching actual live-action (not cartoon!) musicians, having fun, getting into trouble, and playing instruments together. This was something I had to know more about. Around the same time, I remember walking to the next block—a big step!—and passing by a garage where I could hear a band rehearsing inside. I stood at the door, transfixed, knowing that someone inside was making actual music, just like The Beatles and The Monkees, and they were doing it right there in real time, just for themselves—and for me. This was something else I had to know more about!

The transistor AM radio allowed me to hear all the right stuff. Motown, The Who, James Brown, Cream—they were all at my fingertips and became my buddies, the things that slid into my solitude and imaginary world, intermingling, and informing my world. I didn't have many friends, no neighbor kids I hung out with (aside from my Monkees pals across the street), and I didn't play sports. It was me and the radio and my handful of Beatles records. My mom did a great job of keeping me safe, giving me love, and providing a foundation around me, but she was just a kid herself (she was twenty-two when I was born) trying to eke out a living, have some fun, and maybe meet a guy who could help her raise a kid.

I know that my mother harbors some concern, even today, that my childhood was impaired by not having a live-in father or by me being a latchkey kid. There was indeed some loneliness, some nascent melancholia, but in exchange I got the kind of freedom that still boggles my mind today. I'd get on my red Schwinn three-speed bike and ride the two miles to a record store on the Miracle Mile that sold records that went beyond the basic pop hits that I'd find at May Company. This store proudly displayed visually alluring album covers like *Tommy* and *Disraeli Gears* and *We're Only In It For The Money* on the wall, and it spoke to me like semaphore from another world.

Had I been surrounded by a more traditional family, rambunctious playmates, and a social world that needed navigating, I may not have been able to open my mind to this world of art and possibility and creativity at such a young age. The upside? I wrote hundreds of songs, made dozens of records, toured the world, and was able to call making music my day job. As my friend Peter Buck says, 'I won the lottery.' The downside? I was a little stunted in my abilities to learn to play with others or to socially navigate—in short, I didn't develop a lot of the proper people skills, and that provided social challenges for the rest of my life.

But I'm getting ahead of myself...

———

To paraphrase Johnny Cash, my daddy left home when I was three, although he left neither an old guitar nor an empty bottle of booze.

My parents got divorced in 1964, and the only memory I have of him living in the same apartment as me and my mother was watching him standing and peeing in the bathroom and wondering how that all worked. That's it—that image is all I have of us living together.

I have no memory of being sad or angry or scarred or resentful about the split. My parents separating and divorcing when I was so young always seemed to me like one of those things that happened but wasn't all that big a deal. It's just the way things were and—like the weather, what's on the radio, a blown tire, or what's in the fridge for dinner— it had an impact on daily life but was just part of the tableau of a life moving forward. It was something I brushed off, something I joked about, something that defined me in as much as it didn't happen to everyone. But it was also something I never complained about. I would find out as I got older that it had indeed had a major influence on the way I viewed relationships, problem-solving, and personal conflict.

It wasn't the only divorce I'd navigate in my life. Far from it. My father and mother each married four times. My grandfather married and divorced five times. My sisters had six marriages and five divorces between them. Stepsiblings came into my life and then disappeared, leaving a mark but no trace. Boxes were packed, and new homes and lifestyles followed the trajectory of connubial change.

So, why did I view all this as just a fact of my life and not rue my situation and everyone and everything that put me there? I give full credit to my mother and father, who not only made a point to get along and raise me without incident but in fact remained close friends from the time of my earliest memories to the day my father died in 2012. My mother stood mournfully at his hospital bedside along with me, my sister, and two of his other wives as he breathed his last.

The revolving door of new family members has been a subject of jokes far more than expressions of anger in my family. This husband, that husband, this wife, that wife, which husband, which wife, almost playing like an Abbott & Costello routine, and the fact that it's been played for laughs is far superior to the horrors that I know other kids endured. I'm grateful for that. But it left a mark, more stealthy than cataclysmic.

My father and mother met in 1958 at the Packworth apartments on La Cienega Boulevard, just north of Pico. My mother lived on the second floor with her mother, who had recently divorced from my grandfather.

My father was the notorious playboy divorcee who lived on the ground floor. He had two young daughters from his first marriage, and they visited on weekends, but for the most part, his guests were comprised of women in the building and others from the outside world. My grandmother warned my mother about him. She did not heed her mother's advice and I'm glad for that.

My parents, Earl Wynn and Marlene Robbins, married in 1958. I like to joke that their one mission as a briefly married couple was to bring me into the world. That noble mission was accomplished when I was born at St. John's Hospital in Santa Monica on February 21, 1960. Within two years they were separated. I often wonder what caused the passion and commitment to come and fade in such quick succession. My mother has, over time, given me some information that has provided clues more than direct answers, as is often the case when things don't work out. I think he was a guy in his late thirties who saw the onset of the sexual revolution and wanted to navigate it as a single man. My mother wanted another kid, he didn't, and that meant it was time for him to leave. My mother's telling of the story is that one day he said he wanted a divorce and she simply said, 'Okay.' She claims it was that simple, devoid of drama, and inevitable. I was there but I wasn't there, being too young to remember any of it. I'll accept that it was that seamless, which is preferable to imagining the sadness, melancholy, and guilt they may have been feeling but chose not to show around me.

For the most part, I lived with my mother six days a week and then went to my father's apartment in West Hollywood on Sundays, usually spending the night. Whereas my mother was guarded about which of her dates she would bring home and allow me to meet, my father and his decidedly 60s bachelor pad were often accompanied by the woman he was dating at any given time. Unlike my mother and I, he had a pool at his apartment complex, so I enjoyed going over there and splashing around.

The other memory is that, because I would arrive at his place on Sunday morning after whatever festivities and parties may have gone down the night before, there were always vinyl records out of their sleeves and empty record covers strewn about. My main chore when I arrived each week was to match each record with its sleeve and put them back, alphabetized, in the stacks. Thus, a music fan, a record store clerk, a person fascinated by not just music but cover art was born. It was a job I loved so much that, a decade later, I would see my minimum-wage job in record stores as a dream come true.

The records were mostly what you'd expect from a bachelor of the time—mostly jazz-tinged music, with a touch of bossa nova and Latin elements. It was the soundtrack to his life and the way he viewed himself. I can still conjure album covers by Wes Montgomery and Cal Tjader and João Gilberto if I concentrate. I knew how to look for the label on the vinyl and match it with the same label and logo on the cover. Kapp Records, Dunhill Records, Blue Note Records—I had those all down even when I could barely read. I'm sure that the care and concern I continue to take with my own album covers and packages comes from that early vinyl-and-cover-matching gig.

My father was in his early forties, enjoying the life of an eligible bachelor and settling into a growing career as an automotive part-and-supplies manufacturer's representative for sales to retail outlets. He had long been in the automotive world, running Wynn Brothers Auto Parts on Hawthorne Boulevard before I was born. Some of my friends who grew up in Hawthorne—Phast Phreddie Patterson and the McDonald brothers of Redd Kross, in particular—have fond memories of shopping there with their parents.

Strangely enough, he wasn't a gearhead or a car aficionado in any way. It's just the field that he knew, and he was a great salesman. He was always a good listener, and he asked questions. Those two qualities go a long way in achieving success, and he was all about success. He didn't take slackers lightly. His father—the only other member of my family who had been a musician or songwriter, and who died when I was four—often drew ire from my father as a guy who just didn't try all that hard or have much business sense. My Grandma Anne told me that her husband, Matt, once turned down fifty dollars from Irving Berlin for the copyright to one of his songs. Maybe he was too proud to give up ownership and songwriting credit, or maybe he thought he was being lowballed.

My mother was twelve years younger than my father and just doing all she could to put food on the table and pay rent with the help of the minimal alimony and child support my father could muster in the days when he was still struggling for her and her kid. No bachelor pad, no jazz records strewn about—dating wasn't about exploring the new sexual freedom of the decade but rather trying to find the right guy with whom to build a new family. As an adult, I truly admire her resolve and determination to find a good life for us.

Both of my parents ended up remarrying in 1969, and they both left their city apartments for homes in the hills. They remained close friends, and their spouses got along and didn't begrudge them in the slightest for staying tight with their ex; the new spouses both had kids from previous marriages as well. New terrain, new siblings, new parents, new homes, all at the age of nine. But all of it still seemed like a backdrop for what really mattered to me—records, radio, and my guitar.

1.2
MY FIRST GUITAR

A whole lot of life-changing things happened in 1969, the year I turned nine years old. It's funny how, as adults, we view someone that age as a kid, and if they manage to have focused ideas and thought-out plans, we think it's precocious and cute. Maybe that kid is showing signs of great potential down the line. If we hear about a pop sensation combo of pre-teens—take Hanson, for example—we wonder how they managed to have the presence to come up with such fully-formed ideas—or, more likely, who put them up to such things.

Nine was the age when I got my first guitar, took my first lesson, wrote my first song, started my first band, did my first gig, saw my first rock concert—both live onstage and on film—and bought my first record with my own (saved-up allowance) money. And every one of those things was cataclysmic but also seemed to be the natural course of events in the way that I saw my life progressing. I was on my way; I had big ideas and big plans, and I wasn't about to be slowed down or sidetracked by anyone. Anyway, being a loner, living inside my own head, there was nobody to tell me that I was too young to be doing the same things I saw onscreen when I was watching *Woodstock* in a movie theater. I would be simultaneously awed, captivated, and left thinking, *I could do that.*

I don't remember getting my first guitar. I wish I did. I do know it was a nylon-string acoustic guitar that my mother and my soon-to-be stepfather got for me. There's a picture of me where I'm blissfully playing an acoustic guitar but my left hand isn't even touching the strings, so I'm obviously play-acting. But it was clear from moments like that, and from my obsessiveness over music and records, that I wanted to learn to play, and that my mother and/or father and/or stepfather (I'm not sure who had the idea and inclination) felt it was a good idea to get me a guitar and to start me on lessons.

I learned 'This Old Man' at my first lesson and 'Tom Dooley' at my second. The teacher taught me one-finger versions of the rudimentary chords, a C being just my left index finger on the first fret of the second string, a G being that same finger on the third fret of the first. It made playing easy and not too daunting, and I'm grateful for that. You can play countless tunes with just those two chords but throw a more difficult D or A or E (three fingers each!) into the mix and the world is your oyster. My teacher, Mr. Foreman at the Foreman School Of Music, operated out of a building behind a parking lot on Pico Boulevard. He was an older gentleman (although likely much younger than I am as I write these words) and had a strong German accent, comfortingly not unlike that of my great Grandparents who, for all I know, might have been his neighbors back in the old country. He was easygoing and encouraging, and he didn't pressure me. He just gave me the tools, a few songs, and encouraged me to have fun. Plenty of kids start with scales and formal training and learn classical pieces. That may have deterred me from continuing. I'm glad I was given the framework to find my own way and learn to play on my own without being backed into a narrow corner.

One week I showed up to my lesson and Mr. Foreman (I'm pretty sure he didn't have a first name) had a dozen records that he said his kid didn't want anymore, and he thought I might like them. I wish I could remember what they all were, but two stand out. One was an album by the post–Van Morrison version of Them called *Now And Them*. But the one that really got me excited was *Magic Bus* by The Who. This record was heavy and wild and weird all at the same time. My young ears and sensibilities latched on to the silly novelty 'Bucket T' at first—but it was the title track that really pulled me in. I found myself more intrigued by what Pete Townshend was doing with his right hand—the rhythm!—than the left. It was fast and wild and unregulated and filled with adrenaline.

Right around that time, I bought my first album—*Willy & The Poor Boys* by Creedence Clearwater Revival—at the record department of the May Company department store on Wilshire and Fairfax. May Company was housed in one of the more famous architectural landmarks in Los Angeles, the gold-laden Art Deco building that now is the home of the Museum Of The Academy Awards. I'm sure my mother took me there many times growing up to buy clothes and pick up housewares. But if you left the front door of the building, walked down Wilshire, and crossed the street, you'd find yourself at their entertainment annex, and that's where you'd find the record store. And THAT was where I wanted to be. I hung out there all the time, looking at the record covers, and finally, when I had the $1.99 saved up, I was ready to buy my first record. 'Down On The Corner' was a hit on 93 KHJ at the time, and I dug the sound and the mysterious record cover with a bunch of long-haired guys rocking out on a street corner.

Creedence was probably the first band that felt like My Band. The Beatles belonged to everyone, but I felt somehow that CCR was *my* secret passion, despite their ubiquitous presence on the radio. And my connection was only heightened when I went to get a five-dollar money order so that

I could put it in the mail and join their fan club, which operated out of some faraway place called Piedmont, California. I didn't know what or where Piedmont, California, was, but a few weeks later I got a newsletter, a CCR button, an eight-by-ten photo, and a certificate saying I was in the fan club. I belonged! When the next album, *Cosmo's Factory*, came out just a few months later—bands didn't wait too long between releases in those days—I picked it up right away and scrutinized and memorized it, every lyric and every note.

Both The Who and Creedence played at Woodstock. I wasn't there. Wrong age, wrong coast. But my sister, Lindy, and her husband, Johnny, took me to see the movie when it came out just a few months later. They also took me to my first rock concert around the same time—Delaney & Bonnie & Friends at UCLA's Royce Hall. I remember that somehow I knew that Eric Clapton was part of their scene and that there was a chance that he would be part of the gig, and I was disappointed when he didn't show up, aware enough to be hip to that fact but not quite enough to know that the backing band was the band that would eventually be the core of Derek & The Dominoes.

Those two concerts—one in person, one on film—hit me in a very visceral way. Previously, the only times I had seen actual musicians playing in an actual band were in sanitized and truncated performances on TV shows, but this was different. This was wild and untamed and cool beyond anything I could imagine. It was loud and noisy and seemed dangerous and was something I felt but couldn't fully understand. But I wanted to try. Suddenly, just being a music fan wasn't enough. I wanted to make music of my own. I wanted to be in all the bands I loved, and I couldn't really see any reason why that couldn't happen.

I started meeting the other young musicians at Roscomare Road Elementary School with dreams of starting a band. I befriended Philip Haldeman, who not only had and played a drum kit but also had parents who would let him play in their living room. Philip's dad had died in a car accident shortly before we met, and this may be what accounted for the permissiveness. Maybe it didn't. All I know is that I started going to his place and jamming with him on whatever songs my fingers could manage. We started a band called The Light Bulbs, which was pretty much Phillip on drums and me on acoustic guitar, with five other kids all singing along. Yes, that was our band.

I remember we played 'Hey Jude' (not the easiest song—I must have been practicing!), which was a good showcase for our band of minimal instrumentation and maximum vocals. I also remember that one of our singers was a girl named Dinky Grant. Dinky lived around the corner, and we got along well. Years later, she married DJ Bonebrake from X, and in the early 90s, when DJ and I recorded and toured together a little bit, Dinky and I got to hang out together. We never discussed a Light Bulbs reunion, although I have seen a video (no sound, alas) of us playing at a birthday around that time. We seemed to know what we were doing.

That same year, I also met a kid named Chris Taylor, who lived within walking distance. Chris had long blonde hair and a Farfisa organ, and he knew how to play it. Much like Kris Kimball, who I would meet a few months later, Chris Taylor exists in my mind as a full-grown adult, like Rick Wakeman or something. He and I played together regularly, mostly Doors songs, as those were friendly and enticing for an aspiring rock keyboard player in those days. I remember playing long versions of 'Riders On The Storm.' If The Light Bulbs was more like a kids' club—something cute and inclusive—my jams with Chris were more like the kind of thing I saw on the movie version of *Woodstock*. I felt very grown up.

We moved to Bel Air in the summer of 1969, not long after my mother married David. I'm sure it was very exciting for her to have the security of a husband who had enough money to buy a house up in the hills and own a Mercedes. I never understood how he made his money or what he did for a living. He had a company called Medi-Lease and an office in a penthouse in Beverly Hills, but nothing seemed to be happening whenever I'd visit him there. He was swarthy and olive-skinned and wore aviator shades, and all my friends assumed he was in the mafia. Maybe he was.

I was happy for my mother and happy that I was able to have a dog. Gabby was a German Shepherd/Labrador mix who would let me put her tail through the pee-hole of my Andy Warhol tomato-soup-can pajamas, which I would place on her backward for best tail placement. She was a very patient dog and a new best friend. We had a swimming pool in the backyard, too, bordered by a wire fence and a steep incline that led up an ivy-covered hill to Ed Asner's house. I'd see him now and then, leaning down the embankment, waving to me and asking, 'How's it going?' in that Mr. Grant voice. One of my 'jobs' for my allowance was to clean up Gabby's poop, and although I was supposed to put it in a bag and dispose of it properly, I would usually just toss it surreptitiously into Mr. Grant's ivy hill. He never found it, or, if he did, he never said anything.

Overall, though, I was not happy with the move, larger house and dog and pool and Ed Asner notwithstanding. I had gone from living on the flat land of the heart of Los Angeles, where I could come and go and ride my bike and explore and go record shopping as much as I wanted, to a place that was remote, several miles from the nearest thoroughfare and record store, with no friends nearby. I needed my mother to drive me if I was to go look at records or get together with a friend. I escaped further into myself and my records and my guitar playing.

My favorite days were when my mother and David would take me to the Woodland Hills branch of Wallach's Music City, about a twenty-minute drive from our home. The joke among Angelenos is that if you ask how far away something is, you inevitably get the answer 'about twenty minutes . . . with traffic,' no matter how far or without any idea of what 'with traffic' will entail, since traffic is the great X-factor of living in LA.

Wallach's was a magical place. They had records. They had an eleven-by-fourteen yellow printout of the top albums and singles, which I would snag and memorize. And they also had musical equipment—my first encounter with electric guitars and amplifiers. I remember the excitement of seeing a Kustom tuck-and-roll amp, just like the groovy padded one that John Fogerty used. And I drooled over a Crown Guitar knockoff of a Gibson Les Paul.

I finally got an electric guitar when I turned ten. It was cheap and had terrible 'action' (the distance from the fretboard to the strings, and thus the difficulty to play). But I did my best, and it was the electric guitar I played until I was fortunate enough to get the nepotistic deal on the blonde Telecaster a year later.

The other life-changing thing that happened that year happened in August. I remember bringing in the *Los Angeles Times* from the front porch and reading about a horrific murder that happened in Benedict Canyon, just a few hills and valleys from where we lived. The actress Sharon Tate and several others had been killed, and nobody had been caught. For the next few months, while the crime remained unsolved, I heard sounds out my window—the imagined snapping of a tree branch, a creaking that felt like footsteps—and was terrified. And, as with many things that terrify, I was also entranced. I still find city living to be much more comforting and safer than the silence and isolation of living in nature. Maybe it's due to those earliest memories of the unsettling fear of what was to be known as the Manson murders.

With the isolation, the loneliness, the fear, the excitement of discovering live rock music—onstage, onscreen, and in friends' living rooms—the obvious next step for a precocious kid like me was to write my own songs. It was a way for me to become my heroes. It wasn't enough to mimic John Fogerty or Pete Townshend or John Lennon. I wanted to become my own version of them, and that meant creating my own universe, where my music existed on the same level and in the same way as theirs.

Songs were my way of finding my place in the universe, and they were also my newest imaginary friends. Every song I wrote became a way of me saying, 'This is what I do and therefore this is who I am.' I wrote my first song, 'Sing My Blues,' in 1969, that magic year when I became me.

No one there to walk with us
No one there to talk with us
No one there to sing with us
No one there to cling with us
No one there to play guitar
No one there from near and far

No one there to wear my shoes
No one there to sing my blues
Sing my blues
Pay my dues
Or watch me lose
Sing my blues.

1.3

'I'M GONNA GET THAT SONG PUBLISHED FOR YOU, BOOGER'

Aside from the time I once saw Micky Dolenz on a chaise longue at a Palm Springs motel when I was seven years old, Mac Davis was the first famous person I ever met.

I had written my first song when I was nine, and within a year I was playing it on an acoustic guitar at a party for Mac, who within seconds of hearing it said, 'I'm gonna get that song published for you, Booger.' Mac had yet to become the hit-making solo artist, variety-show host, and blockbuster movie star he would become, but he was already a successful songwriter who had written 'In The Ghetto' for Elvis Presley along with a few other big chart hits.

So, there you have it. That's how things go in Tinseltown, right? You pick up a guitar, meet the right people, take a few lunches, and you're on top of the hit parade. Just like in the movies.

That's not quite the whole story.

My sister Samantha, the older of my father's two daughters from his first marriage, had been involved peripherally in the groovy LA rock scene of the Sunset Strip in the mid-60s, quite literally on the fringes as she sold clothes at the Hole In The Wall, a boutique that, among other things, provided the fashion for the TV show *Hullabaloo*. Everybody shopped there, and Samantha, being a personable, fun, attractive woman barely out of her teens, got to know and hang out with some heavy hitters. I particularly like her story of talking down a disgruntled Neil Young after his bandmate Richie Furay, who was getting married, insisted that Neil wear a suit to his upcoming wedding. Samantha told Neil that Richie was only being fair, inspiring the young songwriter to show up to the wedding in a full Confederate soldier's uniform and bare feet.

One of Samantha's best friends in those days was an up-and-coming songwriter named Mac Davis. She tells the story about Mac getting divorced and how she encouraged him to dive back into the dating world by setting him up on a blind date. After some bristling, Mac reluctantly went on the date to make my sister happy. At 2am, her phone rang. It was a sloppy drunk Mac Davis, railing on Samantha.

'I can't believe I let you talk me into going on that date. It was terrible. But the good news is, I came home and wrote a really good song. Do you want to hear it?'

'Sure,' Samantha said, and Mac proceeded to play the first-ever performance of 'In The Ghetto.'

You gotta wonder how bad a date had to be for a guy to be inspired to write such a brutal and sorrowful song just hours later. But I'm sure he was ultimately grateful to her for insisting that he went on that date.

Around that time, Samantha married an executive at Liberty Records named Ron Bledsoe. Ronnie was a groovy, fun guy who wore great clothes—I look at pictures of them from back then and wish I knew where some of those suede coats ended up. Samantha and Ronnie were tight with plenty of big stars, including Ike & Tina Turner—a somewhat distressing thought, in hindsight. I benefitted greatly from Samantha and Ronnie's relationship in the form of a regular flow of free cassettes. Traffic and Canned Heat stand out as two of the bands I was digging into at a young age, entranced by the latter's eleven-minute 'Fried Hockey Boogie' when most of my friends were listening to Tommy Roe or The Archies.

Ronnie left Liberty around 1970 for a VP job at Columbia Records in Nashville. This meant that Samantha would be leaving her hometown of LA for a decidedly different scene, Nashville being decades away then from the hipster haven it is today. But she settled in well and enjoyed the hobnobbing lifestyle—she once met and kissed Elvis, for God's sake!—and the giddy pleasures of driving around Music City in a Rolls-Royce.

I, once again, benefitted from Samantha's new life when, at eleven years old, I was able to buy a brand-new Fender Telecaster at the very low manufacturer's cost of ninety bucks, due to Columbia's very recent purchase of the venerable guitar company (the smell of the brand-new case looms large in my memory).

That same year, I was invited by my sister to fly to Nashville and spend a week with her and Ronnie. I was in heaven. Ronnie brought me into his office and showed me a record cabinet behind his desk. 'Take whatever you want,' he said. I left with about fifty albums, more than doubling my collection in one fell swoop.

'I'm going to a few recording sessions today,' Ronnie said. 'Would you like to go with me?' Obviously, a rhetorical question. I mutely nodded, barely able to contain my teeming excitement. The first stop was a high-budget session in a big studio, pretty much what I might have expected in my imagination, but I was still stunned and spellbound by what I saw. There was a full band and an orchestra and plenty of engineers and assistants keeping busy. It was a big operation. It was showbiz.

The artist was Al Kooper. I was already a big fan of *Alice* Cooper, but I knew that this wasn't that guy. I didn't know much about Bob Dylan (aside from that he was the guy who sang that weird 'Lay Lady Lay' song on the radio), and I most certainly did not know that I was meeting the guy who played the signature organ part on 'Like A Rolling Stone,' not to mention his work with Blood, Sweat & Tears and *Super Session*.

Al was cutting a version of 'Sam Stone,' a song by an up-and-coming songwriter named John Prine. I didn't know who that was, either, but the song was great, and Ronnie gave me a copy of the acetate they cut for him to take home from the session. I still have it today. My mind was blown. I was speechless. I had that same feeling I'd had when I encountered that garage band in my neighborhood or saw *Woodstock*—this is what I wanted to do!

'Now we're going to go to a smaller session for one of our new artists,'

Ronnie said. I quickly learned that not all studios, not all budgets, and not all artist experiences are the same. This was a shoddy little one-room studio on the second floor of a nondescript building. Just the singer and the engineer, listening to playbacks. There was far less glitz and glamour, and I'm sure that everyone at the session was glad to see the label VP show up to hear a few songs. The singer seemed like a nice enough guy, earnest and eager. His name was Dan Fogelberg. I didn't like his music as much as the Al Kooper song I'd heard, though.

Samantha and Ronnie divorced a few years later but remained friends. She went into some wild years, moving back to LA at the height of the 70s disco-and-cocaine era (she liked the former, the latter not so much) and living with me and my mother. Thus, I started high school living with two newly divorced women who were trying to find their ways.

Samantha stayed in touch with Mac Davis and brought me along to a show he played at Magic Mountain when I was sixteen. He was a much bigger star by then, but we were able to go backstage—a first for me!— after the show. Mac saw me and remembered me and lit up a hundred-watt movie-star smile.

'I'm still gonna get that song published for you, Booger.'

1.4
IMPRESSIONS ON A BLANK SLATE

I see more and more young people at my shows these days, and I try to take a moment to chat with them at the merchandise signing booth at the end of the night. And my question is usually the same: 'How did a kid like you get into my music?' To which I usually hear the same refrain: 'My Dad is a big fan, and your records were always around when I was growing up.' It's comforting and amusing, and it makes me wonder if the father in question might also be several years younger than I am. As the great Nigel Tufnel says in *This Is Spinal Tap*, this might be 'a little too much perspective.'

My stepfather played one of those 'music of your life' stations when we traveled in his car down from the hill into the city. In 1970, the music of your life meant mostly things like the easier, more innocuous tunes from the Sinatra or Bennett catalogue, or some silly numbers from Mitch Miller or Burl Ives. In other words, background music. My mother would listen to classical music, not as an enthusiast or student of the form but rather to set the tone and mood and elevate the scenery a bit. Neither of their tastes nor the bachelor-pad jazz or sultry crooner music that my father enjoyed had much of an impact on my tastes, even though much of it would be something I might enjoy hearing at this point in my life. Funny how that goes.

Most of my mother's enthusiasm for the arts was saved for movies. She'd loved them as a kid, and she imparted that love upon me when I was growing up. The Academy Awards were a national holiday in our home, and by the time I reached my teens, I could recite the top winners from any year in history, even though I hadn't seen most of the actual films. In that era, of course, there weren't DVDs or videocassettes, let alone streaming services, so we saw only whatever was on TV or in the actual theaters, which we would attend at least once a week, enjoying the mainstream movies that, in following decades, would make the highest reaches of most all-time best lists.

The one place where my mother's film enthusiasm did have an impact on my musical taste was *Cabaret*. We saw the film in the theater and soon after owned the soundtrack, and I can hear the influence of the Weimar Republic filtered through Bob Fosse in quite a few of my own songs— minor chords, singalong choruses, beerhall rhythms, and all.

Without parents who were listening to the music I cared about, without any siblings living in the house, and without any close friends in the neighborhood, my earliest musical development, guidance, and enthusiasm came from the radio. At first, the conduit was the Top 40 station 93 KHJ (featured so prominently and accurately in Quentin Tarantino's *Once Upon A Time In Hollywood*, a movie that felt like a time machine love letter from my pre-teen days). The Top 40 music of the day was a wild mix—check out any chart or playlist of the day. The Who lived alongside Perry Como who lived alongside Wilson Pickett who lived alongside James Taylor who lived alongside the Edison Lighthouse. It was a good education. The station put out a free weekly two-inch-by-six-inch 'Boss 30' listing the top singles and albums. I begged for a ride to a store each week to get the latest edition and took great care to study which song had risen or dropped the most places and which tracks were 'hit bound.' I still have all of them today.

But the big shift in my musical sensibilities came with the onset of freeform FM radio around the turn of the decade. One of the first in the country was KPPC in Pasadena, and I listened to it whenever I could, which usually meant from the proverbial transistor radio under the pillow late at night. Suddenly I was hearing songs that went beyond the three-minute-singles format, and DJs who purred rather than shouted, proselytizing about the likes of Miles Davis, The Persuasions, Van Morrison, and Captain Beefheart.

I started buying records whenever I could—whenever my mother allowed me to ride my bike down the steep and winding hill to either Westwood Village on one side or Ventura Boulevard on the other. Westwood Village had far superior record shops, particularly Vogue Records, with its wild black light poster room on the second floor. Ventura Boulevard could only offer up the more mainstream record counter at the Sav-On, but it was a little bit closer. Either way, the ride was about three miles—a brisk and wild downhill ride to get there and a sweaty, painstaking return journey home, pushing my bike with a new record in hand. No bike lane, no helmet, perilously steep incline, no worries. Different times.

At that age, music connected in very profound and indelible ways, leaving marks that lasted a lifetime. I was at my father's house on a Sunday night and heard 'Top Of The Pops' by The Kinks and waited pen in hand for the DJ to back-announce his set so I could hear what it was. I loved the song—it was wild and snarly and loud but also funny and kitschy and it connected, even though I didn't fully understand or care about the cynical tale of the mechanics and pitfalls of the music business.

I've just come in at number twenty-five
I'm oh so happy, so glad to be alive

Following the protagonist as he makes his way to number one was a vicarious joyride. I saved up the $1.99 to buy *Lola Vs. Powerman And The Moneygoround* from the Wherehouse in Westwood within a few weeks by shoveling dog shit onto Ed Asner's hill and weeding the front lawn with even more fervor and promptness than usual, anxious to earn the allowance that would turn immediately into more vinyl records.

Another time I was down on Ventura Boulevard on my way to Sav-On with no money in my pocket, merely the desire to see what was new and on sale. I found a five-dollar bill on the sidewalk out front and couldn't believe my luck. I rushed in and bought *Every Picture Tells A Story* by Rod Stewart and still had enough change for a lime-flavored Slurpee at 7-Eleven.

My godmother and my mother's childhood friend, Myrna, had become a secretary at Warner Bros over in Burbank. We would meet her there for lunch a couple of times each year, and we were allowed to shop in the employee record store with Myrna's discount. I would plan my purchases for these lunches weeks in advance. I can't remember how I knew which records were on Warner Bros and Reprise, but I made sure to find out, and I had my list in hand for the usual four or five albums I would buy. Neil Young and Alice Cooper were the big favorites, but I also remember buying records by Deep Purple and Frank Zappa, neither of whom I liked all that much (and still don't).

Along with the radio, there were embryonic rock magazines like *Circus* and *Creem*. I subscribed to the former and tracked down the latter whenever possible, dying with curiosity to hear the stars I was reading about. Most of them got played on KPPC, so I'd hear them all eventually, and then I would plan a long-term mission to get a copy of whatever record I knew I had to have. Both The Beatles and Creedence had disbanded, so my favorites shifted to The Rolling Stones and The Who; *Sticky Fingers* and *Who's Next*, respectively, became staples in my slowly growing collection.

My biggest assistance in satisfying my hunger for rock'n'roll music was my sister Lindy, the younger of my father's daughters from his first marriage. Lindy and her husband Johnny liked to go to live rock shows, and, knowing my enthusiasm, were kind enough to bring me along sometimes. In the years between my first show in 1969 and 1976, when I started driving and had more independence, Lindy and Johnny took me to see concerts by The Beach Boys, Led Zeppelin (twice!), Alice Cooper (three times!), Queen (twice!), Chicago (three times!), Elton John, Leon Russell, and The Who. Lindy is ten years my senior, and I'm somewhat shocked—and eternally grateful—that my mother allowed me to go off with a couple barely into their twenties to stay out until midnight and often spend the night at their house, where sometimes friends would drop by for a drink or to smoke some weed while we listened to records into the wee hours. I didn't share the details of that last part when I got back home the next day.

Seeing live shows was where it all came together for me. It was like a magic trick to see and hear the sounds and mental images from my transistor radio or my record player coming to life before my eyes. I had already begun playing music with friends, so I could relate just a tiny bit to the mechanics of playing in a band—enough to make me even more curious and enthusiastic to do more of it. Once I started playing with Purple Passion/Sudden Death when I was twelve, Lindy and Johnny would even allow us to set up and rehearse in their tiny Burbank apartment. The neighbors must have loved that.

I sometimes wonder how my musical development and taste and enthusiasm would have been different had I lived in current times, where the entire history of music is available at the tap of a finger to be easily streamed without having to pay a single cent. I do know that in those pre-teen years, every live show, every record purchased, every new song discovered courtesy of a stoned late-night DJ was a tiny morsel of heaven in my lonely yet wildly imaginative youth. And the electrical shock of every new song or record or concert that connected with me had the distinct effect of making me think, *I want to do that.*

THE MOTIVATION IS THE MUSE

You've probably read accounts of rock stars who admit that they formed a band to meet girls. Plenty of awkward, nerdy, insecure, maladjusted kids became instantly desirable merely by joining a band—some volume, a record deal, a few catchy songs, and, most importantly, an elevated platform from which to perform and tower above an audience, which instantly makes you just a bit larger than actual life.

That primal motivation didn't factor into my early musical endeavors, nor was that the impetus to start The Dream Syndicate or any of the other groups I played with over the years. The need to mirror, replicate, approximate, and feel like I was on an equal playing field with my favorite records and songwriters was the primary and somewhat narcissistic guiding light, a light eventually followed once I started making records and touring. I just wanted to just keep the dream going.

My motivation to write songs as a pre-teen? That's another story.

Like a lot of American kids of the Jewish faith, I was sent to sleepaway summer camp when I was young. I'm sure my mother and stepfather enjoyed the two-month break from parenting and a vacation of their own while also thinking it would be a good experience for me. The five summers I spent at Camp Scotmar were indeed fun and a big boon to my growing independence and autonomy. Most kids embraced the chance to hang out and play with other kids. I pounced on the chance to be alone even more often, skirting the constraints of adult supervision with ease.

The camp was started by Bert Stern and named for his two kids, Scott and Marla (get it?). In the first two summers, 1970 and 1971, the camp was in Upland, California, just at the foot of Mt. Baldy, where Leonard Cohen would end up escaping to live a monastic life a few decades later. That location was close enough that my mother and stepfather could visit a couple of times during the stay. But in 1972, the camp moved to an isolated plot of land outside of Durango, Colorado, where I found myself much further from home, the only contact being periodic postcards from my mother, many of which were written on the cards enclosed in the original *Exile On Main St.* package. I still have a few of them. I was blissfully independent and removed from any reality I had known in Los Angeles.

I was left shockingly to my own devices while in Colorado. Not a fan of the cafeteria food, I would often go to the lake that was on the premises and catch fish that I would later slice open, clean, and cook over a fire I built myself. As I type these words I hesitate, almost not believing that this was something I did. I don't recognize myself in that story. If someone asked me to do the same right now, I wouldn't know where to start. How did a kid with the same name in this same body ever figure that out? But it did happen, and it meant I could spend more time on my own, lost in my own thoughts, and that was enough reason to make the effort and figure it out. I remember the fish tasted pretty good.

There were activities, some of which I enjoyed: horseback riding, various arts and crafts, and, strangely enough, the religious studies and weekend services. The denomination at the camp was conservative, whereas the temple I went to at home was reformed. These were all interesting to me and, much like with *Cabaret*, the Hebrew songs, with their sad, mournful melodies and reliance almost exclusively on minor chords, ended up having as much an influence on my songwriting and sensibilities as anything else.

But there were also girls. Girls! I may have been antisocial, but I also was entering puberty, and the idea of hanging out and maybe even making out with a girl superseded any need to be alone. Now, this was the swinging early 70s, and most of the attendees and counselors were from California where free love was ordinary and the kids of polyamorous adults were doing much more than just making out—many of the kids just barely in their teens were having sex, undeterred by the supervision of counselors who were mostly teenagers themselves.

I was way too shy for such things. An occasional game of *truth or dare* was as exciting as it got for me. Many of the girls liked me, just 'not in that way.' I was sensitive, a good listener, and benignly non-threatening, but the biggest ace up my sleeve was that I played guitar and wrote songs. I was regularly invited into the girls' cabin at all hours to serenade the sirens. If I couldn't manage to get them to show interest otherwise, things changed when I had a guitar in my hand.

They liked it when I sang songs by Cat Stevens or James Taylor, but they were most enthralled by my own songs. 'Did you really write that?' they asked, and in most cases I had not only written the song but had come up with it earlier that same day, just so I'd have something new to play. Fueled by burgeoning testosterone, I was cranking them out. There were silly, almost vaudevillian numbers like 'Roller Derby Star,' but most of them were wounded, sensitive numbers like 'In My Own Way' and 'Rock And Roll God,' the former a wrenching, breakup song and the latter a multi-part Townshend-esque mini rock opera about dreaming of one day being a rock star. Heady stuff for a twelve-year-old, and enough to get me noticed by girls, if not actually enough to have a girlfriend.

How did I write these songs? How does anyone write songs?

To be honest, I'm often surprised that people *don't* write songs, especially musicians. To me, it seems like a natural extension of playing and loving music. You hear stuff, you're inspired, you sing a melody, you have something on your mind, something eating away at you; you add those words to your melody, and *voila!*—you have a song. I've easily written about a thousand of them, and yet I have many friends and bandmates who have performed music for decades and never written a single song.

Possibly the bigger question is *why* I write the songs. Maybe it's something akin to when you look in a magazine at a model wearing a snappy outfit and think, *I wonder how I'd look in that?* Upon putting down the cash, you realize you look nothing like the model, but hopefully you've approximated something that is pleasing and thus elevated yourself in the process—at the very least in your own self-esteem. I've always been most inspired when I hear some other music that excites me. I hear a song or album that blows me away and think, *I want to do that too!* Much like the person who buys the outfit that looks good on the model, my rendition doesn't entirely resemble the inspiration, but it ends up looking good and natural on me. And then I stand back and think, *How about that! I wrote a song*, and hopefully I like it enough to feel compelled to share it with other people.

My earliest songs came primarily from whatever record was exciting me at the time. In some of them, I can hear echoes of Leon Russell's *Carney*, the original version of *Jesus Christ Superstar*, and Neil Young's *Harvest*, but the biggest influence on me, and the record that consumed me the most at that young age, was The Who's *Quadrophenia*. Pete Townshend captured the sad, melancholy cockiness and anger of being a lonely, maladjusted teenager driven equally by the misanthropy that kept people away and the raging hormones that wanted them closer. I felt like he was singing directly to me. Those songs went into my head, whirled around for a while, and came out as slightly derivative remakes with my own melodies and lyrics.

The other record that had a profound effect on my writing and singing was *Tonight's The Night* by Neil Young. I remember when the needle got to the end of side one and hearing 'Mellow My Mind,' where Neil's voice cracks agonizingly as he tries and fails to reach the highest note. I didn't know you could sing like that. I thought you were supposed to always sing well, achieve perfection, and hit the right notes. It made me laugh at first, then it made me feel uncomfortable, and finally the vulnerability and shocking wrongness made the album resonate with me in a way that fluffy AM pop just couldn't.

I never performed them in the handful of bands I played with back then. But at the end of every summer, when the camp would have the annual talent show, I would, as Pete Townshend would say, pick up my guitar and play, winning first prize every time and watch the girls swoon, disappearing into their own shared sadness and insecurities. It was enough for me.

———

THE SPORTSWRITER

Almost overnight, around the time I turned fourteen, my interest and focus and obsession shifted from music to sports, and to baseball in particular. I still bought records, listened to the radio, and got excited about bands and songwriters. I was still a music fan. But following and eventually writing about sports became my focus. I barely touched my guitar or wrote songs the entire time I was in high school.

How did this happen? My mother was never a sports fan. My father enjoyed watching football on Sunday. I was never an athlete, I didn't play Little League or T-ball or Pop Warner football, and, due to my lack of athletic ability, I did all I could to get out of gym class. I remember my elation at finding out a minor stumble had caused a hairline fracture in my foot that didn't hurt or hinder me much but allowed me to miss several months of suiting up for PE. I would sit on the bleachers during the appointed hour and read instead of embarrassing myself.

Maybe it was because of my friend Mark Schreiber. Mark lived about a mile down the road, and we were hanging out more and more. His dad was the manager of KFWB, the biggest news radio station in Los Angeles, and they had season tickets to the Dodgers, right behind home plate. Mark and his dad took me to games, and the proximity to the action and excitement—as well as having a friend with whom to share this newfound enthusiasm—may have been just enough to turn me on to the game.

Baseball and its reliance on statistics provided an appealing sense of order and ranking and history and that was exciting to me, much in the same way studying the Top 30 charts had been in the years before. *Sports Illustrated* and a company called Strat-O-Matic had dice-based baseball board games based on actual players and statistics that I would play not only with Mark but also for hours and hours on my own, meticulously logging results and updating statistics that I would then pore over as if they were actual real-world stats (which I would pore over and memorize as well). We'd get together and play catch or various games like Over The

Line, which could be played with only two people—very important, living in a neighborhood where I didn't know many kids.

My love for playing music truly peaked with that junior high school show with Sudden Death Overtime. It's fair to surmise that having a brush with the applause, the adulation, and my first-ever sensation of being cool and admired for being in a rock band would have made me hungry for more. But that wasn't the case. Instead, I signed up for journalism class and worked on the *Emersonian*, our junior high school newspaper. It became clear that I was a decent writer, and I was also driven and ambitious. I was given plenty of opportunities to write about school news, politics, music, and sports. The brief flirtation with being a rock star had given way to the thrill of seeing my byline in print over an article I had written, knowing that hundreds of other kids were seeing it as well.

There were other big changes around this time as well. I was too young to fully understand the dynamics of adult relationships, but I was presented with a buffet of information and clues to process. My father and stepmother Sam were openly affectionate and playful, and at some point, I knew that they had parties with other couples and individuals that went beyond cocktails and parlor games. They were full-on swingers, enjoying The Lifestyle. My mother and stepfather, on the other hand, had reached a point of chilly avoidance. I remember getting up for water in the middle of the night and seeing my stepfather either sleeping on the couch in the den or just sitting there with his cigarette glowing in the dark, much like in a Carly Simon hit from around that time.

My mother and stepfather separated and eventually divorced when I was fifteen. The six years of living up the hill in Bel Air, the pool, the yard, Ed Asner, the fancy cars—all over. And I couldn't have been happier. We were moving back down to the flatlands of the city, into an apartment just blocks away from the fabled Pico and Sepulveda intersection, just down the road from McCabe's Guitar Shop, where I bought my first proper acoustic guitar in 1974, and where I would both shop and perform in the decades that followed.

The reason for this excitement was that I could suddenly do whatever and go wherever I wanted. In that year before I got my driver's license, I rode the RTD, LA's bus system, everywhere—to the beach, to the ghostlike Downtown LA, to Dodgers games. I remember shopping at my favorite sports memorabilia shop on the Miracle Mile and meeting an older gentleman with whom I struck up a conversation about baseball, after which my mother let me take a bus downtown and go to a game with him. This, like many other things in my childhood, would make a modern helicopter parent shudder in horror, but it's the kind of freedom and sense of wanderlust and travel and adventure that set me on my road ahead, so I remain eternally grateful, even though I often chide my mother, telling her the stories of 'what she let me do,' to which she'll often say, 'No, I didn't.' But she did.

I went to University High School in West LA, a public school whose list of alumni in the music and film world reads like a West Coast equivalent of the immortalized Fame school in New York City. Marilyn Monroe, Elizabeth Taylor, Judy Garland, Nancy Sinatra (and Frank Jr.), Randy Newman, Ryan O'Neal, Jeff Bridges, James Brolin, David Cassidy, Danny Elfman, Kim Fowley, Annette Funicello, John Densmore and Robby Krieger, both Jan AND Dean, Jeff Bridges, Nels Cline, and Kim Gordon all went to Uni.

It was a dumpy construction site of a school when I attended because, from 1974 to 1977, the auditorium and cafeteria were closed for renovation, which means we were given open-campus privileges not afforded to most students in the LA City Unified School District. Even though I was no longer playing music, I remained a fan, and I would spend most of my lunch hours walking the two blocks to the Licorice Pizza record store and sitting on one of their beanbag chairs, listening to whatever they were playing, which was usually something wilder and more underground than standard Top 40 fare.

I started dating, had my first girlfriends, and hung out with a guy named Mike Block who lived up in Mandeville Canyon, where he often hosted wild parties. He was part of the theater group clique, as were most of his friends, so the parties involved dancing, improvisational play-acting, and other exhibitionistic displays. This was exciting to me, even as I shyly watched from the sidelines while they spontaneously performed 'The Time Warp' from *The Rocky Horror Picture Show*. It was from these parties and from my admiration of these cool weirdos that I gained a love for art rock.

The Rocky Horror Picture Show was fun, but it didn't fully do it for me. But then one night Mike put on *Country Life* by Roxy Music and my mind was blown. This record was everything that I'd wanted to hear—it electrified me, it told me about sex and desire and distant worlds and romance and decadence in ways I had never heard before and couldn't fully understand. Roxy Music was the first 'weird' band I ever connected with, and I was hooked. I voraciously devoured all of their records and anything connected to their world—not only Eno and Bryan Ferry and Phil Manzanera records but even distant cousins like the first album by Split Enz, simply because Phil produced it.

In fact, the first show I ever saw without being chaperoned by my sister Lindy was a 1976 show that Roxy Music played at the Hollywood Palladium. I went with Mike Block, and it was thrilling. I remember being disappointed that they didn't play my favorite song, 'Prairie Rose.' The excitement of the show didn't make me want to pick up my guitar again—not right away—but it gave a fresh reboot to my love and curiosity for music. As fate would have it, the bass player for Roxy that night (and for many of their shows in the 70s) was Sal Maida, my good friend and neighbor these days in Jackson Heights and my bandmate in, yes, a Roxy Music tribute band. Sal was also the bass player for Sparks, whose 1977 New Year's Eve show at the Santa Monica Civic (with Van Halen opening) I heard, standing outside listening through a gap next to the stage door because I couldn't afford a ticket.

Getting my driver's license and my first car—a red AMC Gremlin that had belonged to my stepmother Sam—meant I could drive around LA and listen to cassettes or just sit in the dark in my bedroom and watch the glow of the Marantz 2020 receiver listening to *The Who By Numbers* or *For Your Pleasure*. I remember my ears perking up late one night while listening to KPPC and hearing a song that sounded like Van Morrison but better than anything he had been doing lately.

'That was "Backstreets" by Bruce Springsteen,' the DJ said, 'from his upcoming album, *Born To Run*.' I had a new favorite to add to the list. Springsteen would have a profound and very direct influence on my shift back to being a musician.

I think that maybe some of the disenchantment with the idea of playing music came from a changing music scene that had shifted away from the intimacy and rawness and primitive spirit of the music I had first loved and moved toward arena-rock and prog-rock bands. Performers became distant, unattainable giants, and the very idea that I would somehow exist in that world was unimaginable. I went through a period of listening to bands like ELP and Yes and Jethro Tull—probably a by-product of my curiosity about expansive art-rock bands. I could dig what they were doing, but it was as far from my skill set as playing shortstop for the Dodgers. The guitar stayed under the bed—for now.

In the meantime, my star as a sportswriter was rising. I was fourteen years old and just starting my first month in high school when I heard about a new project called *Student News*, a TV show that would be written and anchored by a mix of students from all over the LA school district. I went downtown for the audition and got the gig. The project was well-funded and coached by people who had worked for local network news programs and had access to professional film cameras and editing facilities to produce a weekly live thirty-minute broadcast. I quickly became the sports editor and was regularly on camera as well. I have a VHS tape of a thirty-minute sports special that I wrote and hosted. My fluffy, feathered, blow-dried hair and silk patterned shirt are a thing to behold.

At the same time, I was throwing myself fully into the high school newspaper and was editor-in-chief for both my junior and senior years. I was so single-minded in my endeavors that I even chose to take a print shop class so that I could learn how to operate and maintain the archaic Linotype machine and set the hot lead that would be used to print the run of each week's paper. Now I was writing, assigning, and typesetting my own stories.

Everything else in school felt incidental. I did well enough in my other classes to graduate, most of my enthusiasm being for math classes, in which algebra worked well alongside my love for statistics. Much like they say about Pete Rose, I was able to compute the change of a hitter's batting average in my head as he ran to first base for a single. I also used my advanced placement in math classes to be allowed to access and learn to use the primitive binary card-punching computer system. I devised a program that could generate a complete baseball game with announcements, commercials, and a full nine innings of action.

I felt I was on the fast track to becoming a sportswriter. I was good, and I knew it. In my senior year I was submitted in two sports categories for a citywide journalism competition—for a previously written story that had appeared in the school paper, and for an article written on the spot from a press conference with all the selected attendees. I won both categories, and I felt like it was only a matter of time before I'd be writing for *Sports Illustrated*. The notion of being a musician had gone completely by the wayside.

I applied for studies at the University Of California-Davis, a school that was appealing because they had a respected rhetoric program, and I felt that would be even more valuable as a writer than would being a journalism major. I mean, I honestly felt like I already had the journalism thing aced! I was accepted, which meant I had to wrap my head around moving from LA, where I had lived my entire life, to a small town of fifty thousand people a few miles down the road from the state capitol, Sacramento. I visited the campus in the summer of 1977, just a month before starting my studies, and made a beeline for the offices of the *Aggie*, the campus paper. I was armed with clippings of my articles, stories about me winning my awards, and recommendations from my various teachers and mentors. The paper's editor was blindsided and amused by this cocky kid.

I began my freshman year as sports editor, covering the varsity football team. Things were moving along just as I'd hoped and expected.

And then came punk rock. With the speed of a Dee Dee Ramone one-two-three-four count-off, my sportswriting dreams and ambitions quickly, completely, and forever fell by the wayside.

I was a good candidate and in the right place for discovering the burgeoning punk rock and new wave scene when I was in my senior year at Uni High in 1977. My favorite bands were The Who and Roxy Music. The influential and infamous Rhino Records store was just a mile down the road, but I spent more time at the decidedly more hippie-dippy Licorice Pizza (bean bag chairs! incense!) just around the corner. My fourth-period Spanish class with Mr. Gomez was interrupted every day by a wild-looking kid with peroxide-blond hair and a boom box blasting *Aladdin Sane* who would walk into the classroom, write 'Bowie' on the chalkboard, and walk out. One day he came in, sans boombox, and wrote, 'Bowie is dead.' He never came back. The impudent Bowie proselytizer's name was Jan Paul Beahm until he changed it to Darby Crash the following year when he formed The Germs with his Uni High classmate Pat Smear.

Michelle was my girlfriend in my senior year of high school. She was wild, rebellious, and fun, and she liked a lot of the music that I liked. As with many music fans who drank the elixir of the coming musical revolution, one could find plenty of records in both of our collections that showed we were ready to see the light of Joey Ramone, but there were also plenty of records we'd want to hide a few years later. I dug what I dug, but I also had a soft spot for Stevie Wonder and Boz Scaggs (still do). Michelle shared my love of Roxy and other art-rock bands and was also into the Stooges. I didn't connect to them right away, but I did get her a copy of *Raw Power* for her birthday.

After I went off to UC-Davis, Michelle ended up being close friends with Darby, and she is prominently featured with him in scenes from the LA punk-rock documentary *The Decline Of Western Civilization*. I came back home once on a break during my freshman year and went out with the two of them to see Warren Beatty's *Heaven Can Wait*. They both took a handful of pills before the movie started, and we all got thrown out of the theater in the first hour. That's my Darby story.

It was 1977. I was seventeen years old. I was on my own and living four hundred miles from home in the campus dorms. That untethered freedom allowed for reinvention, and for the sounds and culture (although not the sartorial style) of punk rock and new wave to connect with me, instantly and profoundly.

The offices of the *Aggie* were in the basement of the campus center in Freeborn Hall, just a few steps from the fifty-thousand-watt college radio station, KDVS, and the campus record store, Zapple Records. That basement was a good place to hang out. As the sports editor and a doggedly determined and aspiring journalist, I spent a lot of time down there. The sports desk was right next to the entertainment desk, where promo LPs from record labels were delivered every day. I figured it would be nice to get some free records and write a few reviews, and I was told I'd have to talk to the paper's main rock critic, Tom Gracyk, a junior who had locked down the main reviewing gig for some time.

Tom ended up being my roommate, my best friend, and quite possibly the biggest musical influence I'd ever have. He was from just down the I-80 in Fairfield and had immersed himself in underground music, listening to freeform radio, reading rock mags, and absorbing more than I ever had, not only in rock'n'roll but also in jazz, bluegrass, country, and just about every kind of music. He also had a weekly radio program on KDVS. He was outspoken and knowledgeable, and I thought he was the coolest.

Tom also proved to not be territorial. He was happy to divvy up some of the promos with me. I still have the clippings of the articles I wrote during my first quarter at UC-Davis, and I can see a steady progression in the records I reviewed—from The Doobie Brothers and Chicago and Todd Rundgren to Dwight Twilley, Iggy Pop's *Lust For Life*, and Cheap Trick. When we received a promotional hanging mobile from Sire Records, announcing its new wave promo campaign with Day-Glo writing and covers by the Ramones, Dead Boys, Richard Hell, and Talking Heads, I snagged it and proudly hung it in my dorm room, much to the bemusement of my jock roommate, who mockingly dubbed me 'the punk rocker.'

Tom and I traveled together in my AMC Gremlin to San Francisco to cover the Sex Pistols' tour-ending show at Winterland in January of 1978—we agreed he would do the concert review and I would write the human-interest feature story. You can see Tom's face among the crowd on the inside cover of *The Great Rock 'n' Roll Swindle*. It was a weird show— Sid Vicious couldn't and mostly didn't play, Johnny Rotten was bored and antagonistic, but Steve Jones and Paul Cook were as solid as they were on the album, which I knew inside out by the time of the show. I preferred the opening acts, The Avengers and The Nuns, the latter of which included a young Alejandro Escovedo, with whom I would become friends just a few years later.

The ride to and from the gig was where Tom and I really became friends. I quizzed him about becoming a DJ at the station. Back then, you had to take an exam to get the license needed to do an on-air shift. It wasn't easy, but I put in the work and passed the test. Tom was the station's music director, and, with his help, I procured a weekly 2am-to-6am show. I was thrilled. The station had an incredible library of records and a listening room, which I commandeered whenever possible. I had a voracious appetite for anything that smacked of new wave or punk rock, and I gave myself a crash course, also fueled by weekly hour-long drives to Rather Ripped Records in Berkeley, where an employee named Ray Farrell kindly took me under his wing and recommended bands he knew I would like. Devo? Pere Ubu? Alex Chilton? Yeah, you gotta have those. Ray went on to be an A&R man at Geffen, signing Sonic Youth, among others.

At the same time, I was becoming disenchanted with sportswriting, and with sports in general. There was no room for any kind of personality in a sports world that was strict and bland and featured coaches who actually said things like, 'On any given day, any given team can beat any other given team.' I can't put all the blame on the coaches and the jocks. I was under the spell of a whole new world, and it was shocking how quickly my focus and priorities changed. By my second quarter, I had stopped writing about sports and put most of my focus on writing record reviews and planning my graveyard shift radio show. My studies were something I pursued just enough so that I could pass my classes and stay in school.

I made the hour-long drive back and forth between Davis and San Francisco almost every week, sometimes to see shows like Iggy Pop (with David Bowie on keyboards) at the intimate Old Waldorf, where I also saw John Cale a few months later. But mostly I went record shopping in Berkeley. I bought whatever 'Rather Ray' recommended, or just picked up a record with a cool cover or a connection to another band I already liked. I quickly absorbed and adored the punk rock building blocks of the Pistols, Ramones, Buzzcocks, and The Clash, and then voraciously dug deeper into everything else from the scenes that were happening around the world.

We also had a club right on campus in the same Freeborn Hall that housed the newspaper and radio station. It was called the Coffee House because that's exactly what it was. During the day it was a nondescript place to get cappuccino and sandwiches. Gigs happened several times a month; the tables and buffet trays and coffee machines would be pushed out of the room, a stage was built, a PA desk rolled in, and it became a 250-capacity venue. The club was run by a guy named Peter Afterman who knew his stuff and had a knack for booking bands on their way up, always seeming to know the ones who would be popular by the time their gig arrived. Our little local club with the foot-high stage hosted gigs by Elvis Costello, The Police, Devo, the Ramones, Iggy Pop, John Cale, Talking Heads, Rockpile, XTC, and many others. These bands would move down the road to San Francisco the next night and play in a much larger venue. None of the bands complained or had an issue with our dinky venue aside from Ultravox, who were mortified by the intimacy and lack of frills and had to be cajoled into fulfilling their contract.

The band that connected with me most and got me thinking about playing music again was Talking Heads. I loved The Clash and the Pistols, but nothing about them allowed me to superimpose myself in their image and imagine I could be up on the stage doing what they did. But Talking Heads? They were just ordinarily dressed, preppy, solid but not flashy musicians. They sang about ordinary things—buildings, government, love, art—and even their angst came from internal neuroses rather than the threat of anarchy. I watched them and thought, *Hmmm . . . maybe I could do that.* My blonde Telecaster was still in LA, and I hadn't touched a guitar once in my freshman year, but I told myself that I'd bring mine back with me after I went home to LA for the summer.

I made another friend that freshman year. I was in a rhetoric class that involved just a handful of students sitting in a circle of chairs and talking about feelings and impressions, almost like something I thought I had left behind in LA. But I started talking to one of the girls in the class about music, and the subject turned to the show by The Jam I was going to see the following week at Winterland.

'I really want to see that show,' she said. 'Can I get a ride?'

I was excited to have a new friend and a new ally in my obsession, and I said yes. We went to the show (which, in true Bill Graham history of perversely mismatched bills, also featured Be Bop Deluxe and Horslips) and hit it off immediately—not romantically, but merely as allies in a very small but very solid scene that was developing around Freeborn Hall. I soon found out that my new friend worked at the radio station as the head of public affairs programming. Her name was Kendra Smith, and she would play a very big part in everything that followed in my life.

I had gone in twelve months from absolute certainty that my future life would be as a sportswriter to caring about little more than punk rock, new wave, buying records in independent record shops (or, better yet, getting free promos from record companies), and spinning those records in the middle of the night across the airwaves of Davis, Sacramento, and beyond. My sportswriting days were done, and my full attention and time was shifted back, once again, to music. I had no idea what I would do with this reignited love and obsession, but I was having fun and was not concerned with where it would all lead.

—

VALIUM, NOSE JOBS, AND THE BOSS

I went back home to Los Angeles the summer after my freshman year a very different person than the one who had loaded up the Gremlin and left for Davis nine months earlier. I had left sportswriting in the rear-view mirror somewhere along I-5, and I was now a graveyard shift DJ, punk rock and new wave enthusiast, and somewhat distracted college student. I couldn't wait to get back to start my second year of college.

Home wasn't home anymore. My mother had married for a third time, to a Beverly Hills doctor named Martin, and had moved into his apartment in Marina Del Rey. There was no sentimentality, no memories, no familiarity with this new place I'd be calling home for the summer, and as much as I was happy to spend time with my mother and father, I also wasn't really returning to anything that felt like home.

Martin had entered my life a few years before when he and my mother had started dating. Much as her previous husband, David, had ingratiated himself with that gift of a Beatles album, Martin won my favor by discreetly leaving a pack of condoms for me at the counter of the pharmacy where he practiced, knowing I had a steady girlfriend at the time and that they might come in handy. I was fifteen and my girlfriend was fourteen, but Martin was right, and he saved me from the awkward rite of passage of mumbling and stumbling through asking for them myself at the drugstore. My mother was none the wiser.

Martin also gave me a Valium when I was sixteen. I don't remember why, but that seemed like an odd thing to do at the time, and it still does. Fortunately, I didn't like it all that much, and I didn't feel the need or desire to try it again. Similarly, he also facilitated my first brush with inebriation at a Passover seder that same year, when my girlfriend and I downed most of a bottle of Manischewitz and made out in a spare bedroom. Again, I didn't get too worked up over the buzz of the booze (the make-out session was another story), and I didn't get drunk again until I was out of my teens.

Another thing that Martin thought was a good idea was that I get a nose job, feeling it would be good for my confidence and future. He sent me to a doctor friend of his who looked me over and showed me what I could look like with some nips and tucks. He made a good case, especially for a teenager going through all of the usual insecurities of that time in life, but fortunately I didn't take the bait.

Valium, cheap wine, and nose jobs. You may be getting a bad impression of the guy, and, based on how things ended with my mother about five years later, you would be right. But he was a smart guy with a good sense of humor. He made my mother happy for a few years and allowed her to shift back on the rags-to-riches-to-rags-to-riches rollercoaster, which provided much-needed newfound security. They had a nice apartment—a good enough place for me to spend a summer while I hung out in record shops, went to shows, and drove around LA. But it wasn't home, and I was already looking forward to August and getting on with things.

One thing happened that summer that would change my life: a Bruce Springsteen concert at the Forum on July 5. I went with my childhood pal Mark, the only pre-Davis friend with whom I'd stayed in touch. We were both avid fans of Springsteen's first three albums, as well as *Darkness On The Edge Of Town*, which had just been released, but nothing could have prepared us for the live show. It's easy now to see his live routine as schtick—a comfortable format he has honed and repeated in the decades since—but at the time it was revelatory. All of Bruce's patter and storytelling felt like it was being conjured in real time, as though the giant arena was a backlit coffee house where Bruce was talking to a handful of friends, while the music itself was larger than life: mythic, heroic, with arrangements that jolted the system with surprise. It was an *I didn't know you could do that* experience, and it got me thinking more seriously about playing in a band again. He even played a Telecaster like I did!

On the way out of the Forum, I saw on the back of someone's tour T-shirt that Bruce was playing at the Sports Arena in San Diego the next night. I decided I was going to drive down on my own and see that show as well, somehow knowing that I could get a ticket at the door. Maybe I called first, but it wasn't sold out, and if I remember correctly, the ticket was under ten bucks. Before I left for the three-hour drive down south, I remembered that my new friend Kendra had gone to her family home in Coronado for the summer. I gave her a call to see if she'd want to go with me. She said yes, and I picked her up on the way.

Kendra was as impressed and overwhelmed as I had been the night before, and as I was driving her home, we started talking about being in bands and doing the kind of magic trick that we had seen Bruce and The E Street Band perform that night. I told her I had played guitar in some bands when I was younger. She said she sang in the school choir. That was all I needed to hear.

'We should start a band when we get back to Davis,' I said, and Kendra agreed.

Years later, on a tour supporting The Black Crowes, Chris Robinson told me that he, his brother Rich, and drummer Steve Gorman had seen The Dream Syndicate open for R.E.M. in Atlanta in 1984 and decided to form a band while they watched our set. I told him I could relate.

1.9
SMALL FISH, SMALL POND

I drove back to Davis in August, this time with my blonde Telecaster in the back seat. Tom and I had stayed in touch over the summer and decided to get a place together when the school year began. We found a two-bedroom apartment about a mile from the campus that we planned to share with two other guys we knew for sixty-two bucks each per month.

At the end of the six-hour drive, I was in the parking lot of my new pad and loading in my suitcase, some books, the records I had bought over the summer, and my guitar, along with everything else I had moved down from the dorms—stereo, a few kitchen items—from the year before. I didn't have a ton of possessions, but it was enough for four or five trips up and down the stairs from the Gremlin to the second-floor apartment.

At the end of the move, I thought it would be nice to play some guitar and break in my new home and my new life. I opened the Fender case and found not my Telecaster but rather several wood blocks in its place. Somebody had stolen my guitar from the parking lot and ingeniously replaced it with something that would give the case a sense of weight so I wouldn't suspect a thing until later. I was crushed.

This also put a crimp in my plans to start a band right away, so I needed to get a job. There was a record store in town, part of a Northern California chain called Eucalyptus Records. This was nothing like the stores that I would frequent in Berkeley or Los Angeles. They sold the hits of the day, plus some meat-and-potatoes catalogue items, along with band T-shirts and a whole lot of drug paraphernalia. Bongs and pipes and scales and vials lined the walls behind the counter and the area near the register. They hired me, and I was suddenly $2.75 an hour, twenty hours a week richer than I was before. After a few weeks, I went to a pawn shop in nearby Sacramento and bought a red 1964 Fender Mustang, a guitar that would be worth several thousand dollars now but cost me less than a hundred bucks in the fall of 1978.

Much as I had done before the summer break, I spent all my spare hours in the listening booth at the radio station, devouring everything in the voluminous stacks of wax. I was getting to know more and more of the enthusiasts of punk rock and new wave. Tom and I staged a coup, edging out the 'old hippies' who in retrospect were listening to the kind of music I love today—Can, Neu, Faust, Keith Jarrett, Miles Davis, the (gasp) Grateful Dead. But the lovers of The Clash, Buzzcocks, The Jam, and Elvis Costello had taken over, and I now had a prime-time weekly radio show on Wednesdays from 6 to 9pm called *Three Minute Rock And Roll* (again, a little ironic, given my eventual tendency towards longer songs).

One of the members of 'our gang' was a guy named Russ Tolman. He, like Tom, was a junior who had already entrenched himself in the station before me. Russ and I became friends, and once I found out that he played guitar, we did what guitarists do and agreed to get together to jam at his apartment. I remember sitting in his room on the bed and playing 'Just

What I Needed' by The Cars for several hours, and that was enough for us to decide that, along with Kendra, we had the nucleus of a band.

We put an ad in the local paper and got replies from exactly one bass player and one drummer, so they were in the band. Gavin Blair was the drummer. He had hair down to his waist and a scraggly beard and was mad about Hot Tuna—not exactly part of our newfound movement, but close enough, plus he could keep time and was a nice guy. The bass player, Steve Suchil, was ten years older than us and was far more seasoned, having been in bands that had played actual gigs in actual clubs, and was a better musician as well. What's more, he had a great record collection; he was well-versed in musical history; and, most importantly, had a house with a garage where we could practice. We were a band, and we were ready to start playing.

We called our band Suspects and, like many a garage band, we started off by learning a bunch of covers. The songs we chose were evenly divided between songs by favorite bands from the 60s and more recently released new wave and punk rock songs, reflecting the same mix of music that Russ, Kendra, and I might have played on our KDVS radio programs. This was the music we loved. It was out of fashion in a small college town like Davis, and it was music that we felt people should know about. If we weren't the most musically adept messengers—none of our covers would be mistaken for a better version than the original—we were sincere and enthusiastic and hell-bent on bringing our record collections to life in person and in real time for anyone who would listen.

Here are some of the covers we played in our first months together:

'I Can't Reach You,' The Who
'Don't Come Close,' Ramones
'Whole Wide World,' Wreckless Eric
'20th Century Fox,' The Doors
'Do Anything You Wanna Do,' Eddie & The Hot Rods
'Don't Back Down,' The Beach Boys
'19th Nervous Breakdown,' The Rolling Stones

I would hear my wife Linda drum on some of those same songs when she played with Golden Smog at the Bowery Ballroom almost thirty years later. For music geeks of a certain age, these were our standards. Despite having Kendra on lead vocals, each of our cover choices were songs sung originally by male singers.

I also had started writing songs again, something I hadn't done since I was thirteen. Much like our choice of covers, my songwriting reflected the music I was listening to and was excited about. I can look back on the songs I was writing at the time and say, 'Ah, that's my *More Songs About Buildings And Food* song, and that one is my *Squeezing Out Sparks* song, and those other ones are Nick Lowe, Devo, and The Jam. Oh, and then those other ones? Those are definitely *Nuggets*.'

I found a copy of *Nuggets*, Lenny Kaye's collection of regional hits and near misses that graced the lower reaches of the charts in the mid-to-late 60s, in the cutout bin of the campus record store just down the hall from the radio station for $1.99. It changed my life, my songwriting, my musical taste, everything. It was the perfect nexus of my love of bands like The Beatles and The Who and the Stones crossed with my more recent embracing of punk rock. It was fun, it was wild, it was disposable, it was essential, and, most of all, it was a reminder that sometimes things that are slightly wrong are better than things that are polished and perfect. Maybe The Knickerbockers were better than The Beatles. Maybe The Standells were better than the Stones. Better is not always best. There is a crack in everything—that's how the light gets in.

I bought up the ten copies in the store and gave them to my bandmates and other friends. I was a veritable Johnny *Nuggets*-seed.

My secret weapon as a songwriter was (and probably still is) my inability or lack of patience or interest to accurately copy my inspirations. I might have heard a song on the radio or on an import seven-inch single and say, 'That's great! I want to write a song like that,' and by the time it filters through my mind, fingers, imagination, and execution, not to mention the interpretation by my fellow musicians, it ends up sounding nothing like the song that sparked the process. I can tell you the song I was trying to rip off on every track on *The Days Of Wine And Roses*, for example, and not have even the slightest fear of being sued.

The songs came frequently and quickly. And if the music came directly from my record collection, the words came from inside—a snotty mix of arrogance, social awkwardness, sexual frustration, and a loner's litany of rants and grievances. Upon reflection, years later, I have often wanted to apologize to Kendra for some of the things I made her sing, but she was always a good sport, delivering my words in a bouncy, peppy, effervescent way that would stand in stark contrast to the cooler, more mysterious persona she would adopt in years to come.

Gigs were hard to come by. The few clubs in town showcased bands with better chops, playing either Top 40 fare or Grateful Dead covers (I remember a Dead cover band called Phydeaux—pronounced 'Fido'—that was pretty big on the local scene). Instead, we talked our way into performing in the dorms or at a campus swimming pool or bike shop. We knew we'd have to have a demo tape to start getting booked into proper clubs, so we found a recording studio in Sacramento that specialized in jingles and commercials. We knocked out three of my songs—'Talking Loud,' 'A Year Ago,' and 'I Got A Right'—and the tape got us a few opening slots at a club in Sacramento called Slick Willy's.

Slick Willy's was a biker bar that had started dipping their toes in the new wave waters, just a toe or two at a time. The club booker liked us, most likely because we were happy to play for almost nothing, and maybe because we had a girl singer. The drinking age in California was twenty-one, and they played things by the book, so the club insisted that Kendra and I stay backstage every minute we weren't onstage, and that we had to be personally escorted when we needed to use the bathroom so they wouldn't get in trouble with the cops.

But it was a real gig, and other real gigs followed, largely facilitated by Russ's girlfriend Connie, who also worked at the radio station and had taken on managing the band. Before long we were invited to play fourth bill on a Tuesday night at the Mabuhay Gardens in San Francisco. This was a very big deal to us—the 'Fab Mab' was up there with the Masque in

LA and CBGB's in New York as a pioneering American punk-rock club. We didn't mind that we had to drive Gavin's truck (to haul the gear) and my Gremlin (to haul the band) ninety miles to and from San Francisco to get paid $25 to play at 8pm to a smattering of people. This was the big time.

The club's booker, Dirk Dirksen, seemed to like us—we worked cheap, we were eager and bubbly and endearingly innocent—and started to give us regular gigs, including opening slots for established acts like Chrome and Nico. We didn't build much of a regular fan base, aside from a smartly dressed college student named John Silva who came to all our shows, had a crush on Kendra, and would later become my close friend and one of the most successful managers in the world.

My studies had become low on my list of priorities, and I found a way to do just what needed to be done to pass my classes. At the time, tuition for a state resident at a UC school was shockingly cheap. I think I paid about $1,000 a year for classes and maybe another $500 for books. My monthly rent was minimal, and we drank powdered milk and ate a whole lot of fried liver, grilled cheese sandwiches, and Kraft macaroni fortified by StarKist tuna to keep our grocery bills low.

My focus, instead, was on the band and songwriting, along with record-shopping excursions to Berkeley, my weekly radio show and working at Eucalyptus, where I had also managed to get jobs for Kendra and Russ. Most of our days at the store were spent selling Journey and Pablo Cruise records, along with metal screens for hash pipes, which ran three for 25 cents. What a nuisance! After a while, I just stopped ringing them up on the cash register and instead would pocket the quarter, since the low-cost item wasn't monitored by store inventory. The in-store music had to adhere to a strict playlist handed down by the central office, and it was rare that a record that I liked was a big enough seller to make the list, so I would play those few records over and over and over. Let's just say I don't need to hear *Get The Knack*, *Candy-O* by The Cars, or Nick Lowe's *Labor Of Lust* ever again.

At the same time, I had pushed my way into a job as program director at the station, which meant I scheduled the DJ slots. Tom was the music director, choosing the records that would be added to the rotation. Our putsch of turning KDVS into a station playing the 'modern music' we loved was now complete. Russ, Tom, Kendra, and I all had prime-time shows and a far-reaching fifty-thousand-watt signal to spread our gospel. We were courted by record companies who kept us supplied with free records and occasional tickets to shows in the Bay Area.

And those shows! The anticipation that simmered on that now-familiar drive to San Francisco made the shows even more exciting, and the giddy recap of the show on the way back committed what we had seen firmly to memory. One show that stands out above all others was The Clash at the Fox Warfield on Market Street, just a few months before *London Calling* came out. The confidence, swagger, playfulness, sense of purpose, and majesty, mythological and at the same time approachable, and the ear-shattering volume dug deep inside my soul. It remains one of the best concerts I've ever seen.

Besides perks like free records and guest-list spots, we also had a phone at the station that allowed us a free and open line to call anywhere in the world on the university dime. One day, Tom, our friend Peter, and I decided to call directory assistance in London to see if any of the musicians in our favorite bands might have listed phone numbers. We made our way through several bands with no luck until we started naming members of XTC, whose first two albums were staples of our playlists. Success! Bass player Colin Moulding's phone number was listed. We called the number, and it turned out the band was on tour, but his wife was glad to talk to us and give us a long-distance connection to a scene we could only imagine. We called her often, and she would always say, 'Oh, it's the boys from the radio.'

Suspects was a good apprenticeship and taught us some of the skills we would need and use in the years ahead. We were never a band that would set the world on fire, but we were good ambassadors for the music we loved, and we managed to get better and more confident over time. We finally reached the local pinnacle of playing the Coffee House, where we had all seen shows that had changed our lives. The first gig we got there was as part of a local new wave showcase that also featured The Twinkeyz, who have in the years since built a strong cult following for their lysergic, gauzy recordings. They were great and like nothing I had ever heard before. And the other time was opening for The Specials, which pretty much felt like the biggest gig we would ever play in our lives. They talked to us, hung out with us, and, most of all, seemed to acknowledge us as peers.

Much like the classes I was taking, anything that wasn't music was of secondary concern. I didn't watch TV, I avoided movie theaters, and I looked down on anything that smacked of mainstream entertainment (I've still never seen *Star Wars*, which, of course, was all the rage at the time). And while I dated a little and had a few girlfriends at the time, it was still far less important to me than making sure I had the new Buzzcocks single with a non-LP B-side. One girl I went out with for a short time dumped me on the same day that I had heard the import copies of *London Calling* would be arriving at Rather Ripped. I licked my wounds, made the three-hour round trip to buy the record, and sat in my dark bedroom playing the album from start to finish in absolute rapture. By the time I reached the end of 'Train In Vain,' I had completely forgotten about the girlfriend.

The longest-term relationship I had was with a woman named Carolyn. She later inspired one of my more well-known solo songs. We broke up amicably in my junior year, and she started dating a local kid named Scott Miller. He and I got along right away, especially as he was a fan of my band and my radio show. He also played guitar and wrote songs and did a bit of home recording. He played me a tape of a few of his songs and I was blown away. Not only were the songs complex, artfully written, catchy, and already fully formed and executed, but they were also a dead ringer for Big Star, a band that was almost completely unknown at the time—and, thanks to Tom, had been placed on my radar and had become my favorite band.

'Ah, I see you like Alex Chilton as well,' I said to Scott, and he said, 'Who's that?' I was shocked. The musical and especially vocal similarities were so pronounced. Within a few days, I went to the cutout bin at the campus store and bought him a copy of the import double-album set of Big Star's first two albums, which ended up being a big influence on his records with Game Theory and The Loud Family—two bands that, in turn, became seminally influential groups of their own.

There was another local musician about three years our junior who came to all our shows. He had hair down to his waist, played guitar as well or better than me or Russ and he became our roadie, a luxurious thing for a band like us to have. We even did our one overnight road trip for a gig in his original hometown of Ridgecrest and stayed with his family and friends. His name was Guy Kyser, and he would end up forming Thin White Rope, a band that would become part of the extended American underground rock family in the following decade.

At the same time, I was starting to feel a bit claustrophobic, living in a small town and being part of such a small scene. The novelty was wearing off, and I was hungry for more. I started thinking about moving back to LA and transferring to UCLA. But things were going well enough for the band that we all agreed to give it just a little longer to see what would happen. We went to a studio in San Francisco and made a single with two of my compositions, 'Talking Loud' and 'It's Up To You.' We sent it out to every college radio station that was in the KDVS directory, tried to hustle it into stores on consignment, and kept playing gigs. Outside of a few stations that took up the cause and a few curious customers who took a chance on buying the single, most of the records remained unsold and unplayed. We were still playing early on weeknights at the Mab, I was still hiding backstage at Slick Willy's until our forty-five minutes on stage, and I was still wearing deep grooves in the stretch of I-80 between Davis and my favorite record stores in Berkeley.

It was June 1980. I had lived for three years in the only city besides LA or New York City that I would ever call home. I had learned a whole new style of music and expanded the knowledge and language of music that would shape my tastes and writing and playing for the rest of my life. I had made friends that would remain in my life and my musical sphere for years to come. But I was done with the small-town life. It was time to go home.

My father was living on Sunset Boulevard, just a few blocks from UCLA, where I would be starting school in the fall. The house had a musty basement apartment with a shower, sink, tiny kitchenette, and independent access via a gate on the side. Most importantly, my father agreed to let me live there for free while I was going to school. There was room in the driveway to park my white Honda Civic (the Gremlin had finally given up the ghost), and I could walk to and from my classes in under a half-hour. I had free rent and inexpensive tuition, and I was no longer distracted by being in a band or my duties at the radio station. I switched my major from rhetoric to English literature, and it seemed that I was back on the course to dive into my studies and get my degree in the next year or two.

But I still needed a job, if for nothing else than to keep buying new records, which remained a high priority. Naturally, I gravitated toward another record store job—something for which I was qualified, and which would also get me significant discounts to feed my vinyl fix. I knew about and had shopped at a store just over the hill in Sherman Oaks called Moby Disc, which was far hipper than the chain store where I had worked in Davis. In the same way as I had gone for a full-force blitz to get the sportswriting gig in Davis three years earlier, I went to the store armed with clippings of my record reviews, recommendations from Eucalyptus Records, lists of my fifty favorite records, and even the Suspects single. Bryan, the store manager, was just about a year older than me and seemed visibly bemused by all my effort just to get a minimum wage job. He hired me on the spot. I had just made my first tiny step into the far bigger, more daunting LA music scene.

Working at Moby was a dream. I could play any music I wanted in the store, and we carried all the brand new imports and independent releases. If not as cool as my favorite Berkeley stores, it was an environment much more in sync with my tastes and passions than the very mainstream Eucalyptus had been. One similarity remained, however. We sold a lot of drug paraphernalia. Not only bongs and pipes and screens but also cocaine gear. We had scales and vials with little spoons, as well as some kind of compound that would help you cut your coke, reducing its potency and density. All of these items, even if not advertised for their intended use, were completely one hundred percent legal to sell and own.

One of our more regular customers was Sherman Hemsley, who played George Jefferson on *The Jeffersons*. But the Sherm who would amble up to the counter could not have been more different from his TV alias. He would talk slowly in a low, gravelly voice, had red eyes, and would come to Moby Disc for both paraphernalia and prog-rock records. Let me tell you, it was a shock the first time I had George Jefferson walk up to me and croak out, 'Hey, you got that new Keith Emerson record? I think someone put it on hold for me with the new PFM and Gong records behind the counter. Oh, and I'll get a couple of those vials over there by the register.'

Another customer was Sal Valentino of The Beau Brummels. Sal had apparently been instrumental in helping Warner Bros sign Rickie Lee Jones, who was high on the charts at the time. As he wasn't a salaried worker, Warners would reward him for his efforts by loading him up with multiple promo copies of whatever their biggest hits were at the time, which he would trade for cash at a store like ours. Every so often, one of my coworkers would say, 'Hey, can someone open the back door? Sal's there with a hundred copies of the new Doobie Brothers album.' It was good for us, good for Sal, and I don't think Michael McDonald was any the wiser.

I no longer had my radio show or my band, and I missed both. I played guitar regularly in the basement, jamming along with free jazz records like Albert Ayler's *Love Cry* and John Coltrane's *Ascension*, both of which were unstructured enough to allow me to find my own way to learn to play the best and most interesting version of 'anything I wanted.' Along with attempting to learn every lick and solo on 'Marquee Moon,' I developed an approach to lead guitar that suited and excited me more than replicating blues licks and scales. If everything was right and nothing was wrong, then my version of what was right was whatever pleased me the most, whatever connected to me emotionally. It worked for me, and it still does.

When I was at KDVS, I learned to work the quarter-inch reel-to-reel broadcast-quality tape recorder they had in the station's production studio, and I would occasionally record bands that came through as well as demos of my own songs. Once I was in LA, I no longer had access to this kind of college-funded studio, so I saved up to get a Teac 3340 four-track reel-to-reel recorder at a discount store in Downtown LA. This was my first experience with sound-on-sound recording, and I was entranced. I began regularly recording my own songs and weird takes on covers like 'Faith In Something Bigger' by The Who, 'Here I Am (Come And Take Me)' by Al Green, and 'Somebody's Watching You' by the Sly Stone protégée Little Sister. Weird stuff to be covering, but songs that somehow fit into my curiosity in learning how to work and master my new toy. A new piece of recording gear will usually result in a bunch of new songs. Rather than study a manual, I just dive in and the trial-and-error leads to a period of inspiration.

There was a venue not far from my father's house called Club 88, a fixture on the punk and power pop circuit, and every Sunday they had an event that was a mixture of open mic and battle of the bands. The club placed cans at the front door, each labeled for a member of a band—singer, guitarist, bass player, keyboardist, drummer. You paid a dollar to put your name in the can that represented the instrument you'd want to play in a band that would be randomly drawn from the slips of paper later in the evening, at which point you'd have ten minutes to huddle with your new bandmates for the evening, come up with a name, and choose the song you would play. The winner at the end of the night would get all the money that had been paid for the slips of paper. I went often, and I seem to remember that 'She's About A Mover' by The Sir Douglas Quintet was usually the song that I'd suggest. I don't think I ever was in a winning band.

Eager for more chances to play music with other people, I would scan the pages of the local buy-and-sell weekly, the *Recycler*, to see if there were any bands that I might want to try to join. The only time I called a number and went to an audition was for a band called Jane & The Cage, whose ad spoke to me for some reason. Jane answered the call in a low, smoky voice and told me to come and check out their set at the Hong Kong Cafe downtown, to see if I'd want to audition.

I went to the show and the band wasn't great, but Jane was stunning. She was about six-foot-four with platinum blonde hair and bangs and cut a very Nico-esque figure. As I found out when I spoke to her after the show, she was also a transsexual and a professional dominatrix, which only made me more intrigued to audition. I met up with the band a few days later and got the gig. After a month or two of rehearsals and one performance on the influential TV show *New Wave Theater* (good luck finding a tape of the performance!), I realized I wasn't digging the music and told Jane that sadly I would be quitting.

'Oh, that's a shame,' she said. 'I was going to offer you the job of watching my sessions behind a one-way mirror to call the cops or step in if I ever had an unruly customer.' I hated to miss out on that gig, but my mind was made up.

Even with the record store job and my brief forays into the local music scene, as well as practicing guitar and home recording, my focus remained on my studies for the first few quarters at UCLA. As it turned out, Kendra had also transferred to UCLA. Being the more social of the two of us, I managed to make friends that were part of her 'north campus' scene—an area of the school that was mostly focused on creative types. This was a nice way of keeping in touch with musicians and artists and actors and making some interesting new friends. It also gave me companions for nightclubbing in a new, unfamiliar scene. Before going to Davis, my concert-attending experience in Los Angeles was mostly limited to arenas and theaters. I had entirely missed the entire first wave of punk rock in LA, never once setting foot in the Masque, LA's pioneering punk venue, for example. That scene, the bands, and the clubs were far from my radar. But with the help of Kendra and another north campus friend who went by the name Ella Black, and who led a no wave-cum-funk combo called Ella & The Blacks, I started going to gigs and DJ events at the hipper clubs in LA. I was still under twenty-one and still drank no more than the occasional beer, so my navigation of the scene was limited to all-ages shows or clubs whose doormen would look the other way and wave me in when I said that I didn't have my ID with me. That barrier disappeared when I reached legal age six months after moving to LA.

I had an unrequited crush on Ella, and I really liked her band, so I would regularly go to her shows at a Hollywood basement venue called the Cathay De Grande, where her band played often. She helped me get to know the people who ran the club, including a genial gentleman named Dobbs, who a few years later started the bar and venue Raji's, where The Dream Syndicate recorded a live album. Despite not having any romantic interest in me, Ella enjoyed my company, my nerdy enthusiasm for underground music, and, most of all, that I would let her park her car at my father's house every day and walk with her to our classes at UCLA.

The Cathay had an event every Friday called The Veil, where they would play art rock, punk, goth, and a new style of music called 'New Romantic' that I didn't fully dig but that had become all the rage. Most of all, it was a place to socialize, people-watch, and hang out with Ella and Kendra, and I was there every week. I would also go to shows at the Roxy and Whisky A Go Go, but the Cathay was the place where I felt like I belonged.

One night, I asked Michael, the other owner of the club, if they ever needed someone to DJ.

'Sure,' he said. 'We need someone for our Blue Monday shows every week. We can't pay you anything, but you play records between sets from 9pm until 2am and can have free drinks.'

I enthusiastically took the gig, and before long I was behind the decks each Monday for the four-set evenings that would alternate weekly between The James Harman Band and Top Jimmy & The Rhythm Pigs.

You might guess that my studies were taking the same secondary status they had in Davis, and you'd be right. I was still shy and, despite it being my hometown, a little intimidated by the LA scene. But between the record store gig and the weekly DJ slot, I was starting to get to know people and feeling more and more a part of my reclaimed hometown. I finished the school year knowing that I was looking for something and still not quite knowing what it was. As much as I wanted to play in a band, I couldn't imagine anything more than returning to playing at the bottom of the bill on weeknights—something that was a little less appealing at that point than it had been a year earlier in Northern California.

As my first summer after returning home began, I got wind of a deal that Greyhound was offering with unlimited bus travel anywhere in the US for the whole summer for just two hundred bucks. I had a romantic fixation on the music history and imagined lifestyles in Memphis (mostly because of my continued obsession with Big Star), Nashville, and especially New York City. I bought the ticket, got time off from my job, and went to the bus station in Downtown LA with a small suitcase and a desire to see the country. What follows is a story that I've told many times, and which has, in a turn of events that would have shocked me in 1980, ended up in the biographies of both Alex Chilton and Big Star. This is my version.

1.11
ALEX AND ME (A STORY WITHIN THE STORY)

I discovered Big Star at the impressionable age of eighteen, midway through the three years I spent at UC Davis in California. I was there because it was one of the few schools in the University Of California system where I could declare a major in rhetoric. Yes, rhetoric. I don't know, I just figured there weren't many things I would end up doing in life that wouldn't be served by a mastery of that subject, essentially the art of bullshitting, mixing and matching words to maximum effect.

My studies, however, quickly became the least of my priorities. Most of my time was spent buying records, seeing shows, starting a new wave band, and, most of all, being a DJ at KDVS, where Tom Gracyk was like a guru to us all. Tom turned me on to the double vinyl reissue of the first two Big Star records that came out on a UK label called Line. Those records spoke to me the same way they spoke to an entire generation of budding indie-rockers, entranced by the pure pop construction, the yearning, heartbreaking lyrics, and the shimmering production. And the backstory didn't hurt: Alex Chilton, the teenage hitmaker with The Box Tops, following up with a band that, despite the love of critics nationwide, failed to make even the slightest ripple in the charts. It was the beautiful loser story—one that is particularly appealing to a disenfranchised, quietly rebellious, outsider kid, as so many of the band's few but fervent fans turned out to be. The band's name, much like calling their debut album *#1 Record*, smacked of cruel, self-imposed irony.

I played those records quite a bit in 1978, but they weren't life-changing for me. They were just good, well-crafted pop records, a comfort trigger to fans of pop architects like Badfinger or The Raspberries, or even The Beatles themselves. They were a way to champion something cool and unknown—to be in on something obscure while still not drifting too far from the records of our youth.

But then I heard *Third*, and everything changed. If the first two records were a below-the-radar secret society, this one was more like an archeological dig. It was a reissue that was never issued in the first place: a lost record that felt incomplete, allowing you to apply the finishing touches from deep within your own psyche. It felt like it crawled deep inside your head and threw a light on the deepest, darkest, most painful recesses and emotions that you thought nobody else ever felt. It felt like a record that was speaking to you and you alone. It was shattering. It became my salve, my hiding place, and it was a constant listen throughout 1979.

I moved back to LA the following year, shifting to UCLA and moving into my father's basement in Westwood, just a short walk from the campus. I had shifted to the more practical English Literature major by then, but once again, the idea of studying was not nearly as compelling as going to shows, being a DJ in a Hollywood nightclub, playing in various bands, and working in a record store. Those things were my finishing school, the post-grad work that I didn't know I was completing as the preparation from the job I have today.

The summer of 1981 was approaching, and I decided that the real education I needed was out there across the United States and that a cross-country journey on a Greyhound bus was the classroom that would provide that education. I had barely been outside of California, beyond a trip to Long Island with my mom and stepfather when I was nine, and another to Texas around the same time. Greyhound had an offer of a three-month unlimited pass for two hundred dollars. It was cheaper than a similar-length quarter of school, though not by much—state schools were a bargain in those days.

I knew I wanted to go to New York City. Washington DC was on the way, so I figured I'd spend a few days there as well. I had an ex-half-niece-in-law (the kind of familial hyphenate that's very common in my family) who had offered to put me up in Nashville. And, most of all, I had been thinking that I truly needed to go to Memphis and track down Alex Chilton, on a pilgrimage to the mystic, elusive, sweet sad messenger who had delivered his broken music to my very soul. It seemed essential. I needed to meet this guy. I had just read about and acquired a ten-inch single by a band called The Panther Burns. The review said that it was Alex's new band, although the record itself had no credits, merely a street address in Memphis. That was all I needed. I bought the summer-long bus ticket, and this rock'n'roll gumshoe was on his way.

Los Angeles to Memphis is a two-thousand-mile journey, and on the Greyhound you can make that journey in a little over two days if you keep moving. A few brief stops at various stations for a snack from Burger King and back on the road. I loved the ride. I sat in the back with the smokers, the restless kids, the grizzled geezers sneaking sips of Early Times out of a paper bag. I didn't smoke and barely drank but it felt like the place to be. I met a girl maybe a year younger than me somewhere along the highway in Arizona. We made out for about a hundred miles. She left, soon to be replaced by an older Mexican gentleman whose hand was crudely wrapped in blood-streaked gauze. He spoke no English, but through the limits of my high school Spanish, I learned he was trying to get back across the border near El Paso, to get medical attention without drawing attention to his illegal status. We shared some whiskey.

The time moved by just fine. This was before the days of the Walkman, let alone iPhones, so there would be no music. I had a book, conversation with other travelers, and hundreds of miles of scenery, and that was the perfect accompaniment for my trip. I arrived in Memphis around sunrise on my third day, ready for my pilgrimage to start. I had reserved a room at the West Memphis YMCA for seventy-five dollars a week, dropped my bag in my room, and went immediately to the address on the Panther Burns record. Sleep and a shower could wait. I was a man on a mission.

The taxi let me off at 706 Cox Street. I knocked on the door and was received by a pompadoured, mustachioed dandy who turned out to be Tav Falco, the lead singer of The Panther Burns, although both he and the band were unknown at the time outside of a handful of scenesters in Memphis.

'My name is Steve,' I said. 'I just came two thousand miles on a Greyhound bus to meet Alex Chilton. Do you know where I can find him?'

Thirty-seven years later, I cringe at my boldness. If somebody came to MY door with that kind of opening gambit, I'd be counting the seconds until I could find a way to politely shut the door and pray the intruder would never return—that is, if I opened the door at all. But Tav invited me in, offered me an iced tea (sweetened, of course—I was in the South now!), and said, 'Well, he hangs out in the same bar every night. We can go and meet him later.' Jackpot.

Tav was quite congenial, considering I had come to the address listed on the record of the band that turned out to be *his* project—a band in which Alex was a sideman, playing guitar and serving Tav's songs and vision. But feelings weren't hurt, egos weren't ruffled, and Tav, ever the Southern gentleman, offered to drive me to the bar later that evening. I was thrilled.

We walked into Zinnie's. It was empty. Country songs were playing on the jukebox. And the one person sitting at the far end of the bar was indeed the object of my cross-country search.

Alex Chilton greeted me with the bemused, wary, but also openly curious smile that I would see again at various times in the week and the years that followed. He seemed neither worried about nor particularly impressed by the lengths I had traveled to track him down. And I don't remember if he asked me to buy him a beer or a pack of cigarettes or if I just sensed that it would be a good idea, but I did indeed lay out a few of my tightly budgeted dollars to set him up. It would be the currency of our friendship, the underlying contract between us for the week to come.

We sat at that bar and talked for many hours. He was a good conversationalist, a good listener, open to this eager stranger about ten years his junior. He was enthusiastic about literature and philosophy, Wilhelm Reich in particular. I had never heard of Reich, but I later found out that he was a philosopher guru who particularly explored the boundaries of sexual musings—quite likely the key attraction to his writings for Alex, who also espoused on love and relationships. We talked as well about music, although mostly music made before I was born and before Alex's tenure in The Box Tops. But Alex's music? I learned quite quickly that his music, and especially Big Star, were topics non grata. At one point I made the eager puppy-dog mistake of asking him if Big Star was going to make another record.

'That's just what the world wants—another record by Big Star' was his cagey but also piercingly bitter response. I left it there.

Alex seemed to take a liking to me. Or maybe I was just someone to talk to in a bar. There's always that. Or it could have been the cigarettes and beer (the former seeming to be of more interest to him than the latter). Either way, he gave more of his time and attention than required, certainly more than I would likely give someone in later years in a similar circumstance, if truth be told. At the end of the evening, I hopped on a city bus back to the Y, and we made plans to meet again the next night.

I filled my days with the wide-eyed tourism that a music devotee would want on his first visit to the birthplace of rock'n'roll. Over the course of the week, I made it to Graceland and Sun Records and also tracked down a giant warehouse filled with knee-high piles of 45s that sold fifteen for a dollar. I climbed across piles of vinyl to come up with a few dozen rare and mysterious goodies.

The second night I was back at the bar and Alex was in the same spot at the end. He seemed happy to see me, and we picked up where our conversations had left off. At some point in the evening, word got around the bar that Jerry Lee Lewis had just been rushed to a nearby hospital and was quite likely near death. Bear in mind this is 1980 and that he lived for another four decades. But the threat seemed serious enough, and Alex said, 'Let's go buy some beer and sit outside the hospital. We need to pay our respects.'

We picked up a six-pack at a convenience store, sat on the sidewalk outside the hospital, and drained a beer each while we discussed the lofty merits of the Killer's records, antics, vocals, and piano playing. After an hour of such reverie, Alex said, 'You don't have to go back to your hotel. I live nearby and I can put you up.' I was very likely even more excited by the fact that I wouldn't have to get back on the bus than I was at the invitation to stay at the house of my hero, albeit maybe just slightly.

It turned out that the place that Alex was calling home at this point was his parents' house. It was a modest two-story home with a bedroom and living room downstairs and a couple more bedrooms upstairs. The first room I walked into was the dining room. LPs leaned against the wall, and I remember Neil Young's *Harvest* being at the front of the stack. I looked up and giddily spotted a gold record for The Box Tops' 'Cry Like A Baby' framed on the wall. Yes, I was a little stunned at the turn of events but also quite tired. He showed me my room, a small bedroom on the second floor, and we called it a night.

The next morning, I woke up and followed the scent of cooking downstairs to the kitchen and found Alex standing by the stove, stirring something in a saucepan.

'Hungry?' he asked. 'I'm making grits.'

Southern California was the extent of my exposure to Southern culture, so grits was something I'd never encountered. Turns out they're pretty bland and made tolerable mostly by the presence of butter and salt. But the fact that it was new, that it was exotic, and that it was being made by Alex made it my new favorite dish (I would go to great lengths when back home in LA to find stores that stocked grits so that I could cook them for my morning meal for months to follow.)

Alex was a great host. He didn't have to do any of that. I don't know if I thought about it very much at the time. It just seemed like something that somebody does when a stranger comes to town, just part of the way life unfolds. I know better now. Maybe it was the openness of the South; maybe it was a different time when conversation and new experiences and personalities were an end in themselves. Who knows? Maybe it was the beer and smokes. But he still did not appear to be tired of me and told me that The Panther Burns were going to play later that night in a small club not far from his favorite bar. I told him I'd be there.

The show couldn't have been less of an event. A small room, just off from a café and bar. I think there were about five other people there watching the band. Alex played drums the entire night, the echo and reverb from his primitive beat ricocheting from concrete wall to concrete wall. It was a mess—a beautiful mess, but a mess nonetheless. And I was a little surprised and more than a little disappointed that Alex never sang or touched a guitar. But he did seem to enjoy his role as the caveman timekeeper more than he had enjoyed talking about any of his music in the previous two days. It was good seeing Tav again, and I also met Ross Johnson, who replaced Alex on drums for a few songs here and there, sang a few others, and banged on a guitar at other times. We got along great— he had an unaffected, welcoming style that put me at ease, relieving me of the underlying need to be cool enough to be worthy of Alex's time. It turned out that Ross worked in the Memphis State University library just a few blocks from my hotel, so I told him I'd drop by and visit him the next morning on my way into town.

The next morning I was there at ten and we got along, talking about music and about Alex as well, Ross being generous with some background and perspective on Alex's reticence to talk about or revisit his past, all things that are obvious in hindsight—a beautiful loser in a failed band is romantic to a starry-eyed teenage music devotee, but a little less glamorous to the one who has to live out its minutes and hours and days. After chatting, I bade Ross farewell and caught the bus back to the Downtown Greyhound station, where I planned to get on a Mississippi riverboat tour. I was still a tourist in an exotic land, after all.

The boat ride was cheap, short, placid, and scenic. I was happy to find there was a bar on board, and a couple of beers made it easier for my mind to aimlessly drift into various Tom Sawyer reveries. By the time I got off the boat to head back to catch my bus, I was feeling lazy, slow, and spaced out, truly sliding into the speed and temperament of most of the people I had met in Memphis. But I was also a little bit off my guard when a guy approached me around the back of the bus station.

'Hey, you want to buy some weed?' he asked, grabbing my hand and placing a thinly rolled joint in my palm. 'Ten bucks,' he said.

'No thanks,' I said. I had neither the money nor the desire.

'Hey, man,' he angrily replied, 'you already took it. You owe me ten bucks.' Before I could reason my way out of a neatly laid trap, he pushed me against the wall and said, 'Give me your money.'

I had about seven dollars. I gave it to him. My afternoon high was squelched, and I felt the adrenaline rush and sense of violation that goes with such a sudden intrusion. He was gone and I was broke.

I wandered over to Tav's house, which was only a mile or two away, and told him the story, still shaken up and lacking even the bus fare to get back to my hotel.

'That's terrible,' Tav said. 'Let's go find him and get your money back.'

Yes, that's what he said and yes, against all reason, that's what we set out to do. Naturally, and luckily for us, we didn't find the guy, but Tav was all fire and brimstone and ready to do battle with my assailant. The confrontation never came, but I did get a ride back to the Y, where I was able to cash a few traveler's checks. I was back in the money and ready for another night in the bar with Alex. By that time, he had heard about my little mugging incident. He was sympathetic but also betrayed a bit of the feeling that it was all part of my education and that I should have been able to spot that outcome from a mile away. I felt the first pangs of having overstayed my welcome, but Alex was still welcoming, and I was still laying down the one-dollar bills for beers and smokes, as well as the occasional quarter in the jukebox.

After a night of Bud, cigarettes, and Tammy Wynette, Alex kindly offered a ride back to the hotel, but said he needed to stop by his pad first. No overnights, no grits, but he did offer me a beer—one of the leftovers from our Jerry Lee six-pack.

'Look,' Alex proudly stated, 'there are still four there! I didn't have any of them.' I'm not sure if he felt he had to prove something to me or to himself, but the point was made, and I wasn't surprised when I heard a few years later that he had given up drinking.

My week in Memphis was ending. I was starting to feel very much at home and was trying to decide whether to put down the money for another week at the YMCA or just move on down the road to Nashville, Washington DC, and New York City. I decided one more night at the bar would give me some kind of clue, sensing that my novelty as the new kid in town was, understandably, starting to wear off.

Alex was at his usual spot. I wandered over and sat in the seat next to him. He was as welcoming as usual, and he asked if I was having a beer which, I knew, was code for a request for me to buy a couple for us to drink. I had checked my remaining funds and estimated what I needed for my trip ahead, and I was a little alarmed that I was not hanging on to as much money as I had hoped to have for the coming weeks—especially in those days, before you could extract money from a wall with a mere piece of plastic and a few remembered numbers. I knew that my days as the deep-pockets barfly needed to come to an end.

'Alex,' I said, 'I hate to say it, but I really can't afford to keep buying you beers and cigarettes.'

'Well, you don't have to stay neither, do you?'

I knew it was time to go. The next morning, I was back on the Greyhound and moving down the road. I had time on the long drive to finally take in what had happened. One of the main reasons for my journey was to find the person who had created the music and words and sounds that had had such a profound and devastating effect on my malleable psyche. And find that person I did. But I also found a person who, despite his openness to strangers and experience and conversation, was bitter and disparaging about the very music that had put me on that bus in the first place. I couldn't understand how anybody who had conjured up such honest and beautiful and, to my ears, perfect music could also hold it in such low regard.

I would meet many musicians in the years to follow who felt let down by their dreams despite their good fortune in continuing to be able to make records and deliver their music from town to town. Heck, it had even happened to me for moments here and there, although my experience in Memphis in 1981 taught me to never become bitter about the thing I loved the most.

My own time of making records and touring was still a year away—a lifetime at that age. In my suitcase on that trip was a cassette of a song called 'That's What You Always Say,' which I had made before my trip on the Teac 3340 myself in the basement of my father's house. The words were unfinished, the vocal was just a stream of mumbled sounds, and the beat came from a tiny Boss Dr. Rhythm drum machine pattern, but the song was unmistakably the same one that I would end up recording on each of my first two records and which remains a regular part of my live show. I had thought I might play it for someone along the way, to what end I didn't know. During my time in Memphis, it never seemed right or appropriate. I didn't even mention it to Alex—if he didn't want to know about his own music, why would he care about mine? Now that I look back, I think he may have liked it. It wasn't *all* music that he had grown to dislike, merely his own. I couldn't make that distinction at the time.

The trip continued. I tried unsuccessfully to seek out traditional country & western bars in Nashville. 'Why would you want to hear that corny old music?' I was asked more than once. I burned my way through museums and observed sessions of the government in action in Washington D.C., even stopping by the Library Of Congress to see the card for the copyrights I had submitted a few months earlier for a handful of my songs. Seeing my name and songs on a card in a library in Washington D.C. was exciting. I felt like it legitimized my standing as a musician, even though, truth be told, anyone with a handful of dollars, a cassette tape, and some postage could have done the same.

A few days later, I ended up at Port Authority on 8th Avenue in New York City at 4am, beginning three weeks of concerts, museums, endless walks, slices of pizza, sleeping at the YMCA on West 34th Street, and the beginning of an intense love affair with the city that continued until I finally moved there in 1994 (and where I live today). I had also spent all but my last few dollars and had only that tiny bit of money and my bus ticket to get back to LA. It wasn't the greatest feat of budgeting, and I knew I would have to make the last three thousand miles with no breaks and almost no food or drinks. But I also knew that I'd be traveling via Memphis.

I wasn't about to intrude on Alex or Tav again, but I did have Ross Johnson's number. I called him up, and he said, 'Get off the bus when you get to Memphis. I'll pick you up, give you a home-cooked meal, and put you back on your way that night.' Yes, one meal in three thousand miles, aside from a few carefully doled-out Burger King cheeseburgers along the way. It was a very good meal.

And then I was home. That was the end of my search for America, adventure, and Alex Chilton. But my brushes with Alex Chilton didn't end there or in the summer of 1981.

Just two years later, I was on tour with The Dream Syndicate, a few months after the release of our first album. Things were going well. It was that heady time, that first rush of being some version of the Next Big Thing, and I'd come a long way since riding around on the Greyhound with a rough cassette of a new song in my pocket, harboring dreams that it might end up on a self-pressed 45 someday (which it did, just a few months after my Memphis trip, under the moniker of 15 Minutes—a project name reflecting my belief that it would be the last record I'd make before getting on with my life).

We were playing at a club called Tupelo's in New Orleans. The band and I pulled into the club in the late afternoon for soundcheck and began the night's ritual. Gear out of cases and placed onstage, afternoon beer consumed, shake out the cobwebs from the night before. As I got ready to step on the stage to get a guitar sound, our tour manager came up to me and said, 'I'm not sure, but I think that guy over there sweeping up the room might be Alex Chilton.' Sure enough, it was Alex, sweeping up remnants from the night before, tidying up a very untidy club.

I walked up to him.

'Alex. It's me. Steve. I met you a few years ago. I took a bus to Memphis and hung out with you for a week.'

He gave me that same wry smile but also had the look of someone who has no recollection of the person that he's talking to. Just a polite 'Oh, hi. How's it going,' and truly not much of an invitation or encouragement to take the conversation any further. At the time, I truly believed he had no memory of me whatsoever but, in retrospect, it's possible he just felt a little defensive and embarrassed about our roles at that very moment—the headliner ready for a hot show ahead and the guy who was making a few bucks sweeping up to make the club presentable for the night. Whatever the truth might be, it furthered my feeling that although I still liked his records immensely, I didn't hold him in the same hero status as before. That was not very sporting of me and maybe even a little harsh, but at twenty-three years old, I wasn't exactly swimming in perspective about such things.

I did avoid Alex when given the chance to talk to him in years to come. In fact, I learned to avoid meeting any heroes, something I still tend to do, unless I'm working with or touring with one of them. I certainly had chances to talk to him over the years. I saw him play live a few times in Hollywood. We were even labelmates on Big Time Records for a year or two and shared many friends in common.

I didn't encounter Alex again until years later, in 2007, when we played a festival together in Norway called Down On The Farm. He was there with a reunited Big Star—he had made his peace with his history at that point—and I was playing in a reunion tour with my old pal Dan Stuart under our old aliases of Danny & Dusty. It was the last date on our tour. The band was the same as the one who had recorded our second record a few months earlier—Bob Rupe and Stephen McCarthy from Gutterball, Chris Cacavas from Green On Red. My future wife, Linda Pitmon, was sitting in on drums on the tour for Johnny Hott. In other words, old friends and family together on the road. We were in a celebratory mood, if a little fried from the ravages of travel and late nights and long shows.

Dan knew Alex from the old days, and they chatted on the bus. I avoided him, lost in that weird place where shyness, aloofness, and avoidance all hang out together. But I was excited to see their set. It was fantastic, Alex and Big Star's original drummer, Jody Stephens, augmented by Ken Stringfellow and Jon Auer from The Posies. It was perfect, it was beautiful, and I believe I exchanged a 'nice set' and a 'thank you' with Alex in the break after they finished and before we played. That was good enough for me. We had a good set, and then The Flaming Lips played after we finished, ringing in the midnight hour in a psychedelic haze that shifted to a very real rainstorm, shortly after I had watched Robyn Hitchcock and John Paul Jones jam with Chip Taylor, the writer of 'Wild Thing' and 'Angel Of The Morning.' They played deep in the Norwegian woods by a campfire until 3am. Truly the mixing and matching and unexpected pleasures of a festival—one of the reasons I still love playing them.

The next day we were understandably exhausted. Linda and I dragged ourselves to the airport to catch a plane to Italy and start another series of shows in Reggio Emilia. As we were walking toward our gate, we heard a Southern drawl very out of place in the Oslo airport say, 'I think you all are at the wrong airport.' It was Alex. He seemed very happy to see us, and we started chatting—about the festival, our respective sets, where we'd been, and where we were going. And he asked us both the same thing he asked me when we first met that first night at the bar in 1981: 'What's your sign?' Anyone who has ever known Alex can hear his voice asking that very question. We told him. And then he asked, 'What year were you born?' We answered. He hesitated for a minute, laughed, and then shook his head. 'You guys aren't supposed to be together.' So much for words of wisdom from my hero.

Alex said he was on his way to Paris for a six-week vacation at a friend's house. He showed us his boarding pass and said, 'Do you know where this gate is?' Linda looked and said, 'You're headed in the right direction, but you better hurry—your plane leaves in four minutes.' He smiled and walked off slowly and lazily, bringing his Southern pace to a Scandinavian airport. I don't know if he made his flight, but I hope that the plane was late taking off, for his sake.

My encounters with Alex ended just a few years later. Big Star were booked to play a show at the Masonic Lodge in Brooklyn. For whatever reason, Linda and I didn't even know about it, but Ken Stringfellow, who had become a pal in the years that followed our first encounter in Norway, had invited us to the show. I think there was a moment of hesitation about going, unfathomable to my twenty-one-year-old, Greyhound-riding younger self. And we did indeed realize that we would be fools, near heretics, to not get on the 2 train from the Upper West Side to Brooklyn. And what a show. There were about seven hundred people, the room was packed, the band was fantastic, and Alex seemed to be having fun and at peace with his 'failed band' (things had changed) and his legend.

We were invited backstage by Ken after the show, and this time Alex remembered and was happy to see me. We found a quiet spot and settled into a leather booth in the backstage area and talked for about an hour, catching up on life on the road, music, politics, and more, and yet still not once mentioning our first encounter back in 1981. It just seemed best to let that one lie.

I told Alex that I was planning on visiting New Orleans a few months later. He wrote down his phone number and asked me to call him when we came to town. I was touched and felt like the story had come to some kind of peace and closure I didn't even know that I needed.

Alex died suddenly from a heart attack a few months later at the age of fifty-nine. He was getting ready to go to Austin for a Big Star show at a South By Southwest showcase where he would be received as a hero and legend of the indie movement, a far cry from the bitter and invisible days when the band existed the first time around. It was just a few weeks before our New Orleans trip. I still had his number in my wallet, though I can't find that slip of paper today. Sometimes the memories are better than the artifacts themselves.

PART TWO
THE WORD FROM OUTSIDE

2.1
THE BIRTH OF THE DREAM SYNDICATE

My cross-country adventure was done, and despite feeling just a tiny bit more worldly now than when I stepped onto that Greyhound bus in Downtown LA two months earlier, I returned to life exactly as I had left it—my father's basement, my record store job, and the beginning of a fifth year of college looming ahead. I really had no idea what the future might hold, but I was certain that my days of playing in a band wouldn't have a very big role in it. I still enjoyed messing around with the tape machine, writing songs, and playing my black Les Paul in the basement through my tiny Fender Champ amplifier, for my own amusement and nothing more.

Let's talk about guitars. After my childhood Telecaster was stolen in the summer of 1978, I went rapidly from one replacement to another. At the time, electric guitars weren't the high-value collector's items they are now, and I could go to a used guitar store and trade whatever I had at the time, throw in an extra hundred dollars, and get something a little better than what I had before. It was a transaction I repeated regularly over the next few years, and I never owned more than two electric guitars at one time until many years later.

During my time at Davis, one of the few other bands playing 'the new music' was Mumbles, led by a slightly older guy (he might have been in his early twenties!) named Richard McGrath who was easily the best guitarist in our scene. He would later form True West with my Suspects bandmates Russ and Gavin. Richard played one of those clear Dan Armstrong guitars, and I would stand in awe as he channeled Tom Verlaine and Keith Richards with seemingly little effort. One day he told me he was selling the guitar and wanted to know if I was interested. I jumped at the chance. Finally, I could sound like Richard!

What I didn't realize was that Richard sounded like Richard because he was Richard. It's the singer, not the song—or, more accurately, the axeman, not the axe. That's one of the most beautiful things about guitars—the same two players can play the same series of chords in the same way on the same guitar through the same amp, and each will have their own sound and feel.

Upon moving back to LA, I found a tiny guitar shop on Fairfax and Wilshire, just across the street from the May Company store where I had bought my first records. The store was called Norm's Rare Guitars, and over time it became one of the more well-known used guitar shops in the country, partially due to supplying and being credited for the guitars that Nigel Tufnel proudly displays in *This Is Spinal Tap*. They always had great items that rarely went for more than three hundred bucks, all of which would be worth at least ten times that amount today. Over the course of my first years in LA, my red Fender Mustang and clear Dan Electro became a black Les Paul and the 1964 sunburst Jazzmaster I played in the first year of The Dream Syndicate. By 1984, I had bought and sold two Jazzmasters, a Fender Jaguar, the Les Paul, an Epiphone Riviera, and a black Telecaster, never paying more than a hundred dollars plus the trade-in value of the guitar I was ditching. One of the few regrets in my life is that I didn't keep all of those guitars.

Despite the occasional dalliance with other manufacturers, I have always preferred Fender electric guitars. By rough count, I've owned about twenty over the years. Maybe it's because of the Telecaster I got when I was a pre-teen. Maybe it's the thin neck, easy to whip around, or the seemingly indestructible body—I've tested this latter attribute many times over the years. But most likely, it's the sound. Fenders, especially Telecasters, slash and rip, like a switchblade or an icepick, as Telecaster devotee Albert Collins once described his sound. If Gibson guitars roar and ooze and bludgeon, Fenders are more likely to weave and bob, jab and retreat. It's the difference between, say, Sonny Liston and Muhammad Ali.

The cassette of my home recording of 'That's What You Always Say' had traveled the country with me, but my dreams of 'playing it for the right person' hadn't gone beyond Ross Johnson hearing and liking it when I was in Memphis. I thought it was a cool recording—a primitive but nicely overdubbed mix of my Boss Dr. Rhythm drum machine, my rudimentary bass playing, and my guitars and vocals both processed heavily through an Electric Mistress chorus pedal. The bass guitar was a white Fender Musicmaster that Kendra had bought in Davis when she played in a band called The Icons. I borrowed it from her for my recordings and ended up using it to create many of the new songs I had started writing since moving into my father's basement.

But what to do with all these new songs, recordings, and other basement experimentations? My brief time playing with Jane & The Cage hadn't been much fun, and I wasn't in any hurry to hunt down any more strangers for rock'n'roll blind dates. It just seemed disheartening and even a bit pointless. All I really wanted was to find a way to release 'That's What You Always Say,' so I decided that I would put it out as a single myself, allowing me to forever look back and say, 'Well, at least I made one record that I liked,' and maybe show it to my grandkids someday.

I had recorded another song in Davis with Scott Miller and his band Alternate Learning (which also featured my previous and his current girlfriend, Carolyn). 'Last Chance For You' seemed like a good B-side. I decided to call the record and project 15 Minutes, since it felt like it would be my personal fifteen minutes of (non) fame. I found out about a pressing plant in Santa Monica called Rainbo Records, and I placed an order for two hundred singles. Lord knows what I thought I would do with them, but that was the smallest run that they offered.

Around the same time, I had gotten to know two sisters named Kristi and Kelly Callan who would often shop at the record store. They told me they had been writing songs and playing together and asked if I would listen to the tape that they had recorded. I took it home and was blown away, mostly because they reminded me of The Shaggs, whose *Philosophy Of The World* had been in steady rotation on my turntable since Rounder Records had reissued it a few months earlier. The Shaggs had a primitive way of writing songs and playing that felt equally amateurish, broken, and at the same time completely fully formed in the lexicon of their own way of hearing music. The Callan sisters had that same quality. Songs would change speeds, keys, and moods on a dime, in a way that simultaneously made no sense and all the sense in the world.

I said, 'I love your tape and I'd love to play in a band with you.' I also told them that they reminded me of The Shaggs. They didn't bother to follow up by listening to the band to whom I'd compared them for another few months, but when they finally did, they were angry. 'We don't sound anything like them! They're terrible.'

We'd get together in the basement and play some of their songs and some of mine, and I would record them all on the Teac. We called ourselves Goat Deity. We didn't think much beyond just playing together for fun—our one and only gig was in their mother's living room for family and friends. I don't remember ever talking about trying to go out and play live shows.

After a while, we decided that having a bass player might round out the sound of what we were doing. Our ad in the *Recycler* may have mentioned The Shaggs—I can't remember. But the description of what we were doing was enough to draw the attention of a guy named Karl Precoda, who came by the basement one evening to play bass with us. He was friendly, nervous, and impossibly skinny, and he had a cool rock haircut, equal parts 60s mod and 70s Stones. He said he had been playing in Hollywood with the performance artist Johanna Went, and the fact that he had been playing actual Hollywood clubs put him about two steps ahead of anything we had been doing. The rehearsal went well, and

I walked him to his car at the end to see if he'd like to come back and join us again sometime.

'Wow, they're awful,' he said. 'But I really like your songs. We should play together on our own. I'll bring my guitar next time.'

Over the next few weeks, we were together all the time. We jammed in the basement, sometimes playing 'That's What You Always Say,' sometimes a cover like 'Suzie Q,' but mostly just grooving on an E or D chord for hours on end. There was a chemistry and kinship in our playing from the very start, and we both had equal patience for hypnotic, droning, distorted music that didn't really bother to go anywhere. It's as if we mutually freed each other up to not expect music to be any more than just a mood and a sound and a psychedelic place of being. 'Where are the songs?' and 'What's the arrangement?' or 'What are we trying to do?' were not in our lexicon. Jamming, talking about records, and then usually a drive down the road to Arlene's Donut Shop for chili fries and an apple fritter was good enough for the two of us.

Around the same time, I learned about an opening at the Rhino Records store on Westwood Boulevard, much closer to my dad's house and far cooler than Moby Disc. I applied and got the job, which at that time felt like the greatest thing that had ever happened to me, like getting invited to play with The Rolling Stones or something. This was the big time. There was a certain fame that came with working at a store like that. I started getting recognized at shows, and I felt like a local star in my own right.

My studies continued, but with less enthusiasm, as I got more excited about working at Rhino, playing with Karl, and continuing to DJ at the Cathay De Grande. The one class that did happen to particularly enthrall me was called 'Death And Dying,' a study of death and literature. I chose to write my term paper on Gary Gilmore, with a particular focus on Norman Mailer's *The Executioner's Song* and Gary's brother Mikal's articles in *Rolling Stone* about their interactions and his attempts to halt Gary's execution. Morbid stuff, and I was pretty wrapped up in learning as much as I could to serve both my curiosity and the grade on the final paper.

Imagine my surprise when, upon my first day at Rhino, I was getting my schedule and lowdown from the store's boss and saw that the employee list included the name Mikal Gilmore.

'Is that THE Mikal Gilmore?' I asked the boss.

'Yes,' he quickly responded, 'and we don't talk about that here.' Not wanting to rock the boat on my new job, I kept my mouth shut. I got to know Mikal as we shelved records together by day while writing about him at night once I got home, the two activities never overlapping. I believe I got a B+ on the paper, though I'm sure with a few choice quotes from the source of my studies that grade may have been a notch or two higher.

Much like when I was working at the radio station three years earlier, I was getting a more comprehensive education in the things that would aid and abet my future vocation by working at Rhino than in any college class I could have taken. The employees at the store were a notoriously caustic, cocky, and cranky bunch who each had their own area of expertise. There was John, the boss, who knew everything about reggae and had an inside line on getting the rarest of white-label twelve-inch singles directly from Jamaica. There was Sam, who was the expert in folk music. Richard Grossman not only knew all there was to know about jazz but was also a pianist who had made several well-regarded records of his own. There was Jon who went by the nickname of Otis, greased his black pompadour with Tres Flores, and made sure we were stocked with the best blues and rockabilly records. I liked and admired him greatly, and when he turned me on to the joys of drinking bourbon whiskey, I took to it like a diving duck.

My usual workmate behind the counter during the day shift was Nels Cline, a guitarist who had also made highly regarded records, including some with Anthony Braxton. This made Nels the most famous and accomplished and respected musician I had ever met. Nels didn't listen to much rock music, just the occasional Stones record and *Marquee Moon* and Tom Verlaine's solo albums, which must have connected to him because of Television's ability to soar like a great jazz improviser. A few decades later, of course, Nels would be one of the top rock guitarists in the world with

Wilco. I'd like to think that some of the rock records I was playing in the store when we worked together had some minor impact on his foray into the non-jazz world.

I had the dream job of ordering and stocking our indie and import rock records. While I was learning about jazz and blues and reggae from my colleagues, I was also dutifully scanning the pages of *NME*, *Melody Maker*, *New York Rocker*, *Maximum Rocknroll*, *Flipside*, and any other fanzine to come through the store. I wanted to know about every record that was coming out—even the ones I didn't particularly like—so I knew what to order. My biweekly conversations with local importers and distributors were approached with the same fervor that a guy at the track might place on reading the racing form. Nothing gave me more feelings of pleasure and accomplishment than going out on a limb to order twenty-five copies of the twelve-inch of 'Poison Arrow' by ABC and watching them fly out the door in a matter of days.

Bands would come in and ask if we would take their seven-inch singles and self-pressed albums on consignment, and I would not only say 'yes' but make sure to listen to every one of them. Neither of us remembers the encounter, but my friend and bandmate Peter Buck and I are both pretty sure that I would have been the guy behind the counter when he came out to LA and brought in five copies of the first R.E.M. single for us to try to sell for them. I'm sure it went on the front rack, not far from the prime spot where I had placed my own 15 Minutes single, which I would try to foist on customers who came into the store and purchased anything that seemed to fit alongside my homemade record.

Karl and I continued to get together, and at some point I told Kendra, 'You oughta come play with us sometime. I mean, your bass is already living full-time at my place.' She started joining our jam sessions, and she was a perfect fit, equally desirous of long, formless, trippy explorations and happy to lay down a sultry groove that would repeat over and over. The three of us started hanging out all the time. Once, after a Fleshtones show, we were invited to one of their infamous 'Blue Whale' parties (named for the cocktail they would make in large quantities in a garbage can liner) back at the notorious Tropicana Motel in West Hollywood. We hung out until dawn, drinking and having fun with actual record-making, touring musicians, and being accepted as part of the gang (again, being the kid at Rhino may have opened some doors). We drove back as the sun was coming up, and for the first time, we said, 'That kind of life sure looks like fun. Let's do it!'

This is where things start happening very quickly. I started writing songs to fit the music we were making—songs that would have a series of chords that would repeat over and over and build hypnotic circular effects. 'Some Kinda Itch' was one of the first, along with 'When You Smile,' a song I had written when trying to approximate the B-side of a Soft Boys single called 'Strange' that I really liked at the time. Karl came up with one of his own called 'Sure Thing,' which, like the two other songs he ended up contributing to The Dream Syndicate, felt like a perfectly formed distillation of the things I was trying to do with my own songwriting at that particular moment. He found the center while I was testing the fringes.

I met a guy at the store named Randy who said he was a drummer. We needed a drummer, so that was good enough for us. Randy started playing with us. He was as amateurish as we were, but, unfortunately for him, drums are the one instrument where you want a steady hand. There are plenty of bands who can make magic with limited musicianship as long as they have a drummer who has the groove, the swagger, the propulsion. Randy didn't have any of those, but he was a nice guy, and we enjoyed his company.

One day, after Randy left a rehearsal, Kendra said, 'I know the drummer of Human Hands. His name is Dennis. I saw him at a party and told him what we were doing, and he seemed very interested. Should we give him a call and invite him to play with us?'

Should we give him a call and invite him to play with us? Are you kidding? The Human Hands were a known band. I had seen them open for The Feelies at the Whisky a few months earlier. They had a record out (that we sold at the store) on an actual record label, Faulty Products. They were part of a scene in Pasadena that also included Wall Of Voodoo and BPeople, and they were peripherally connected to 45 Grave, who I really loved. All those bands were on the *Darker Skratcher* compilation album, which I owned and played incessantly.

Should we give him a call? Sure, why not, but why on earth would he want to play with our band? It's not that we didn't have confidence or believe that what we were doing was good. On the contrary, we thought we were making the greatest music ever known to man, but we were equally confident that it was a music that nobody else in the world would like. Nothing in LA's musically segmented scene of punk, power pop, art rock, ska, and rockabilly seemed to have a place for our music, which drew upon garage rock, 60s music, psychedelia, and repetitive drones—all things that seemed very much out of favor. But we called him, and he said he could come out on December 27, 1981.

To quote the start of many a bad novel, it was a dark and stormy night. Dennis drove the full hour from Pasadena to my dad's place and loaded in his drums. We were a bit nervous and still pretty blown away, but being the cocky kids that we were, we decided just to do our thing. We played hour-long versions of 'Susie Q' and 'That's What You Always Say' and maybe a few of our other originals. None of us said much—we just jammed. Dennis recorded the whole thing on cassette on his boom box, before at some point quietly saying, 'Okay, I guess I'll go home now.' I helped him pack up, and after he drove off, we were all laughing: 'Well, I bet he's regretting that he drove two hours in the rain for *that.*'

Out of politeness, I called Dennis a few days later to thank him for coming out and playing with us and asked if he had happened to listen to the cassette he made of the rehearsal.

'I've listened to nothing but that cassette in the last few days,' he said. 'It's the best thing I've heard in a long time. I'd love to play more with you guys.'

We had a band.

———

NAVIGATING THE POST-PUNK WILDERNESS

To fully understand what happened in 1982, it might help to know a little more about the musical landscape in 1981.

The fervor and constant surprise of the earliest punk rock days had calcified and subsided. Some bands, like the Sex Pistols, The Jam, Buzzcocks, and Television, had either broken up or were on their last legs. Others, like The Clash, Ramones, and Talking Heads, had evolved out of their edgier beginnings into exploration and solidification that would make them as much a cornerstone of the rock music scene as bands like the Stones and The Who. Their releases varied in quality and reception, but they could never replicate the boldness and surprise of their opening salvos.

Punk Rock Mk I was dead and was replaced by a more macho and sometimes worryingly racist version that repelled rather than appealed to me. The underground had fractured into subsets of rigidly regimented scenes like power pop, ska, rockabilly, goth, and New Romantic, each with their own specific fashions, rulebooks, scenes, and fans and a comfort in not blending into what anyone else was doing. If you were part of those worlds, you played by the rules, didn't ruffle feathers, and were rewarded with a specific and marketable fan base.

I had been more excited about bands that blurred the lines and had audacity and ambition and the desire to evolve and surprise. What's more, these new bands were incredibly manicured and avoided unruly, confusing, rough edges that would endanger their placement in their scene. Guitars—those messy and sprawling messengers of confusion and rebellion—were tamed by pedals and processing and a gradual lowering or elimination in the mix of records that were being made in the new decade.

I was able to find some bands that spoke to me and that aspired to more than just belonging to a scene and getting signed. I was intrigued by the music coming from Hoboken, New Jersey, and a club that loomed large in my imagination called Maxwell's. So many of my favorite bands—The dB's, The Bongos, The Feelies—were regulars there, and I dreamed that someday I could be as well. Over in the UK, Echo & The Bunnymen, The Teardrop Explodes, Joy Division, and the bands that recorded for the Scotland-based Postcard label, like Orange Juice and Aztec Camera, excited me as well and pointed to a way forward. But my favorite band of all was a band from Manchester called The Fall. Their music was so ramshackle and broken, so amateurish, and at the same time moved and grooved irresistibly. The singer, Mark E. Smith, had more in common with the raps on the Sugarhill Records twelve-inches than any pop records. I listened to their early classics *Dragnet* and *Grotesque*, the *Slates* EP, and the singles that came out in that period more than any other band at the time.

One thing that all those bands shared was a debt to The Velvet Underground.

I knew Lou Reed's music a little bit growing up from 'Walk On The Wild Side' and the *Rock 'n' Roll Animal* album, both of which got some play on the radio. But I never knew or heard about The Velvet Underground until 1979 in Davis, when I showed up to our bass player Steve Suchil's garage ahead of the rest of the band and he said, 'I want to play you a record that I think you're going to like.' He held in his hand a plain white cover with a banana on the front, pulled out the vinyl, put it on the turntable, and lowered the needle. The moment I heard 'Sunday Morning,' my life was changed. I can't think of a moment in my life when music spoke so strongly and directly to me in an instant. That album's seemingly simple formula of mixing classic, hooky songwriting, intelligent lyrics, and a fearlessness to sabotage both of those elements with noise and dissonance made sense, appealed to me, and, perhaps most of all, seemed like something I could do and something I would want to do.

In 1981, the Velvets were somewhat under the radar in both in the mainstream and the underground (much like Big Star, The Stooges, The Modern Lovers, and more recent bands like The Only Ones, Soft Boys, and Gun Club—all of whom I loved, and all of whom would end up being seminal, influential bands over time). It was so rare to hear a band that sounded like or even got compared to The Velvet Underground that I would seek out any band whose record was likened to them in *New York*

Rocker. I remember buying the Human Switchboard album, not getting it, trading it in, and eventually buying it again just because they kept getting the VU comparisons in reviews.

Garage rock and the *Nuggets* influence also loomed larger and larger once I moved to LA. And, once again, I found it hard to find new bands who fit into that sound and style. If a band sounded like the Velvets, I wanted to hear them, and if a band sounded like The Standells or The Seeds, I felt the same way. The Fleshtones from New York certainly fit the bill, and I became a fan. There weren't many others around although there were two combos in Los Angeles that were on the scene, ably rocking the garage sound.

The Last had a single on Bomp Records called 'She Don't Know Why I'm Here' that felt like a 60s band filtered through CBGB's played in the heart of a nuclear power explosion, and their live shows had that same mix of catchiness, classicism, terror, and devastation. They were managed by Gary Stewart, a guy I knew from shopping at the Rhino store before I began working there. He knew I was a fan and let me know one day that they were auditioning guitarists to play rhythm and sing in the band. I met up with the members of the band at a Shakey's Pizza Parlor, and we got along well enough that I was chosen among the three finalists who would be invited to audition. One was me. One was David Roback, who would end up achieving cult and then mainstream success with Rain Parade and Mazzy Star. And there was also another guy. *Another guy* got the gig.

The other band purveying the garage sound in LA, although with a little less popularity than The Last, was The Unclaimed. They were a bit more purist in their love for the stylings and sounds of the genre, mostly resembling a mix of the Music Machine and Byrds in both look and sound. They put out one four-song seven-inch EP, and there's no denying that 'The Acid Song,' written by the band's guitarist, Sid Griffin, had a big influence on me, as evidenced by the obvious similarities in chord change and overall groove to my own 'That's What You Always Say.'

I got wind of a gig at the Cathay, where Sid Griffin and Keith Streng of The Fleshtones would be having a party to celebrate their shared birthdays.

I was determined to be the DJ that night, and I was thrilled when the club owners gave me the gig. Oh, how I culled and studied all my garage records and B-sides ahead of that night to impress them. And, sure enough, I was visited regularly throughout the evening by the members of both bands, all of whom were in attendance. They dug my taste and knowledge of their music as much as I dug their bands. Friendships were forged, and shortly after that, when The Unclaimed broke up, I approached both Sid and lead singer Shelly Ganz to let them know I'd be up for being a part of whatever they did next. To my surprise, they both said yes.

I had to make a choice, and I went with Sid. Our personalities melded better, I found him a little easier to talk to, and I preferred his slightly more panoramic, less parochial style. We started getting together at his tiny Hollywood rehearsal studio with a solid rhythm section of seasoned locals Barry Shank on bass and Matt Roberts on drums. Sid was generous enough to encourage me to play a few of my own songs in the group, opting for more of a Beatles approach of multiple writers and singers than the focused frontman that he'd had in The Unclaimed. I brought some of my growing love of the VU's feedback and dissonance to their cleaner 60s sound, which may have thrown them for a bit of a loop but was also accepted and encouraged.

This was all happening at the exact same time that Kendra, Karl, and I had started playing together. So, I found myself struggling to balance two very exciting embryonic bands with my thirty hours a week at the Rhino store, along with my DJ gigs at the Cathay De Grande and a dwindling handle on my studies at UCLA. Something had to give, and right about the time that Dennis joined me, Kendra, and Karl, I got together with Sid and told him I had to quit his band so I could focus more on the other group. He was stunned. After all, he was known on the scene, had made a record, and could easily get shows, yet I was choosing a much lesser-known entity. But I knew that I was choosing the band making music closest to my heart and to my tastes. Also, I wanted to be the predominant writer and lead singer in what I was going to do next. Sid and I stayed friends, and shortly after my departure, he found a replacement in a talented and mostly unknown Virginia transplant named Stephen McCarthy. With that, The Long Ryders were born.

Around Los Angeles, other unseasoned and unknown musicians, not members of any local scene, were also trying to reconcile their love of 60s music, garage rock, and the echoes of punk rock and new wave in a way that seemed unfashionable but spoke to their desire to make music and mix styles and sensibilities that, like me, they weren't finding anywhere else. In the final days of 1981, a scene was rapidly bubbling to the surface, and we would all quickly find each other in the new year ahead.

2.3
FIRST GIGS, FIRST RECORD

Dennis, Karl, Kendra, and I had, to various degrees, all paid our dues over the years, slogging it out in clubs and bars, parties, dorms, and social gatherings, rarely making money, facing indifference, and hungrily greeting every small victory as manna from heaven and down payment on the long shot hope that a few more small victories might be in store. That's just the way it is for most bands and musicians in the world. On the other hand, The Dream Syndicate never paid any dues, at least not in the conventional sense. We went from zero to sixty in no time.

Consider the first month after that rainy night rehearsal with Dennis. In a little less than four weeks, we came up with our name, learned and rehearsed a full set, recorded a four-song demo that would become our first EP, and managed to book and play a gig opening for an internationally touring act at a sold-out show in a prestigious local club. And, at the time, nothing about that rapid start felt strange or unexpected. It all happened too quickly to feel like anything other than inevitable.

Choosing a name is usually the hardest part of starting a band. Every option sounds terrible, and the more options considered, the worse they all sound. Eventually, however, no matter how awkward or silly or convoluted the name of a band, it ends up sounding normal, just a moniker for something that evokes more than its literal meaning.

Still in the throes of my cross-country trip, I wanted to call the band Big Black Car for the song on Big Star's beautifully unvarnished third album. It seemed like a good name—rhythmic, evocative, a cool but obscure reference point that would alert a potential fan to our hip tastes and what they might expect to hear at a show—an easter egg for those in the know.

Nobody else in the band liked the name. Karl was dismissive, Kendra was ambivalent, two sides of the same responsive coin, guaranteed to take the wind out of the sails of any action or proposal in the context of band politics. Dennis being older and far more experienced in band dynamics knew that saying no wasn't enough—it was best to have a better idea.

'How about The Dream Syndicate? I have a record by a guy who played in Faust named Tony Conrad, and one of his records is called *Outside The Dream Syndicate*. I always liked that title and thought it would make a good band name.'

Because we were still a little bit pinch-me shocked that Dennis wanted to play with us and wanted to just choose a name and get on with it, we said, 'Okay.' It didn't seem like *that* big of a deal, and it had to be done if we wanted to get a gig. Having Dennis in the band made such a thing seem like a possibility and a goal for the first time since we had started jamming. It was just a name for now. Not forever. I certainly wouldn't have imagined I'd still be making records and playing shows under that name forty years later.

We also didn't know—not even Dennis—that The Dream Syndicate was a band that Tony Conrad had with John Cale immediately before Cale and Lou Reed started The Velvet Underground. That knowledge and revelation would come later.

So, we were The Dream Syndicate. The next step would be to get a gig. Dennis felt confident that he had enough connections via Human Hands to get local clubs to at least check us out and take us seriously. We would essentially be selling ourselves as 'Dennis Duck's new band.' But we needed a demo tape, a way for the club bookers to hear our music before we could expect to get any gigs.

Dennis knew a guy named Tom Mehren who had a home studio in Pasadena. He said that Tom would charge $100 for a full day's work. He also thought it would be a good idea to spend another $100 to bring in his friend Paul Cutler from 45 Grave to engineer the sessions since he had worked with Paul and felt he would get better sounds than Tom would on his own. Two hundred bucks was no small amount of money, but we also felt it was worth doing properly and would help us get shows.

We booked the studio for the second week of January. We chose our four favorite originals: 'Some Kinda Itch,' 'When You Smile,' 'That's What You Always Say' (already an 'oldie' for me, and on its way to being the well-worn, well-traveled song it is today), and Karl's 'Sure Thing,' which he had written for me to sing. Karl had no interest in being a singer in the band. As for me, aside from a song or two with Suspects, I had never been the lead singer, but it was never even questioned that it would be my role in The Dream Syndicate. I had the 'right wrong' voice for the music we were making. And, no getting around it, I sounded a bit like Lou Reed, which was never my intention or a studied decision, just my choices and sensibilities and phrasing, and the way my vocal cords happen to vibrate together.

I'm pretty sure we recorded every song in one take. Everything, including my vocals, was done live. The rest of the band played in Tom's living room, and I sang in the kitchen so that my voice would be isolated enough to stand out in the mix. If you listen closely to the last moments of 'Some Kinda Itch,' you can hear that I don't sing the final few words, because I had to step out of the kitchen and away from the microphone to poke my head into the living room and cue the end of the song to the rest of the band.

By the end of the day, we had a mixed, four-song demo tape. Paul did a great job, given the studio and time limitations, and we were happy with the results. It sounded like we sounded, and we very much liked the way we sounded. We joked at the time that we were a band that would be loved or hated and not much in between. If extended, repetitious songs with distortion and feedback and an untrained but earnestly instinctive non-singer were your thing, we might be the band for you. If not, sorry, there's another band down the block. We had no desire to compromise what we loved, and, in fact, it was never even discussed or an option. We were immediately our own favorite band, the kind of band the four of us had all been hoping to find but hadn't in that current musical climate. And our first recording was everything we had hoped it would be.

Dennis rushed a copy of the tape to local impresario Brendan Mullen, who had run the Masque and now was booking a new, trendy venue on Sunset Boulevard called Club Lingerie. Brendan was friends with Dennis and liked what he heard on the cassette. He needed a support act for a show the following Saturday by Brian Brain, a new band led by Martin Atkins, the drummer from Public Image Ltd. The show had been sold out for weeks, so there was no need for the opener to sell tickets or draw fans. Brendan had the luxury of doing a favor for a friend.

Were we nervous? Did we think about and strategize the best way to make an impression at our coming-out party? Hardly. We just showed up and did our thing. We got some of our friends on the guest list, including Sid Griffin, who admonished me for, at one point between songs, grabbing a slice of pizza that I had in a bag behind my Twin Reverb and sneaking a few bites onstage while introducing the next song. 'That's not professional,' he sputtered, and he was right. But little that we did or tried to do in the year ahead would be done with any desire to be professional or to be loved or to become famous. And, among other things, that was likely one of our strongest advantages.

Choice gigs followed immediately. We played a few weeks later at the On Klub in pre-hipster Silverlake, opening for 100 Flowers, a new version of the punk-pop band Urinals. Wall Of Voodoo, who were beginning to gain popularity with their first EP, were getting serious airplay on KROQ. They asked us to open two nights at the seven-hundred-capacity Country Club in Reseda. The Minutemen brought us down to Dancing Waters on their home turf of San Pedro. And, for our first road trip, 45 Grave asked us to open up for them in Phoenix. They said we could cut costs by using their drums and amps for the gig, which allowed the four of us to pile into my Honda Civic with just our guitars and a few overnight bags.

When Alex Gibson of BPeople asked if he could get a ride to Phoenix as well, we said, 'Sure, hop on in.' Five hundred miles in a Civic with five people crammed in. No problem. Nobody complained, although we were glad that Alex The Stowaway decided to stay in Arizona, which meant we'd only have to have the four of us on the way back.

We had become more and more enamored with our demo tape, and at some point, we decided to just put it out as an EP. If we liked it so much, we reasoned, maybe other kindred spirits would like it as well. I had already done a self-pressed record with Rainbo, so I knew the ropes. We used a grainy photo from that first Lingerie show on the cover. Dennis and I were big fans not only of jazz music but of the artwork on jazz records from the 60s, particularly the ones on Impulse. We went through our collections for inspiration, and Dennis showed me one by Yusef Lateef called *Psychicemitus*. We both liked it so much that we appropriated the design, part and parcel, arduously doing the rub-on letters ourselves and getting help putting it all together from Dennis's close friend Tom Recchion, who, years later, would be a Grammy-nominated art director for Warner Bros.

Making a record is one thing, but trying to make people hear about it is another thing altogether. Nonetheless, we had serious advantages from the start.

One, of course, was that people knew Dennis and Human Hands and were receptive to checking out his new band. Another was my job. I spent hours and many thousands of dollars each week buying records from all the big local and national distributors of independent and import music. We had good working relationships, got along well, and they counted on those Rhino orders for steady income. If the kid at the store putting in the orders also happened to have a band that needed distribution, they were happy to take on more copies than they would have by the average Joe on the street, and they would give it a little extra push as well. (And, as it turned out, they would always pay on time for what they sold, not wanting to incur in kind any late payments from Rhino.) What's more, one of my jobs at the store was to report our top ten bestsellers each week to the *LA Weekly* for its 'New Wave Charts.' I had no shyness about making sure we were on that chart every week—and it was an accurate report. The record had sold well from the get-go at Rhino.

We also found ourselves with a manager, and one who would help us a lot in those early days. Billy Bishop had managed Human Hands until they broke up, and he remained tight with Dennis. Billy was working as an engineer for Rodney Bingenheimer's popular and influential *Rodney On The Roq* program on KROQ, and thus Rodney ended up playing our record every week on his show immediately after receiving the first test pressing.

I had a big stack of those test pressings, and I would give them to any rock critic who came into the store. I also had the chance to give one to Peter Zaremba of The Fleshtones, who was shopping in the store and remembered me from the DJ night at the Cathay and the party back at the Tropicana Motel. I thought he might like it, and I was beyond myself with joy and surprise when I picked up the next issue of *New York Rocker* the following month and saw that Zaremba had mentioned it as one of his favorite new records. Things were happening.

Of course, all these insider advantages wouldn't have meant much if people didn't like the record. As it turned out, the same thing that got us so sincerely giddy about our own music—specifically that it was the music we loved and had been dying to hear but hadn't been able to find anywhere else on the scene—meant that it had the same effect on other music fans, especially those who were fans of The Velvet Underground, garage rock, and guitar-based independent music, a hybrid and sound that nobody else was mining at the time.

Paying to press up a record on a record store clerk's salary wouldn't be easy. I remember taking my mother to lunch at Du-Par's on Santa Monica Boulevard and asking her if I could borrow $500 to cover the shortfall needed to press a thousand copies of the EP. I wasn't in the habit of borrowing money from my folks, but this was an emergency, and she came through. Thanks, Mom. We sold all one thousand copies of the record almost immediately and pressed another thousand, which sold out right away. Thanks to my connection with the distributors, I was able to get paid quickly, so I could keep up with the demand.

By the time the record came out, we had already started to get our first reviews and features in local periodicals like the *LA Weekly*, *BAM*, and *Music Connection*, and most were over-the-top effusive raves. My workmate Mikal Gilmore was writing about music for the *Herald-Examiner*, the daily paper that was second in circulation to the *Los Angeles Times*. He loved what we were doing—like many rock critics, he loved the Velvets and found in us a band that pushed the same buttons while drawing upon other critic-friendly influences like Bob Dylan, Creedence Clearwater Revival, and Neil Young, all filtered through a punk-rock sensibility and spirit. Mikal wrote a large cover story about us in the *Herald* after we'd been a band for less than six months. More gigs followed.

It was all happening. Fast. Rather than carefully building on our newfound success, we would instead do our best to challenge and confound our audience. We'd play songs twice as long, devoting much of the extra time to ear-shrieking feedback coaxed from Karl's Silvertone guitar through my Champ amplifier. At one early show, Paul Cutler was doing sound for us. At the beginning of 'When You Smile,' somewhere in the third or fourth minute of feedback, people started streaming to the sound booth, asking him to turn down the infernal noise. 'Sure,' he said, only to push the fader louder and louder with a big grin on his face. We lived up to our credo to be either loved or hated, but we sometimes pushed harder for the latter, maybe as a badge of honor, to show we didn't compromise for anyone. As Kendra once said, 'I'm not your monkey.'

We had felt, only months before, like we were making the kind of music that nobody else seemed interested in making. But things were changing. A scene was building from the far reaches of the expansive county of Los Angeles, and my job as overlord of the seven-inch indie singles rack at Rhino provided me with a bird's-eye view of the oncoming storm.

I had a single in stock by a band from San Pedro called Salvation Army who were mining a different side of the punk-meets-60s sound that we had been making. And, one day, a girl named Vicki Peterson came in with copies of a single by her band, The Bangs, to sell on consignment. I flipped out over the record's A-side, 'Getting Out Of Hand,' and said I'd be happy to help them out with anything they needed. I got together with Vicki and the band's other writer, Sue Hoffs, at Tom's, the chiliburger stand on Pico & Centinela, and told them where to buy seven-inch plastic sleeves and other essentials of self-distribution. In a bit of kismet, Sue was also friends with the guys in The Rain Parade, whose self-released single we carried, and who also fit into this new modern mishmash revival of the past two decades. I got a hold of Michael, the singer of Salvation Army, and we all became fast friends and mutual fans and started talking about doing shows together. The first stirrings of our little scene had begun.

2.4
THE PAISLEY UNDERGROUND

If I had to name a date when everything kicked into high gear it would be April 30, 1982. Our EP had come out earlier that month and we were asked to headline a show at the Cathay De Grande, a heady step up from only recently having been the Monday night DJ who worked for free drinks. I asked Salvation Army and The Bangs to open the show, and our newfound collective of bands had its first showcase. Advance hype and ticket sales were great, and we knew we'd have a packed show. It's worth noting that The Bangs were the opening band every time we played together that year—an order of things that would change, of course, the following year, when they became The Bangles.

The club booked another local band, Green On Red, to play the smaller upstairs bar before our show began. I was excited because I really liked their *Two Bibles* EP, which Dan Stuart had given me the summer before, when I was working a temporary summer job in the shipping room at a distribution company called Faulty Products. He had wandered in on his lunch hour to drop off a handful of records for us to sell on consignment, and we had a brief, friendly conversation. I was drawn in by their sound, which tempered punk and art rock with decidedly classic rock piano stylings—something you didn't hear that often. I couldn't have imagined that I'd end up playing with the record's pianist, Chris Cacavas, for most of the next forty years.

I stood by the club's front door, greeting fans and friends while I waited for Green On Red to hit the stage. I was still at the point where more people knew me as the 'guy who works at Rhino' than as a bandleader, and I was happy when one of my favorite customers, the pioneering rock critic Richard Meltzer, came through the door. He said, 'My friend Lester Bangs died today. He would have really liked your band.' That saddened me and took some of the wind out of my sails but at the same time made me want to play a great show for Lester, whose writing I had enjoyed since my early teens.

Green On Red were fantastic. The acoustic piano on their studio debut EP had given way in the live setting to a reedy, psychedelic organ, and lead singer Dan had gone from the mild-mannered, officious guy I'd met dropping off records on his lunch break to a menacing, terrifying singer, coaxing shards of fuzz out of his Gretsch guitar and singing about a seediness, desperation, and romanticism that seemed right at home in a Hollywood club. I went up to Dan after the set to reintroduce myself and tell him how much I liked the set, and he gave me a giant bear hug.

'My brother. You're like Ernest Hemingway mixed with Lou Reed. We should hang out.' My friendship with the charismatic, always larger-than-life Dan Stuart began.

There was still a show to play downstairs. For the uninitiated who are familiar with the music of The Bangles and The Three O'Clock but never saw them before they changed their names, it might be a shock to have seen and heard their early sets. The Salvation Army's set started at top speed and then just kept getting faster, like The Who and Pink Floyd in a blender on the highest setting, nothing like the more inviting, sugary pop band they would become. When I became a big fan of Hüsker Dü a couple of years later, I was struck by how much they reminded me of those early Salvation Army shows.

The Bangs were also wilder, more intense, and more unhinged than the hit-making band they would become two years later. I maintain they were the musicians with the most accomplished handle on song structure, hooks, and stage presence of any of our bands. And their choice of covers was impeccable: Love's '7 And 7 Is,' The Changing Times' 'How Is The Air Up There,' and The Seeds' 'Pushin' Too Hard' all rocked with the cockiness and swagger of the best *Nuggets* bands. They were always fantastic, and even though I very much liked their Top 40 hits (I'm even a staunch defender of the mega-platinum 'Eternal Flame,' which always reminded me of 'The Morning After' from *The Poseidon Adventure*), I was also happy when their reunion shows in the current century saw them returning to a sound and style approximating an even more assured version of shows like the one I saw in the Cathay basement.

After following what were suddenly my three favorite local bands, all operating at top form, what could we do to try to justify our headlining ringleader status—something that would have been unimaginable just four months earlier? Like always, we just allowed our moods, the vibe of the club, and the music to dictate where the evening would go. Kendra and Dennis would lay down an unyielding and unchanging propulsive groove while Karl shot out caterwauling shards of white noise and fractured chords and I did my best to ride and occasionally harness our wild beast of a band. We raced to the finish line like beat-up stock cars driven by monkeys wearing blindfolds. We knew where we were going, but we had no more of a clue than anyone else in the room how we would get there.

This was the setlist that night:

Too Little Too Late
When You Smile
Halloween
That's What You Always Say
Sure Thing
Definitely Clean
Until Lately
Some Kinda Itch

Just a year earlier, Kendra and I had sat in one of the back booths one late night at that same Cathay De Grande blueprinting our thoughts on what made for a perfect band. We realized that all of our absolute favorite records came down to the same four elements and criteria:

1. **SEXY** Not a puerile, suggestive, gratuitous sexy, but rather the sultry swagger of records by Howlin' Wolf, The Rolling Stones, and The Cramps. Music that raised the heat index, leaving you feeling hot and bothered and ready to act on your building and unbridled passion, pulling you into a netherworld groove only to leave you in a helpless puddle at the end. This is the stuff that gave rock'n'roll its name.

2. **FUNNY** I'm not talking about novelty songs here, but rather a knowing, winking sly nod, self-awareness, and levity. We all liked artists who didn't take themselves too seriously, which made it all more serious than if you were just po-faced and posing as some lofty, somber voice of God.

3. **SCARY** Not scary like bargain-basement Dracula goth, which was getting popular at that moment, or doom-laden formulaic metal. Rather, the scariness of letting yourself plumb the deepest depths of your psyche, take off the guardrails, and not have any fear of driving yourself into the ditch, allowing the audience to share the fear of the wild ride. In other words, that 3am feeling when the defenses are down and the bars are closed.

4. **CAN FALL APART AT ANY MOMENT** This was, to me and Kendra, the most important one. There had to be a sense of chaos and things happening in the moment. Over-rehearsal was anathema, and the simple joy of righting a capsizing ship was more interesting than a smooth, expertly built ride. We were drawn to recordings that felt like it was the only time the band members had ever or would ever play the songs in their life. The songs we loved most tended to teeter, wobble, and threaten to fall off the tightrope but never fully plummet from those heights.

Our favorite bands had all four elements, particularly on records like *Exile On Main St.* and *Raw Power* and *London Calling*, and more recently *Fire Of Love* by The Gun Club. *Blonde On Blonde* checked all four boxes. So did both albums by The New York Dolls and *White Light / White Heat* by the Velvets. On that night in a basement in Hollywood, The Dream Syndicate had those four things in spades, and it was why we felt sure that as good as those other bands were, and as much as we loved what they were doing, we also stood alone in our own world—a world in which we found many music fans wanting to sign up for the ride.

Things had changed. I knew enough about the history, and, as Meltzer would say, the aesthetics of rock to know I was part of something very special—something that was happening and growing quickly—and that our music was connecting with people in a very tangible way. I was still the shy, nerdy college student, the eager record store clerk, and the nightly club DJ, but it was getting harder and harder to balance those with the growing demands of being the leader of a popular band.

Something had to give, and shortly after that Cathay show, I walked into a Shakespeare class I had been taking at UCLA for a midterm exam. I looked at the test and realized I couldn't even begin to answer a single question, not even with the bluff-friendly skills I had learned in my rhetoric classes. I walked out in the middle of the exam straight to the admissions office and quit school. I went back to my dad that night and told him what I had done. He said, 'You're twenty-one and you are old enough to make your own decisions, but I think you're throwing your life away.' Years later, he would come around and learn to appreciate my music and would be proud of what I had achieved, although he would nonetheless always say, 'You should record more ballads.'

College dropout, Hollywood rock club headliner, record store clerk with a critically acclaimed EP on the local independent music charts. My life had certainly changed quite a bit in just a few short months.

—

2.5

OUT OF LA, OUT OF MY HEAD

We started getting more gigs out of town, usually in the Bay Area. The routine was always the same: rent a van around 8am from the Budget car rental on Wilshire and 23rd, strangely enough the exact same location where I'd been managing a Fotomat booth as my high school job just five years earlier. I couldn't get a credit card, which meant I couldn't rent a van, but this location was managed by my friend Chris Bailey, who also drummed with various local groups and hung out a bit at Rhino. Bailey was the patron saint of scrappy young bands, renting them vehicles they would have no way of procuring otherwise.

By 9am we'd be loaded up and on our way up the 405, over the mountains of the I-5 leading to the Grapevine beyond, endless stretches of dirt and desert and the stench of cattle near Coalinga and finally into the East Bay, where we played regularly at a club called Berkeley Square. Soundcheck, kill a few hours, hit the stage around midnight, pack up and get right back on the highway and drive through the night to Los Angeles, where we'd arrive in time to qualify for the twenty-four-hour price on the rental, hop in our respective cars, and get to our jobs or beds by 9am. Rinse and repeat.

We did it because we could. We did it to spread the gospel. We did it because suddenly people wanted us to play in their clubs. Our EP was getting press and airplay nationwide, without the benefit of promotion. It was all word-of-mouth. I was not only the singer, guitarist, and songwriter (and graveyard-shift van driver), but I was also the record label, and I had no time for hype and phone calls. In those pre-internet times, word got around via local press, underground rock magazines, college radio, and eager, proselytizing independent record store clerks like me.

Shortly after our record release on April Fool's Day, we got a call from a DJ in Austin named Jody Denberg. He had a specialty show on the local mainstream station KLBJ (owned, as the call letters would suggest, by Lady Bird Johnson). He loved and was regularly playing the record and wanted to know if we were interested in playing a show in Austin. 'Yes' was the only answer we had for such things back then.

We made the two-thousand-mile drive with nothing more than refueling breaks, wired on coffee, classic rock radio, and a few loaves of bread, packaged bologna, and American cheese, making sandwiches as we rolled down the road. Jody generously put us up on the living room floor of his one-bedroom apartment, the four of us lined up like elves in the sleeping bags he provided. The show was great, and we hung out with Jody's close friend Alejandro Escovedo, who I had watched just a few years before at Winterland when he played with The Nuns, opening for the Sex Pistols. He told me about a band he had begun playing with called Rank & File.

Thanks to Jody we had a great turnout of people who knew our EP, made enough to put gas in the tank and buy more bread and cold cuts, and we were back in the van, making a beeline back to LA. It was our first taste of touring, and, despite the hard travel, we all knew that we wanted more.

No longer tethered by my studies at UCLA, my life was now fully consumed by music: record store clerk by day and rocker by night. I was getting a lot of attention for singing and writing and playing gritty songs with an unhinged sound and style that suggested dark themes, chaos, and emotional catharsis. This didn't jibe with the shy, nerdy kid I had been just one year before, and I was starting to get swept away in the thrill of early and rapid success. It was changing me, slowly but surely.

There's a story about Laurence Olivier and Dustin Hoffman talking during the making of *Marathon Man*. Hoffman says that he had been staying up all night and wearing himself down intentionally to get into the character he was playing. Olivier responded, 'Why don't you just try acting?' Many years later, I would realize that the way to shift from your daily Clark Kent persona and become a more interesting Superman onstage was simply to take a deep breath, think about what you want to do, and then just go and inhabit that space. But that didn't occur to me at the time, and I needed a way to become the person I thought I had to be to be the lead singer in an increasingly popular band like The Dream Syndicate.

I found the way . . . and it was alcohol.

Apart from that Manischewitz one-night bender in high school and the very occasional beer, I never touched alcohol in my first twenty-one years on the planet. My Rhino workmates Jon 'Otis' Williams and Dave Crouch would take me after work to a local VA bar on Sawtelle Boulevard called the Tap N' Cap. A shot of whiskey and a beer was a buck, Lefty Frizzell and Hank Williams were on the jukebox, a beat-up pool table was in the corner, and the lights were always very low. I enjoyed it all—the camaraderie with my new friends, the music, and, most of all, the jolting sucker punch of that first taste of whiskey and the attitude-shifting wash of confidence that the ensuing buzz would provide. I was able to feel like somebody else, somebody swaggering, and cool and a bit dangerous—and I liked it.

My pay of free drinks for DJing for five hours at the Cathay De Grande became more valuable as I downed five or six drinks during the evening. My consumption was still far less than that of Top Jimmy (from The Rhythm Pigs) who was often headlining, or Tom Waits, who regularly hung out. But nonetheless, I would get pretty hammered, hop back into the Civic, and drive the length of Sunset Boulevard back to my dad's place, sometimes stopping off midway at Oki Dog, a notorious hangout for punk-rockers and teenage runaways. I'd wolf down one of their signature concoctions of tortilla, hot dog, pastrami, chili, and cheese to soak up the buzz, which, along with covering my left eye with my left hand to reduce the spins, would get me back home. I'm not proud of this last part, and I'm lucky and grateful that I didn't do damage to myself or anybody else.

I was also drinking more at Dream Syndicate shows, often reaching full blackout state onstage, which would often necessitate a call the next day to my old Davis friend Tom, who had moved down to LA and was working at my old store, Moby Disc. Tom came to all the shows and would fill me in when I'd ask, 'How was it? What did we play? Did I say or do anything stupid?' all the while looking at my Jazzmaster pickguard, smeared in the blood I had shed while slashing my right hand against the strings. As much as I drank, I never played the wrong chords or forgot the lyrics, but the irreverence of eating a slice of pizza onstage had shifted to a new, demystifying breaking of the band/audience fourth wall, playfully mocking both ourselves and the audience and challenging their perception and reasons for wanting to watch what we were doing. It was an extension of the knowing, opinionated, antagonistic record-store clerks at Rhino, and many of the things I said onstage about other bands, local writers, and things happening around town were the same things I might have said from behind the counter at the store. I'm sure it annoyed and turned off some attendees, but others came to enjoy this as much as the music itself, at least for a while. It was a way of saying to the audience, 'We're all in this together, we're all just hanging out, we are you'—something that another band, The Replacements, was also doing at the same time, two thousand miles away in Minnesota.

There was no other band on the scene doing quite what we were doing at our lives shows, and we reveled in our contrary, antagonistic, and provocative behavior as much as we did in our actual music. We wanted to take everything further and further with each show. If a song was long, make it longer. If there was feedback, make it louder and more painful. If a song got quiet, make it uncomfortably quiet and embrace the stark dynamics of silence zigzagging with the noise. We lived for confrontation. Pushing buttons with volume, dynamics, snarky stage banter, and even cover choices atypical to our scene and sound (Blue Öyster Cult, Johnny Cash, Eric Clapton, and Donovan come to mind) allowed us to keep ourselves and our audience on our respective toes. We didn't want to ingratiate ourselves, and we felt we were doing more of a service to our fans to confound their expectations.

From the beginning, we would often say that we'd rather be one person's favorite band than a group that a bunch of people somewhat liked a bit. With that credo, we made every show a test. *Oh, you think you like us? Well, try THIS!* Rather than repel those early fans, it made them like us all that much more, and our prickly behavior became part of the reason they would come back for more.

Along with the confidence that came from our fledgling success, I had also transformed with the help of a fashion makeover from Karl, who had begun cutting my hair and advising me on clothes and attitude. He held the view that you must look and act the part, something I hadn't thought about much before. I remember him telling me after my weight ticked up to just a few pounds over skeletal, 'If you're going to get fat then get really, really fat. Otherwise, keep the weight down.' His haircuts were sassy—the best anyone gave me until my wife Linda started cutting my hair years later. He did a great job on me, and along with his own sense of classic-rock look, Dennis's art-rock/café-society vibe, and Kendra's rhythmic sway and beauty, we had a motley but very appealing onstage presence that took me by surprise, never having given much thought to clothes or hair. I credit Karl for all of that.

In the eighteen months that followed my move from Davis, I hadn't dated anyone at all and had been completely celibate. That changed with the rise of the band and my drinking, and the ensuing confidence boost I got from both. I started dating Carmel, who worked at Faulty Products as well as a local distributor with whom I was dealing as both a Rhino employee and through our own record. She was a couple of years older, came from Cleveland, and reminded me of her fellow Ohioan Chrissie Hynde. We went out for a few months and had a great time, but things started fading as summer began, due to alcohol, the changes in my life, and just the natural deterioration of young romance. I was already looking for a way out when Michael Quercio of Salvation Army put together a Fourth Of July weekend getaway to nearby Catalina Island for the members of our bands and The Bangs. I broke up with Carmel the morning of the planned trip so that I could go alone and have fun with my friends.

We showed up on the island with a return trip scheduled for the next day but without having booked any hotel rooms. We walked around, talked, drank, and, when it got dark, hopped a fence and planned to sleep on a golf course. Some of us might have had sleeping bags, but that wasn't a concern. I had gotten to know Sue more at gigs and from lengthy phone chats, and there was a moment that evening on the golf course when she flirted with me, but I was more concerned with hanging out with the gang, drinking and flying solo, having been out of a relationship for all of twelve hours. I politely declined, and she instead connected with Salvation Army guitarist Louis Gutierrez. They ended up being a couple for the next few years.

Our little golf course slumber party was rudely interrupted by sprinklers going off at 4am, and we gathered ourselves and brought our newly solidified scene back on the ferry to the mainland a few hours later. Not long after, Michael did an interview in which he was asked about our collective of bands and called it the Paisley Underground. Much like the Mersey Beat scene of Liverpool, the LA Sunset Strip collective of the 60s, and the CBGB's gang of 1975, we had a name, a gang, and the power of that identity helped all of us to get more attention in the months that followed. The camaraderie, styles, and sounds, and now the moniker of our scene, made it easier for people to discover our music.

The band I was hanging out with most of all was Green On Red. They were also big drinkers, and their music was closer in sync with what we were doing—darker and edgier. Like me, Dan Stuart saw the lyrics as a literary experience, telling tales that owed more to Charles Bukowski and John Fante than they did to Lennon and McCartney or Syd Barrett. Band members Jack Waterson, Chris Cacavas, and Alex MacNichol shared a duplex apartment near Paramount Studios in Hollywood and began hosting weekly Sunday-night barbecues, which increasingly became a gathering point for our paisley bands and slightly newer bands on the scene like The Rain Parade and The Leaving Trains. Hanging out until the sun came up, strumming guitars, replenishing drink supplies, eating burgers, playing records, we forged friendships that would last for life. At one of the barbecues, Dan played me a cassette of songs his band had recorded at a local rehearsal studio. He said they planned to make a hundred copies of the cassette to sell at shows. I heard it and was blown away.

'Hey,' I said, 'I made all the money back on our EP. I'd like to put your record out on my label if you're cool with that.' And, with that, my Down There label had a catalogue.

At the same time, my label was about to lose its first band. The indisputably coolest label in town at that time was Slash Records, which had put out records by X and The Blasters and The Germs. Slash had a subsidiary called Ruby Records, run by Chris D, a thoughtful and intense guy who fronted his own band, The Flesh Eaters. Chris had already put out records by The Misfits and Lydia Lunch, and *Fire Of Love* by The Gun Club, my favorite album at the time. I don't remember any talk of a contract or a budget or promotion or lawyers. Just Chris saying, 'I can get three midnight-to-8am shifts at a good, local recording studio called Quad Tech. We can make the record and have it out in the fall.'

An album on the prestigious Ruby/Slash, less than a year after our first rehearsal, seemed like the culmination of a dream. Of course, we said yes.

2.6
THE SONGWRITER

With the prospect and plan of a first album just ahead, we knew that we needed to fill that album with more songs of original material. This might be a good time to talk about the mystical art, cause and effect, and mercurial pull of songwriting.

It's not a compulsion that afflicts everyone. I've known plenty of dedicated, obsessive, and talented musicians with an encyclopedic grasp of music history who have written only a handful of songs. They, as Leonard Cohen once said, 'live for music' and are deadly serious about their craft and contribution to the overall tableau of a gig or recording session. But if you put them in a room with a one-hundred-dollar bill dangling on a pole outside the door for the taking once a song was written, they would very well leave the building with empty pockets.

As I mentioned earlier, I wrote my first song at the age of nine. Back then, I wasn't writing for a band, and I wasn't writing for an upcoming release. I was writing because I was enraptured by the music I was hearing on my radio, and I wanted to be a part of that world as well. Most of my early songs were written when I was under the hypnotic sway of a record that I had heard for the first time and that had me in its thrall. If I loved the new Kinks or Creedence record, and it inspired me to come up with my own approximation, I would feel like I had become a part of their universe. John Fogerty wrote a song. Ray Davies wrote a song. And then I wrote a song. We were now linked in the songsmith brotherhood. I had created my own universe that was adjacent in the sonic solar system to my heroes.

Lyrics are often the hardest part. My earliest songs were an extension of the loneliness I was feeling, as an only child living far away from the few friends I had. I had things that I needed to say and nobody to whom I could say those things which meant that the song universe became my all-purpose confessional booth. The earliest songs—many of which I can still remember and play today—were pure unfiltered cries for help and connection set to melodies, structure, and arrangements that felt like *Quadrophenia* or *Lola Versus Powerman And The Moneygoround*, two very emotional records that strongly connected to me at the time.

My favorite songs have always come quickly, usually not much longer than the time it takes to play them. Sometimes they come to me fully formed in my head when I'm walking down the street. For all the talk of the muse and the more spiritual concept of God speaking through the music, I think it's more a matter of being open and receptive while also being engaged and excited. That combination will usually do the trick, but one of the sad things about getting older and hearing more and writing more—and, if the cards fall your way, writing songs for a living—is that you have so many things that block the openness, receptiveness, and excitement. Rationality and experience and professionalism can shut down the process and silence the muse.

I've found the best way to silence the noise that leads to creative inertia is to simply work quickly and avoid censoring yourself. Is the song awful? Does it sound like some other song? Who cares? Forge ahead. Don't look down. There's always time to revisit and fix things later. Even the worst or most derivative song can be stripped for parts and rebuilt into a much better one just a short time later. But if you do nothing, you have nothing to fix or revisit.

The songs I wrote for Suspects and in the years that immediately followed were all exercises in replicating my favorite new wave or punk rock music at the time. *A Different Kind Of Tension* by the Buzzcocks really inspired me in the months after it came out. The mix of the raw punk sound and energy with perfect pop hook construction and vulnerable, pleading lyrics connected with me. I have a few songs that I've never released that would have fit right on that album, making me a musical Zelig-like figure, part of Pete Shelley's universe, peering right over his shoulder from the adjusted band photo in my imagination.

By the time The Dream Syndicate came along, the music that most excited me was the music that we were making. Suddenly, the universe I wanted to join and expand upon was our own. I listened to our rehearsal tapes and cassette recordings of our shows that friends and fans had given me over and over. Much like Dennis after that first rehearsal, this was the music I wanted to hear, and that was motivation to write more so that we'd have new songs to play.

One very effective method I used for writing songs in those early days of The Dream Syndicate was to close my eyes, imagine putting a needle down on a vinyl record, and think about what I would want to hear once the sound began. I was so voraciously hungry for the music I loved and wanted to hear that the fantasized version of that music was easy to turn into reality.

At the same time, consciously or not, I was still approximating other things I was hearing to come up with my songs. Most bands' first albums can't help but be a little derivative, squeezing out the sponge that held all the sounds and styles and songs that made you want to make music of your own. And we were no exception. It's just that our inspired amateur approach made it easier to camouflage and hide our sources. But the statute of limitations is on my side, so let's take a little stroll through the songs that we brought into the studio for *The Days Of Wine And Roses*.

'Tell Me When It's Over': this was inspired by the twelve-inch version of The English Beat's 'Save It For Later.' They were part of the new ska scene, but this record felt more like The Velvet Underground. Just a song in D with three chords going round and round and round, building a loop and swirl that entranced and made time stand still. Nobody's ever called me on this one, proving, once again, my 'gift' for not being able to copy accurately and not particularly caring. The lyric came from a show we played in Hollywood with Red Cross (pre-name change), right when our EP came out. We were supposed to headline, but their manager chided us, saying that they had been around longer (despite the bandleading McDonald brothers being fourteen and eleven years old at the time, their first EP predated ours by a year) and we should respect their odd seniority. I acquiesced but was annoyed by this veteran scenester's snobbishness. Please just shut up and tell me when it's over.

'Definitely Clean': definitely The Fall. No doubt about it. Just listen to *Grotesque* and you'll hear this song repeatedly. The lyric came after hanging out with a girl I was wooing and being sent home unceremoniously after dropping her off at her apartment in Venice. The frustration of the evening channeled into the lyrics that I most likely wrote and shouted aloud on the drive home.

'That's What You Always Say': music borrowed from that Unclaimed EP and written on Kendra's Musicmaster bass. It's that 'BUM-ba-BUM' almost straightened out, waltz-style, that felt good to play on bass. It wouldn't have come out the same way if it was written on guitar. It was also one of my earlier minor-chord songs, but far from my last. The lyrics on the 15 Minutes version were just mumbling, wordless nonsense leading to the title on the chorus before slipping back into nonsense. I fleshed it out with more words of missed signals and bad connections when it became a Dream Syndicate song.

'Then She Remembers': all downstrokes. It's not easy to play, and sometimes now I'll cheat and throw in a few upstrokes to keep my right arm from falling off. This feels like *Raw Power*, but I'm not sure if that's what I was listening to then. I know that I was cranking a lot of *Damaged* by Black Flag around the time the band started—Karl and I loved driving down the road and singing along to 'TV Party'—so there's some of that as well. The words are brutal—just a handful of lines distilling some vivid abuse. It wasn't always easy or natural to shift from the guy working behind a record counter to the guy spewing out words like these. Whiskey was the palate cleanser between day (job) and night (gig).

'Halloween': Karl's song, but here's a little secret: I wrote the last two verses. And it's my guitar solo, so that's about half the song as well. I didn't claim a co-write at the time, whereas I might have today. But I was so happy that Karl had written a song, and that it felt so much like the absolute distillation of the kind of band we wanted to be. According to Karl, it was inspired by Jamie Lee Curtis and the movie of the same name.

'When You Smile': the music was from a Soft Boys B-side, lots of Floyd-esque arpeggios, something that R.E.M. were picking up on three thousand miles away at the same time. The words? I know it has become a love song for so many listeners over the years, so I hate to tarnish that appeal, but it was actually a gentle kiss-off to a girlfriend I dated for a few months in the year before The Dream Syndicate. I felt torn between the pleasures and comforts of having a girlfriend and the feeling that there were Big Things To Do. I was reading a lot of Thomas Carlyle at the time, and somehow his message of action and self-determination came out in ending the relationship and writing this song.

'Until Lately': another Fall song, specifically 'C'n'C-s Mithering.' There's a line in that song, as well, about '*500 girl deaths*' which snuck into my '500 Girl Mornings' a few years later. And the classic '*A&M Herb was there / His offices had fresh air / But his rota was mediocre.*' We ended up on A&M just a few months later, as it turns out. Another song I wrote on bass, and that bass line, rather than the chord progression, is what gives the song its shape and movement. Sometimes chord changes get in the way of a good thing.

'Too Little Too Late': in which I write a song for my old lead singer, Kendra Smith, to sing on the record. She certainly wasn't clamoring for a lead vocal, happy to just groove behind our madness. But the Velvets comparisons were already piling up, and I figured snarkily that our first album should have a 'Nico song.'

'The Days Of Wine And Roses': it's 'Tombstone Blues.' I didn't even realize that until the album had been out for a while. But I'm sure Dylan stole that song as well—he's the most fleet-fingered musical thief out there. Our thievery was always well disguised by a band that didn't care or make any attempt to play nice with the source or intent. My little talking blues song—spurred by the simple writing of that movie title on a piece of paper and thinking it would make a good, updated song title—was hijacked by our love of The Gun Club's debut album and Greg Ginn's sprawling, syrupy shards of guitar soloing.

None of the thirty or so records I made over the next four decades would ever have such an easy genealogy of influences. As time went on, I no longer needed to mimic a favorite record to feel like I belonged in the same world as my heroes. I was now a member of the club. Songs would come from other places, sometimes in bunches, sometimes in dribs and drabs, sometimes faster than I could put them on record, and sometimes, agonizingly, not at all.

2.7
THE DAYS OF WINE AND ROSES

We had a date set up by Slash to make the record at the end of September at Quad Tech Studios on the eastern end of Hollywood, bordering on Koreatown. Chris D would produce, just as he had done a year earlier with The Gun Club at the same studio. They gave us three consecutive nights from midnight to 8am. In the forty years since, I've never encountered a single studio that offered this kind of graveyard shift. I'm guessing that it came at a lower rate. Despite the demands on those of us who had day jobs, we were just happy to be going into a real and serviceable recording studio to make our first album.

A few weeks before the session, we had been booked to play Andrea 'Enthal's popular *Two O'Clock Rock* program at the local public radio station, KPFK. Andrea's show, named for its Saturday night/Sunday morning 2am start time, had been a big influence on me in the year before

The Dream Syndicate. She played a lot of the brand-new UK releases from Factory and Rough Trade Records that would have an impact not only on my songwriting and musical aesthetics but also on the records I would order the following Monday morning to carry in the store. It's where I first heard Echo & The Bunnymen and Joy Division—two bands whose first two albums and surrounding singles rarely left my turntable around that time. I can hear echoes of Ian Curtis and Ian McCulloch in my earliest vocals (influences that never cropped up again on any subsequent records).

The timing of our radio appearance seemed great since it would provide a tune-up before going into the studio to make our album, while also giving us a well-recorded document of our live set to examine for notes and preparation. We decided to play the four songs we had released on our EP and a handful of covers, not wanting to play any of the newer compositions for fear that we and the rest of our fans would get overly comfortable with those versions and end up being disappointed by the way they came out on the record. At the last minute, we changed our minds and decided to play our newest song, 'The Days Of Wine And Roses,' and, sure enough, both Dennis and I left the album sessions thinking the KPFK performance was better. We considered using that live version on the album.

We were flying high the day we arrived for the radio session. Our popularity, both locally and nationally, was building quickly, and we had the validation of being signed by the coolest label in town. The station's studio for live sessions was large, capable of holding three hundred people, and it was apparent that even with the late starting time of 2am, there would be no problem filling the room. We had a nice mix of fans, friends, and other musicians from the Paisley Underground. Peter Buck, who was temporarily residing with the rest of his R.E.M. bandmates just down the road at the Oakwood efficiency apartments in Burbank, was there, although we still hadn't properly met. My ex-girlfriend Carmel was there too and wreaked her revenge for being unceremoniously dumped by spending much of the show heckling me. You can hear her multiple times on the album of the show, which came out a decade later as *The Day Before*

Wine And Roses, right up to the point where our manager Billy Bishop picks her up and carries her out as I grimly say, 'Elvis has left the building.'

The confidence and the excitement of playing live on the air—along with the six-pack of Mickey's Big Mouth I'd purchased at a gas station across the street—resulted in the best show we'd ever played up to that point. We focused on the twin elements of our careening punk rock side, influenced by recent records by Black Flag and The Circle Jerks, balanced by our extended, sprawling hippie jam side, with the two elements coming together at the same time on a cathartic, anarchic take on Donovan's 'Season Of The Witch.' I had been fooling around with a little five-note riff reminiscent of Television's early single, 'Little Johnny Jewel.' We decided we would take a chance at our biggest show on live radio and play a song that would begin with that particular riff but with no musical or lyrical road map beyond that and just play it for as long as we wanted. Our friend, the writer Byron Coley, suggested we call it 'Open Hour'; that title stuck until it was changed to 'John Coltrane Stereo Blues' when we were making *Medicine Show* the following year.

That show set us up well for making the album, filling us with confidence and fearlessness. On the other hand, I do remember the sensation once we were in the studio of being near the final minute of what I knew was a good take of a song, thinking and praying, *Oh, man, please don't make a mistake or play a wrong chord or drop a pick and fuck this up.* I've never had that feeling in a studio since, but I knew we were walking on clouds, and I was afraid of looking down or waking up from the dream or of letting the band or our mission down in any way.

Chris D was the perfect producer for our session and his style is one I've tried to emulate when I've produced records in the years since. He approached the session as a fan, as a listener, as the conscience that we needed so that we could barrel through, take down the guardrails, not worry about a thing, be ourselves, and let it fly. He did the worrying—as well as the time and take management—for us, while slowly making his way through a liter bottle of Smirnoff vodka. The house engineer and studio manager, Pat Burnette (the son and nephew, respectively, of the great Johnny and Dorsey Burnette of The Rock And Roll Trio), easily kept up with the pace of the evening. I think we got most of the songs in a single take.

A lot of our sound in those early days came down to the Mutt 'n' Jeff mix of my large, loud Twin Reverb with Karl's tiny Champ amplifier. I would get maximum clang and jangle from my rhythm while Karl skulked about with shards of noise and chaos that sat within the overall sound, instead of standing out in 3-D above the fray. It's not the typical lead guitar/rhythm guitar approach but rather one big, amorphous mess that worked for us and would also be ill-advisedly abandoned when we made our next record.

We successfully captured all nine songs in that first late-night session, wandering out tired but contented at 8am, our eyes blinking off the harsh morning LA sunlight. The following night was spent on vocals and some minimal overdubs—a harmonica on 'Until Lately,' and a foghorn-like sliding note on the solo of 'Tell Me When It's Over' that I had borrowed from a section I'd always liked in the middle of 'Ramble Tamble' by Creedence Clearwater Revival. Otherwise, all the instrumental parts, including solos, were done live that first evening of tracking. On the third night, we mixed the entire album in eight hours—a fast pace. Most mixing sessions I've had since would tackle two, maybe three songs a day, but never as many as the nine songs we finished that night that ended up on the album.

On that last morning, I left the studio at 8am and got into my car with a cassette of the mixes sequenced in the order they would appear on the album. I drove across town to Westwood, where I opened the Rhino store to start my shift and cranked the tape at top volume on the store's stereo system, reveling in the certainty that we had made a record that reflected the music we loved and what went down at our best live shows. I remember thinking, *Well, if I never make another record again, at least I'll know I made one really great one.*

It's rare to finish an album and say, 'I wouldn't change a single thing.' Usually, there's one mix that bugs you, or you have doubts about the sequencing or some fade out that doesn't curve quite as it should. Maybe it's a vocal you wish you could go back to and try one more time. But I knew that our first album was perfection—at least by the standards we had set for ourselves. The only other time I had that hundred percent feeling of satisfaction would come twenty years later, when I made *Here Come The Miracles*.

The Days Of Wine And Roses came out on Halloween, four weeks later, and we quickly found out that a whole lot of people agreed with our assessment of the record. Naturally, it sat on the top rack at Rhino and was our top seller, with sales more than doubling those of the second and third slots, Fear's *The Record* and Richard and Linda Thompson's *Shoot Out The Lights*. Slash was flooded with requests for review copies as well as requests for interviews in *Rolling Stone*, the *Los Angeles Times*, and other big publications in the US and abroad.

I was still in charge of ordering the British music weeklies for the store, so I was delighted to open up the latest issue of *NME* that arrived one day and see a full-page glowing review that concluded, 'There are narratives that tenderly, wistfully long after a kind of normality or stability of emotions that the singer seems to know is not his lot in life. Hard guitars, hard feelings, hard to ignore.' I made a point to place that issue front and center on the store's magazine rack.

I had always devoured music magazines, and I often felt that the interpretation and contextualizing of the music could be as much of an art form and statement as the music itself. It was a lesson reinforced by my studies of English literature, where the writings of a biographer and essayist like John Ruskin or James Boswell could be as worthy of study as the work of their subject matter. Much like my needle-drop imagination school of songwriting, rock criticism helped me to know which musical moves and stage patter and even small details in album packaging and interview responses would make for the most fun and relatability in the music press. It wasn't calculating; it just came naturally, as I could connect to and evaluate what I was doing as a musician, a fan, and a critic, all at the same time.

At the same time, that studied approach was not enough. The X factor was knowing what we knew but also being unafraid to toss it all out the window each night onstage, making up rules and breaking rules as we went along. 'We're lucky,' I said to the *Los Angeles Times* shortly after the album's release. 'What we decided to do was something that people wanted to see at this point. It's not like we sat down last December and made a blueprint with long songs, lots of feedback and lots of yelling. You'd have to be pretty stupid to plan your success that way. We just lucked out.'

Our official coming-out party for the record happened a few weeks before the release at the Music Machine, once again, with Salvation Army and The Bangles (who had changed their name from The Bangs to avoid litigation from another band out in New Jersey), along with the addition of Rain Parade as fourth on the bill. Both The Bangles and Salvation Army (who would shortly change *their* name as well) had new, top-notch records out, and we were all feeling good about our paisley gang. The show sold out in advance, and it was the moment our scene both peaked and began to decline, as we all were responding to demands to take our music out on the road. The death of any great musical scene is success, since you're no longer spending time at home, hanging out together. Your city, your hangouts, your shows, your clubs have now expanded to the rest of the world.

Two weeks after the record's release, we went out on a week-long run opening for The Psychedelic Furs in the biggest rooms I'd ever played by far, including the Santa Monica Civic, where I'd seen The Beach Boys in 1971, and where I'd stood with my ear pressed against the side door on New Year's Eve 1977, unable to afford a ticket, listening to my future bandmate and friend, Sal Maida, play a headlining set with Sparks.

Just one year earlier, I was playing the hell out of the first Psychedelic Furs record in my father's basement. I remember dreaming of some kind of local scene with bands like the Furs and the Bunnymen—something that would happen to give me that same sense of a movement, like the punk rock and new wave explosion that had excited and inspired me five years earlier. And now? We had become the very scene I had imagined, in tandem with similar collectives that were starting to bust out across the country in Athens, Minneapolis, and New York City, and many points in between.

Twelve months earlier, I was someone whose only ambitions and dreams as a musician were to be someone who gets together with friends and jams in the basement. Now I was part of a band that released a record that would be one of the most well-received and written-about albums of 1982. The *Los Angeles Times* and *Herald-Examiner* named *The Days Of Wine And Roses* the 'number one LA album of the year' and called us 'the most important Los Angeles area pop or anti-pop band of 1982,' respectively. I would become accustomed to knowing that I could drop by the newsstand on the corner of Cahuenga and Hollywood and pick up any music magazine on the racks certain that there would be a rave review or feature about our band inside. Those were some incredibly big life and attitude changes for a kid like me, and there would be even bigger changes ahead in the new year that was about to begin.

2.8
THE ART OF THE IMPROVISERS

One night around this time, Karl overheard a snippet of a conversation from a bathroom stall in a club after one of our sets.

'I used to like the Dream Syndicate. Now they're a bunch of hippies.'

We laughed when he told us the story, and that comment became a favorite inside-joke and catchphrase in the following weeks.

The disgruntled, baffled fan was most likely responding to one of our expansive evenings, a night when we would choose to stretch our songs long beyond their original recorded intent. We enjoyed jamming and exploring and the uncertainty and suspension of reality, as well as the psychedelic state that would happen when the three-minute count of a song drifted into double digits and beyond.

Jamming had gotten a bad name, particularly leading up to the punk era, when it meant little more than, *You guys hold down the fort and play rhythm for a long time while I endlessly solo, and then maybe I'll do the same for you.* Meandering, ego-tripping, pointless showing off was usually only interesting to the one who was doing the showing off.

But we had begun in the basement with our own version of the tired form. Our preferred style of improvisation, rather than a showcase for imagined virtuosity, was instead a reflection of our love for the swirling psychedelia of John Coltrane's 'Afro Blue' or 'Ascension,' the numbing drone and repetition of The Velvet Underground's 'Sister Ray,' and the psychic collective elevation of 'East/West' by the Butterfield Blues Band, a track I had played over and over endlessly one night late in 1982 while tripping on acid. It had quite an impact.

We were one of the few bands of our newly hatched independent scene, locally and nationally, who were embracing this decidedly unhip long form of song structure. Some dug it, some didn't. We did, however, and that was all that mattered.

There was a show we played at the end of 1982 in Santa Cruz, a college town with a hippie enclave. I thought it would be geographically appropriate to wear a tie-dyed T-shirt and have us make up most of the performance as we went along. Our hour-long set contained only three songs. We opened with a compact, straightforward version of 'When You Smile' and finished with an equally by-the-book cover of the Buffalo Springfield's 'Mr. Soul.' But in the middle, we played a forty-five-minute version of our freeform 'It's Gonna Be Alright.' We were really feeling it, losing ourselves and also excited, collectively thinking, *They're digging it, they're really digging it,* only to finish the marathon number and see a silently dazed and baffled audience who were seriously nonplussed at best by what we had just done.

So much for understanding the 'what they want' part of 'give the people what they want.'

Back when I was in fifth grade, my teacher presented an interesting experiment to the class one day. She said, 'For the next fifteen minutes, I'm giving you complete freedom to do whatever you want. Anything. I'll be here watching, but just have fun and make up your own rules.' I saw a classmate choosing to use his freedom to paint a picture, a piece of construction paper perched on an easel. Using what I perceived as my own freedom, I went over and mixed up his paints and augmented what he had done. The teacher was scolding and disapproving, saying, 'You used your freedom to stop him from enjoying his.'

This was initially mortifying but eventually instructive—one of those things that stuck with me. It's played into my approach to musical interaction over the years. My freedom, our freedom, your freedom is all great and to be commended while we have our extended workouts, but that freedom should be in support of each other, in harmony and confluence, rather than stealing the narrative and spotlight for oneself.

Good jamming is like a conversation. Imagine all the performers onstage as a group of people having a chat. The lead guitarist might, via his fingers and strings, be saying, 'Hey, let me tell you a story,' while the rhythm section responds, 'Uh huh,' 'You don't say,' 'Tell me more,' 'Wow,' or just nodding approvingly. Sometimes there might be an overlap where another soloist comments, 'Yes! That happened to me, and here's my account'— an overlap of commentary, like in, for example, a Robert Altman film, where voices naturally continue and complete each other's thoughts. Or maybe everyone just talks at once, loudly, almost oblivious to each other, the din of a trendy, noisy modern restaurant—incomprehensible, lacking a narrative, but exciting in its relentlessness.

As an only child, I often find myself trying to read the room, searching for clues in the words and rhythms of other people so that I can fit in and create a sense of family where one might not otherwise exist. This is jamming as well. A good, conversational session with a stranger or friend is memorable and transcendent in a way that a lengthy monologue, a long solo of a one-way conversation, can never be.

One of my favorite activities is to place myself in a new city and wander the streets randomly, looking for clues for the next step, understanding the groove and speed of the terrain and feeling like I've made a new geographical friend after a few hours of getting lost and finding myself again. This is jamming as well, a push and pull with and against the elasticity of a bustling metropolis.

I think improvisation plays into our sense of being emphatic creatures. We're all in an uncertain place, unchartered territory, with the knowledge that it could all fall apart, that we could all end up with musical egg on our face. We're worried, the audience is worried— 'I hope they're going to be okay. I'm so nervous!'—and then when hopefully it all works out, a natural musical climax and resolution has occurred, and we're all safely back into the song structure, there is a sense of relief and even exhilaration: 'They did it! WE did it! We're all in this together! Hooray for us!' which can mean more and deliver more satisfaction for both band and audience than a dozen album tracks played perfectly just like on the record.

The Dream Syndicate has always been, at heart, a jam band and a groove band. We've always been a band that wanders afield, testing the edges, daring ourselves to fall off into darkness, only to rescue ourselves at the last minute and live to do it all over again. It's probably what we do best, and it's one of the main reasons people continue to come see us play after all these years.

2.9
DOWN THERE NO LONGER

One more thing happened at the end of 1982 that took me another large step away from who I had been a year earlier. I moved out of my father's basement. The unspoken understanding had been that I would live there for the sake of convenience and budget while I was going to UCLA. Now that my days as a college student were well behind me, it was time to find a place to live.

An acquaintance and fixture on the LA music scene, Joanna 'Spock' Dean, said that she was renting a house on Crescent Heights Boulevard in the heart of West Hollywood and had a room that was available to rent. I packed up my guitars, amp, clothes, stereo, and two-thousand-plus records, and as the new year began, I was living with Spock and another roommate, Wazmo Nariz, who had made a catchy single a few years earlier called 'Tele-Tele-Telephone' that had been a fixture on my KDVS radio show.

I was now within walking distance of the Roxy, the Whisky A Go Go, and Starwood, as well as plenty of taco stands, donut shops, and liquor stores. Spock had been in the pioneering LA all-female punk group Backstage Pass and knew plenty of people in the local music world. Our pad became a kind of rock'n'roll hangout for musicians, music biz people, and scenesters who dropped by on the way to or from the clubs. Living there made it easier to see shows and meet people in a world that had previously been distant and alien to me. I was gradually becoming less of an outsider looking in.

In early 1983, we were asked to perform at Club Lingerie for a show called *Hot Spots* on the USA TV Network. This meant national exposure, the chance to reach more potential fans across the country. Unfortunately, a few days before the gig, I started having some serious tooth discomfort in my back molars that got worse and worse until I finally woke up in blinding pain on the morning of the taping. I rushed over to my dentist, who told me that the problem was my wisdom teeth and that all four would need to be pulled. He offered to do it right then and there. I was faced with a horrible choice. The pain was so bad I could barely imagine getting onstage and playing a show but, on the other hand, pulling four wisdom teeth was a ridiculously serious procedure to undertake with soundcheck only a few hours away.

'Yank 'em,' I said.

Sedated from Demerol, and with a filled prescription of codeine at the ready, I was feeling no pain and ready to play. I managed to make it through soundcheck and the show by chasing the Demerol and codeine with a few shots of whiskey. We played a brand-new song called 'Still Holding On To You,' along with 'Tell Me When It's Over.' If you watch the clip on YouTube, you can see that my cheeks are swollen like a chipmunk and my eyes are glazed. Dennis handles almost all of the accompanying interview, but the performance itself is actually quite solid. In those days, I had the supernatural ability to be five steps beyond blotto and still remember the chords and words to my songs—a blessing and a curse, since it only encouraged me to test that skill on a regular basis.

Our growing audience and press and radio play led us to gigs we had no business playing. One day we got a call from the Palace Theater on Hollywood and Vine because Toni Basil, riding high on the charts with 'Mickey,' had canceled her show for that evening. They wanted to know if we could fill in on just a few hours' notice. We'd get $500, which was a king's ransom to us at the time—the most any band I'd ever played with had been paid to play a set of music.

We showed up to soundcheck, and the club manager got upset because they had a dress code that didn't allow for Karl's torn blue jeans. Every fiber of our being said to tell them to go fuck themselves, but we wanted the money. We went home to change our clothes, and, at the same time, get extremely drunk. On returning, naturally, there was almost nobody in the audience since everyone had asked for a refund due to the non-'Mickey' show. We were in serious 'don't-give-a-fuck' mode and opened with a serviceable version of a song Karl had recently written called 'Halloween,' and then I started vamping on Big Brother & The Holding Company's 'Piece Of My Heart,' not bothering to change the gender and camping up the lyrics. The house manager was not amused and dropped the curtain on us mid-song. We still got paid, but we were riled up and ready for a confrontation. Rather than take it out on the club—they kicked us out soon after giving us our money—I put my fist through a glass cabinet once I got home. I still have the scar.

Alcohol and other substances started showing up, much as they do when a band starts gaining traction, and they were a natural fit for our confrontational spirit and sound. After learning the joys and accompanying abandonment of inhibition that can come from a few shots of whiskey, I also found that it gave me the confidence I needed to be the frontman onstage. It made me feel like a different person. The more I drank, the more I became that person.

The drinking did, in fact, give me courage and turn me into someone else besides the record store clerk, college student, and sweet, nerdy music fan that I had no desire to be when I was onstage. It was medicinal, it was scientific, it was escapist, but it also set a pattern that would not do me any favors in the following months and years.

Along with drinking, I discovered the wonders of speed, particularly crystal meth amphetamine. We had begun to employ the services of a tour manager and soundman named Pat who was also a casual, low-level meth dealer. To be honest, I can't remember what came first. Did the access and proximity to speed make it more tempting to have him around, at the ready with go-faster drugs? Or, as part of our live music operation, did he get us the speed to help us with late-night gigs and drives? I really don't remember—probably both were true—but he was now part of our team.

Speed was great. It was exciting. It helped me get things done, and, while high, feel great about what I was doing. I loved the jolt to the system, the feeling of suddenly being wide awake and ready for anything. I enjoyed the sensation of mucus mixing with the speed, dripping down the back of my throat as a way of letting me know the drug was taking effect. I even loved the way my tattered and curled dollar bills, which doubled as snorting devices, would for days still smell like the substance that allowed me to stay up later, play and listen to more music, drink more, and keep the party going for just a little while longer. It was a good drug for working, getting things done, and experiencing a little more of everything.

But it was also miserable when the speed ran out. I'd be tired for days, depressed, doubting everything that had made me so excited only twenty-four hours before. This was the downside of the upside. Luckily, even with our new tour manager, I was neither connected nor rich enough to buy the drug regularly, so I was able to resist the temptation to immediately get more and get wired again. I'd just sleep it off and wait the weeks until it would enter my orbit again. It was far easier and cheaper to buy a half-pint of Beam or a two-dollar shot in a local bar.

In the meantime, good news continued to come in for the band. We were contacted by a young agent in New York named Frank Riley, who wanted to add us to his roster of artists comprised of other indie-rock pioneers across the country, like The Replacements, the dB's, The Feelies, Hüsker Dü, and a new band out of Milwaukee called The Violent Femmes. He had cornered that fledgling market, and it felt not only like a good fit but like the only fit for a band like us. *The Days Of Wine And Roses* was taking off, and there were plenty of clubs across the country who wanted to see what we were all about.

In the month before the start of our first cross-country tour, we played a trio of shows in LA. That sounds unfathomable now, in a time when playing the same town even twice in one year can feel like overkill for a band on any level of the touring spectrum. But people went out to shows more back then; we were playing with the hot hand, and we wanted to play it as much and as often as we could. We did our regular gigs at Club Lingerie and the Music Machine, but the big one—the one that felt like the official showcase for the new album—was at the Roxy.

The Roxy was the most prestigious club in town and a new Big Rock frontier for us. I had seen Lou Reed, Richard and Linda Thompson, Television, and Nils Lofgren all play great shows there in the years before, and I had done my best to snag tickets for a surprise Bruce Springsteen show there in 1975, only to find the line stretching over a mile down the Sunset Strip immediately after it was announced. Now we were headlining, and the show was sold out. Our entire label and all the major local rock critics would be there. And, uncharacteristically for us at the time, we played it straight, both chemically and in terms of our setlist and performance. We played the new album, and we played it like it sounded on the album, my snarky comments kept to a minimum. The audience liked it—but I wasn't happy. Standing with Dennis in the parking lot at the end of the night, I said, 'We sold out.'

I wasn't referring to the number of bodies in the room. I was responding to one of the first and only times we behaved like a normal, professional rock band, yet rather than feeling like we had crossed a threshold and made it possible to capitalize on our success—both of which were true—I was embarrassed. I felt like a charlatan. It's the way I tended to think back then. If you expect one thing, I'll give you another. We had built our band

and expectations so firmly on going against the grain and being hated or loved. Nothing in between would do. It would have been a good time to tone down the contrarian brat routine a little bit, to be kind to an audience that was truly excited to take us in as the next big thing, but I had my schtick, which was largely a defense mechanism, and I wasn't ready to play it safe.

What I didn't realize at the time was that our version of playing it safe would still have been way outside of the mainstream, and still plenty challenging. The music, even when played exactly as it was on the album, was still light years outside of what the center held at the time.

As February began, the four of us and road manager Pat were in a fifteen-passenger Econoline, leaving LA in the dead of winter to start a six-week tour across the country and back.

PART THREE
I'VE GOT A PAGE ONE STORY BURIED IN MY YARD

3.1
THE FIRST TOUR

There's nothing like your first tour, and ours was a doozy—a collection of experiences that simultaneously would make you want to be on the road for the rest of your life (which would be the case for me) or make you think twice before ever doing it again (as would be the case for Kendra).

The first of the firsts happened as we were driving across Arizona, and it started snowing. In my first twenty-three years on the planet, I had never seen snow fall from the sky. As we stopped for coffee in a diner in Bowie, Arizona, and watched the flakes come down, the waitress filling our cups asked, 'Are you guys in a band?'

'Why yes,' we proudly replied, 'we most certainly are a band, and we're starting our first tour across the country.'

One of the tough things about being a band from LA is that you're going to have to drive a lot of miles to get started on your tour. San Francisco is four hundred miles to the north. Denver is a thousand miles to the east. In our case, the first show of the tour was fourteen hundred miles down the road in Austin. Speed, coffee, gas-station junk food, and the sounds of John Cougar and Pat Benatar on the FM rock stations helped the time pass quickly.

This was our second time in Austin, and seeing Jody and Alejandro there made it feel like a local show, revisiting old friends and seeing fans who had come to our show only a few months earlier. But after that we were heading into the great unknown, beginning a day later with our first visit to New Orleans. As was the case with most nights on the tour, we stayed in a motel a long way from the center of town to save money. That was fine for Karl and Kendra and Pat, who were all exhausted, but I had never been to New Orleans, and with a night off before our show, Dennis and I took the van into town to have a look.

We ate dirty rice at Popeyes, a chain of chicken restaurants that was at the time unknown to us in California, and it felt like the most exotic thing on earth. This must be real New Orleans food! We went to a seedy bar called the Dungeon, which I have realized since then to be a Bourbon Street frat boy/tourist trap. At the time, it felt like the real deal, something out of a Tennessee Williams play filled with alluring and yet unfathomable late-night creatures. It was all new and mysterious, even to 'big city' kids like Dennis and me. We finished the evening just before sunrise with beignets at Café du Monde, a sweet conclusion to a savory evening. We were glad we had made the late-night trek and were filled with stories to tell our bandmates the next day.

Getting some rest, on the other hand, might have been a good idea, since the New Orleans show was followed by an overnight thousand-mile drive to Atlanta, and then another six-hundred-mile drive to Washington D.C. By the time we reached the fabled 9:30 Club—a regular stop not only for our band but for pretty much every indie band throughout the 80s— we were buoyed by the adrenaline rush of a packed show, free pizza in the downstairs backstage area, and the knowledge that the next day would be a four-hour drive up I-95 for our first show in New York City, at the very trendy Danceteria, no less. New York City loomed large for me as the home of our favorite bands, music scene, and movies, and as the place where I'd had such great adventures only eighteen months earlier. We knew there was some serious anticipation for the show, and we couldn't wait to get there.

The morning after our D.C. show, we woke up in our motel and looked out of the window in shock at all the snow that had fallen in the few hours we had been asleep. Later known as the Megalopolitan Blizzard, the storm dropped nearly two feet of snow in one day, ranking it as the second-largest snowfall to hit the East Coast in recorded history.

We still had high hopes and were hell-bent on getting to our show, but after six hours we had only made it thirty miles up the road to Baltimore, and it became apparent that we wouldn't be playing at Danceteria that night. I was crushed, devastated, inconsolable. In my mind, that was the end of everything. We had killed any chance of a career or future in New York City. Nonetheless, we valiantly pressed on, making it as far as a Baltimore airport-adjacent motel that had only one room available, which we gratefully took, crowding ourselves across the two beds and floor space while Pat called the club to say we wouldn't be able to make it.

'Are you kidding?' they responded. 'Don't worry, there's two feet of snow and nobody's going out tonight anyway. Stay warm.'

My spiraling dread of a canceled show killing our New York City career had been premature and, much like our weary heads, was gently laid to rest.

We managed to get out of Baltimore the next day for our show that night in Hoboken, New Jersey, at Maxwell's, the club that had fired my imagination as I read about it in *New York Rocker*. As magical as it was musically and culturally, the club itself was a nondescript two-hundred-capacity box with a burger joint out front. Despite the snow, we had a decent turnout. The house sound engineer that night was a local named Ira Kaplan who knew about and dug our band and, I'm sure, made us sound good.

The shows were all going great, and people along the way were ready for and receptive to what we had to offer. Our punk songs got punkier, our sprawling jam songs got longer, our covers moved further from what was considered cool in the underground world, and the fans who turned out weren't fazed in the least—they had been prepped by semaphore signals of press and other word of mouth to know what to expect. It was gratifying and even a little unsettling as we realized that we no longer needed to confront or shock to get our music across.

TOP LEFT I think I'm attempting an A-minor chord on the fifth fret, but of course I would have had no idea at the time. I wouldn't start playing for another seven years, but I sure seem happy to be giving it a shot. Maybe one of the last times I played in shorts.

TOP RIGHT A little bit older, a little more comfortable with the guitar, but hand still angling for that magic fifth fret. And what about the bongos—or the sandals, for that matter? So many questions. This is the year that I began guitar lessons. I obviously needed them.

CENTER LEFT I'm faking it well. I was never much of an athlete, but my batting stance looks pretty solid. This was during the high school years when music took a back seat to sportswriting for a little while. My shirt forecasts my eventual migration to New York City a couple of decades later and the New York Yankee team that I support today. Apologies to my LA friends.

CENTER RIGHT My parents, Earl Wynn and Marlene Robbins, made for a dashing couple. They married in 1958 and separated four years later, having just one kid in the process. Very efficient. They remained close friends until my father died in 2012. This was taken on their honeymoon.

BOTTOM LEFT That's me in the top row, second from left, at Page Elementary School, Los Angeles. My mother would drop me off at 8am before work and come and retrieve me at 6pm when she was done, giving me ample time to be bored and my imagination plenty of time to run wild.

LEFT A little beefcake for the photo section. Hey, we're just barely out of the 70s here, and jean cutoffs were still very much in vogue. I seem to be enraptured by Albert Grossman's *Ladies And Gentlemen, Lenny Bruce*, most likely imagining and honing the confrontational patter I would adopt for those early Dream Syndicate shows. *Photo by Tom Gracyk*

RIGHT One of the few times I took my blonde Telecaster out of its case during the high school years when my attention shifted primarily to sportswriting. Apparently, my attention had shifted from barber visits to blow dryers during those same years as well.

ABOVE I went to UC Davis to study rhetoric but ended up doing a master's thesis in undergraduate studies with my band, Suspects. Kendra was the singer, I played rhythm guitar; Russ Tolman and Gavin Blair would go on to form True West. Bassist Steve Suchil was the first to turn me on to The Velvet Underground, and I thank him for that.

ABOVE For a while there, the Paisley Underground was as much a scene as any other musical collective from other cities and times. We hung out and played shows together, we inspired and challenged each other, in some cases we even dated each other. This was the peak moment of our little gang, the twenty-four-hour period when we took a boat to Catalina Island, tried to sleep on a golf course, and deepened our bond. I'm not sure who took this photo, but I'll be sure to tell you all when I find out. Clockwise from top left: Debbi Peterson, Vicki Peterson, Dennis Duck, Kendra Smith, two friends of the Peterson sisters, Michael Quercio, Louis Guttierez, Susanna Hoffs, and me.

LEFT The Inn Square Men's Bar in Cambridge, Massachusetts, wasn't around all that long, but in the early 80s it was a regular stop for bands of our ilk. We played there twice. I liked it. It was an intimate room, always lively, and you could reach the bar from the stage—a blessing and a curse. *Photo by Jim Merrill*

Stereo

the dream
syndicate

**the days
of wine
and** roses

RIGHT One of many guitars I would buy and then trade for another after a handful of months, never owning more than two at any given time. They were all cheap at the time, including this Dan Armstrong clear model, and all of them are worth a whole lot more today. I don't have too many regrets in life, but I sure as hell wish I had some of those guitars again today.
Photo by Tom Gracyk

OPPOSITE PAGE I had the idea of doing a photo session deep inside Topanga Canyon, and photographer David Arnoff was game. It was a pretty incongruous setting for post-punk, psychedelic, paisley urban warriors such as ourselves, but there was always an undercurrent of hippie swamp freaks in everything we did. This became the poster for *The Days Of Wine And Roses*. I have it on my wall at home.

TOP RIGHT Here we are posing as the New York band we imagined we were, despite all of us being native Californians and this fire escape being in LA, not Manhattan. Without thinking about it all that much, we were more inspired by CBGBs, the Factory, and the Village Vanguard than we were by surfboards, sunshine, and the Pacific Ocean. *Photo by Edward Colver*

BOTTOM RIGHT On Halloween 1982, we played a gig somewhere in Hollywood. I forget the club, but I remember—and this photo is evidence— that we thought it would be fun to dress up in drag for the show. In a moment of high-concept genius, Kendra did the 'double drag' as a woman dolled up like a male drag queen. It was impressive. I don't think anyone has seen this photo before. I found it deep in a box in my closet where I probably thought I had hidden it forever.

OPPOSITE PAGE A late-night photo shoot for the *NME* in downtown New York City in early 1983, and our first time meeting iconic rock photographer Laura Levine, whose work I had enjoyed in *New York Rocker* and other magazines in the previous years. I believe that three members of our band had dropped acid, and the other one (me) was merely deep into a night of whiskey shots. Karl and I would end up walking the streets of Manhattan for the ensuing twenty-four hours after the shoot, leading right up to our first NYC show at the Mudd Club.

RIGHT Kendra Smith was the soul of the band, no doubt about it. She had only been playing bass for a little over a year when we started, but her sense of groove and mystery was factory installed from birth. One night, in a dark, corner booth at the Cathay de Grande, we devised a formula that defined every record we loved and the one that we knew we wanted to make. The conversation probably looked a little like this.

LEFT We finished our first European tour in the fall of 1984 with a show at London's fabled Marquee club. So many of my favorite bands had played there, and it was a thrill to sell it out just a few weeks after packing out another London club, Dingwalls, to start the tour. Crossing the pond gave us a new life, a new jolt of energy, and new places to play. We'd end up playing more shows in Europe than in the USA in the ensuing years.

BELOW Dennis Duck and I have been playing together in The Dream Syndicate for over forty years. Here we are early in that tenure, sometime in 1983. Let there be no doubt: the only reason we were able to get out of the basement and secure plum gigs from the start was because Dennis had already been on the scene, in the clubs, and on the airwaves with his band Human Hands. We were 'Dennis Duck's new band,' and it served us well in those first months. *Photo by David Hovland*

OPPOSITE PAGE We knew how to pose. Somehow it seemed effortless at the time. *Photo by Edward Colver*

RIGHT On tour with R.E.M. in the summer of 1984. This one feels more post- than pre-show, based on the variously giddy and fuzzy expressions. We had a lot of fun on the tour—we knew we deserved it, a decadent victory lap. Only a couple of years before, we were both slogging it out on the new wave circuit across America, and this leap to sold-out theaters felt like a vindication of those efforts.

BELOW 1985. R.E.M. had just played their biggest LA show to date at the Greek Theater before decamping to the cozier Lhasa Club in Hollywood for the post-gig party. I lived just down the block and played there often in my earliest days of solo acoustic gigs. Unsurprisingly, a whole lot of jamming ensued, including this rare sighting: Peter Buck singing! I wish I knew what song we were playing. *Photo by Greg Allen*

OPPOSITE PAGE This photo session for the Danny & Dusty band likely took only a little less time than it took us to record our entire album, once we realized our ramshackle thirty-six-hour session was going to be coming out on a major label. Clockwise from top left: Stephen McCarthy, Sid Griffin, Tom Stevens, me, Chris Cacavas, Dennis Duck and Dan. *Photo by Amy Mehaffey*

ABOVE San Francisco, 1984.
Photo by Laura Levine

OPPOSITE PAGE Laura came to visit me in the Bay Area while we were making *Medicine Show*, and unlike the green kid on his first tour that she had met in her photo studio one year earlier, I was now deep into a taxing five-month recording session, drinking a fifth of Jim Beam every day and watching TV preacher Dr. Gene Scott late into every evening. A little off the rails, but it made for some good photos and posing, channeling Dr. Scott here at the foot of Sather Tower on the UC Berkeley campus.

ABOVE Dennis, Paul, Mark, and me, just across the street from Uncle Rehearsal Studios in Van Nuys. Mark and his brother Scott have owned Uncle since the late 70s. It's still around, and I still dive in for a tune-up now and then. Just behind us, and a few steps up the road, is the liquor store where we'd buy cheap beer. I can't tell if we're on our way there or back, but we dug a deep groove in the pathway over the years. *Photo by Tom Gracyk*

RIGHT I celebrated my twenty-sixth birthday at Eldorado Studios while we were making *Out Of The Grey*. Dennis's wife, Amy, baked this cake and surprised me with it on a recording break. It was tasty, and the sugar rush took us late into the night. *Photo by Amy Mehaffey*

We were flying high from the show at Maxwell's when we left to pack up and make our way to the cheap motel down the road in nearby Secaucus, where we'd be spending the next few nights, only to find our van was gone. It had been towed by the city while we were onstage, and Pat had to go to the local impound center to pay the two hundred bucks we could barely afford while, thankfully, he sent the rest of us to the hotel to get some sleep. It had been quite a first week on the road.

Twelve months earlier, our sphere was limited to my father's basement. Six months earlier, our world was the clubs of Hollywood and Santa Monica. Now we were, to quote ZZ Top, bad and nationwide, and we were also seeing the first flickers of interest from overseas in Europe. Geoff Travis at Rough Trade Records had licensed our album from Slash, and I couldn't have been more thrilled, as I was a big fan of the label. We had a day off after the Maxwell's show before what would now be our first New York City gig at the Mudd Club the following night. Rough Trade had arranged a photo session with *NME*, which gave us an excuse to go through the Holland Tunnel into Manhattan on our night off.

The shoot was scheduled for the evening at the downtown apartment and photo studio of Laura Levine, who was the top rock'n'roll photographer in the city. I had seen her work in the *Village Voice*, *New York Rocker*, and *NME*, and it felt like a big deal to be visually captured by such a well-known photographer. Of course, the gravitas of the situation did not cause us to rest up or prepare. Instead, we killed time before heading over to Laura's studio by getting drunk (me) and taking LSD (Karl, Kendra, and Dennis). We were out of our minds by the time we got to Laura's studio, but due to her skills and our youth we managed to nonetheless look mysterious and alluring, and the photo that ended up being used from that night has remained one of the iconic images of that lineup. Laura suggested we close our eyes as though we were—get it?—dreaming. Given our physical state, that was an easy instruction to follow.

As we got in the van around 2am to drive back to our cheap motel in Secaucus and call it a night, Karl and I were not pleased. We wanted more time in New York City, where the bars wouldn't close for another two hours. Pat, still wiped out from retrieving the van the night before, finally got sick of our griping and whining and moaning and said, 'Okay, you two. You want more time in the city? Get out. Soundcheck at the Mudd Club is tomorrow at 5pm. See you there.' We thought he was kidding, but he was dead serious. He'd had enough of us. He gave us an envelope of crystal meth, kicked us out, and drove off. We were shocked but also kind of happy, knowing we could stay up all night and spend some serious time in the city.

We wandered through the snow, got a few drinks, had a cheap diner breakfast in the West Village, and then tried to figure out where to snort the speed. We were a bit nervous and paranoid but, knowing now what I know about New York at the time, I'm sure we could have just chopped out a few lines on a police car and snorted them without any need to worry. It was a wild and lawless city back then. Instead, though, we went to a public restroom in Grand Central Station, one of us standing watch while the other went into the stall to get properly wired.

This might have been as close as Karl and I would ever be again. We had a great time, wandering through the snow in Central Park, drifting into record stores in Greenwich Village, looking at people and buildings. As much as we gave Pat a hard time when we got to soundcheck, we were also happy that he had forced this adventure upon us. The snow, cold weather, and lack of sleep took its toll, however, and we would both end up getting sick in the week that followed.

Like most New York City clubs, the Mudd Club was well on our radar, looming large as a place of rock mythology. It had more of a reputation as a gathering place for scenesters and late-night adventurers, as well as for the namecheck in the Talking Heads song 'Life During Wartime.' And, true to its reputation, it was too cool for school: our set, which began at the vampire hour of 3am, was met, for the first time on the tour, by a seemingly indifferent crowd. They weren't excited or shocked or annoyed, just...bored? Who knows? They might have been tired. Or high. Or both.

But somebody must have liked what they saw, and word must have spread, because by the time we came back a week later for a show at another Gotham legend, Folk City, we opened up the *Village Voice* to the center pages, which were always devoted to upcoming events of the week, and were shocked to find that Laura's picture of us spanned almost the entire two-page centerfold. I had read the *Voice* religiously every week at the Cahuenga newsstand and continued to read it until it folded decades later, and I never saw anybody else get such a strong positioning on those pages. The anointed dean of rock'n'roll writing, Robert Christgau, wrote glowing and ecstatic words about us to accompany the photo. It was hardly surprising when we pulled up for soundcheck and found a line around the block with far more people than could fit in the club. Incidentally, Ira Kaplan booked us for the gig and was our host that night as part of his 'Music For Dozens' series. We drew more than a few dozen that night.

I was sincerely thrilled and flattered by the turnout and ultimately by a great reception, which proved Mudd Club to be the zoned-out anomaly that it was. New York was the city of my dreams, the birthplace of so many of my favorite bands, and we found ourselves being embraced wholeheartedly on that Folk City night.

I should have been giddy and grateful, but at that age, I didn't know how to embrace that kind of adulation or how to deal with it. Instead, I found myself remembering how funny and cool I thought it was when Lou Reed chose to viciously dress down Christgau during one of his raps on 'Take No Prisoners,' and thought it would be fun and bratty to do a similar thing, choosing to recite the words Christgau had written about us in the *Voice* onstage at Folk City in a bored and ironic tone. I cringe now when I think about it, especially since I was actually a big fan of his writing and read his reviews regularly. I'm hardly surprised that not only would Christgau never write much about my music again but also that he would take some seemingly random, vicious jabs at me when he did deign to write about me in the years that followed. I had it coming. Then again, it was not lost on me that Sonic Youth got a free pass with their single 'I Killed Christgau With My Big Fucking Dick' and remained in his good graces for years.

The following weeks were filled with heady adventures. We were equally well received in Boston, a city that, along with New York, would become a place where we'd play as regularly over the following years as we did in our hometown of LA. Our show at Philadelphia's East Side Club was opened by a Boston band called The Dangerous Birds, featuring a singer, Thalia Zedek, who completely mesmerized me and would become a good friend and bandmate a decade later. In Chicago, at Tut's, we had a completely inappropriate opening band who finished their set with a straight, un-ironic version of J.J. Cale's 'Cocaine,' so we came out and opened our set with that same song because, well, that's the kind of bratty thing we liked to do. A few days later, in Minneapolis, we played First Avenue and were told repeatedly through the night that 'Prince is here to see you guys.' We never did actually get to meet him, but I'd like to think we got him started on the paisley journey that he began in the following years.

As it turns out, the greatest threat to the survival of our band wasn't the weather or long nights or drugs or any other potential hazard of touring life but rather a potential threat to the very name of the band itself. We were getting ready to go onstage in Buffalo when someone came backstage and told us, 'Tony Conrad is here tonight to see your show.' It turns out that the former Faust member and leader of the original pre-Velvets Dream Syndicate, as well as the man from whose 70s solo album we had borrowed our name, was a Buffalo resident. We panicked a little. What if he resents our unrequested appropriation? What if he threatens legal action? We were uncharacteristically nervous as we hit the stage yet made sure to deliver the best we had to offer. Tony Conrad must have liked what he saw because, moments after we finished our set, he bounded backstage and said, 'That was a great show—I'm so proud to have you boys carrying on the torch of The Dream Syndicate.' Permission granted, possibly one year after it should have been requested.

The strangest show we played on that tour may have been in Kansas City. Shane Williams wrote for the fanzine *Flipside* and was known as the Rock'n'roll Bank Robber, and, true to that moniker, he was doing time for armed robbery at Leavenworth State Penitentiary just down the road from KC, writing about punk rock and occasionally booking bands to play for the inmates. He knew we were playing close by, so he got us a gig that would fit easily into our packed schedule, since Leavenworth's stage time was mid-afternoon. We arrived early in the afternoon and were told that for security and contraband reasons, we couldn't use our own gear and instead had to rely on their in-house Peavy backline. Peavy would make better gear in the ensuing years, but at the time they had a bad reputation. I remember thinking, *Man, prison is harsh, you gotta play through Peavy amps.*

Despite it being in a maximum-security prison, things seemed surprisingly lax and freewheeling. We wandered down the halls to the auditorium, inmates walking around us, unshackled and paying uncomfortably close attention to Kendra.

I had one of my 'seemed like a good idea at the time' notions to just get up and play nothing but classic rock covers, thinking it would win over the lifers. Here's the set we played:

'Born On The Bayou' (CCR)
'Let It Rain' (Clapton)
'Outlaw Blues' (Dylan)
'Mr. Soul' (Neil Young)
'Then She Remembers' (our song—a little punk rock for Shane)

What I didn't expect was complete indifference. Inmates wandered in and out, checking out a song and then leaving. What else was on their schedule or gig planner that day? The few that stayed for the whole set only had one response to our set: 'Let the girl sing.'

We played our last show of the tour in Denver and then came back home to LA, ragged but also having had an irreplaceable experience. Our first tour of duty was over, and like other such experiences there were casualties and changes, and things would never be the same.

When we returned to that same diner in Bowie, Arizona, six weeks later, the same waitress greeted us with, 'Hey, it's the guys in the band.' We were shocked and amused that she remembered us, but now we were seasoned touring veterans, very different from the kids who had passed through town six weeks earlier.

EXIT KENDRA, ENTER U2

We came back home from our first tour very different than we had been when we left home six weeks earlier. Calloused and battered and exhausted from the long drives, late nights, and minimal sleep, we were encouraged by the places where we had been greeted like royalty (NYC, Boston, Chicago, Minneapolis, DC), but also humbled by places we had played to sparse crowds who hadn't gotten the memo yet (Detroit, New Orleans, Denver). We had become well versed in the routines and rhythms of touring—something that is second nature to me now but was still a wild, unknown mystery when the tour began. There aren't many other jobs where you travel every day and sleep in a different bed every single night, and it's not a life for everyone.

I loved it. And I wanted more. I think Karl and Dennis felt the same. But it was grueling for Kendra. Touring—especially back then, in a more male-centric world—can be much tougher on a woman, dealing with nightly bullshit and condescension, clumsy and drunk come-ons, and environments that don't always allow for hygiene or privacy.

We also had been slowly but gradually shifting away from our art-band roots, the more feminine side of our music that reflected The Velvet Underground's influence of mixing vulnerability and a gentle beauty with noise, and taking on more of a Crazy Horse, muscular, grinding guitar approach. Neil Young, like most of the music we loved, wasn't in fashion at that moment, having just released the head-scratching *Trans*. When it comes to the template of two guitars dueling against a steady rhythm section, one man's Velvet Underground or Television is another man's Crazy Horse. In twelve months, we had made the first step from college students and wide-eyed fans toward being seasoned veterans. That brought on a confidence and a certain heavier and more macho sound and approach.

Before the tour, Kendra had started dating David Roback, who had just left The Rain Parade. As the only one with a significant other back home, she had found herself pining for LA more than the rest of us.

It wasn't entirely surprising when she called me not long after the tour and told me that our upcoming show at the Vox club in East LA would be her last. She was quitting the band. I don't remember trying to talk her out of it. I don't remember having much of a reaction, one way or another. Maybe it's just because things were moving so fast that there was no time to think about what things meant.

'You're quitting? Okay, we'll get someone else. We've got things to do!'

But it did change us. It turned us immediately into another band and severed me from my closest friend and the steadying anchor and soul of The Dream Syndicate—the person most closely tied to our original sound and manifesto. It was the end of a chapter. The band that existed for all of fifteen months and had made the first album and EP was finished, even though we didn't think about that at the time, too caught up as we were in the swelling momentum and excitement and new offers that were already coming along. Nonetheless, I wish I had at least tried to convince her to stay.

At Kendra's last gig, we played a new song called 'The Medicine Show' for the first time. I had wanted to write a song like Big Brother & The Holding Company's version of 'Ball And Chain' from the *Cheap Thrills* album, where they shift dynamics brutally, going from a foreboding whisper to an unhinged explosion and release. Like many of my songs back then, 'Medicine Show' quickly moved away from that intent and inspiration and settled into a grooving, Doors-like slow, burning shuffle.

The other thing I remember about Kendra's last gig was a sweet fourteen-year-old girl coming to our soundcheck with her mother. She liked the band but was all about Kendra, focusing on her the entire time, talking to her, and giving her a cassette of the songs that she and a friend had written and recorded under the name Going Home. Her name was Hope Sandoval, and she would replace Kendra just a couple of years later in the band Opal (née Clay Allison) that Kendra had formed with David Roback after she left our band.

Another big change and shift in our standing occurred when we were approached by a guy named Tim Devine, who wanted to manage us. He had worked at Warner Bros and was well-connected in the music world. He was a fan of our music, saw the critical and underground success we were having, and felt we could take it to that almighty Next Level. We were seduced by the good game he talked, and Dennis took on the unenviable task of firing his good friend and our manager of the previous year, Billy Bishop. It must have been very hard for Dennis, and, sure enough, Billy was heartbroken. I still feel terrible about it, years later. Needless to say, that was the end of us being played on Rodney Bingenheimer's radio show.

Nonetheless, Tim lived up to the promises he had made. Within a few short weeks, we were being courted by major labels, despite still being signed to Slash, and Tim expertly massaged and groomed that interest over the following months. Tim was also very good friends with Paul McGuinness, the manager of U2, whose third album, *War*, had just been released and, thanks to a new TV channel called MTV, was really starting to take off. U2 were aware of our music, thanks to the good work Rough Trade had done in the London music press, and they asked us to be the support band on their upcoming three-week coast-to-coast US tour.

Of course, we said yes. The only hitch was that we didn't have a bass player, and we needed one quickly. The tour was starting in just a few weeks. I remembered Dave Provost from his days as a member of The Textones, a band he had with future Go-Go Kathy Valentine. I had seen them play around town often and always dug his style. I had met him at the record store one time and invited him to sit in with me and the Callan sisters in my father's basement. He added a solid foundation to our amateurish meanderings. I knew he'd be a fast learner, and that he was a good, solid guy. And, what's more, I found out he had played with Al Green for a few years on the San Fernando Valley club circuit, before the reverend's career took off in the early 70s—a nice bonus selling point for the press release. Dave was in, and we were about to embark on our second national tour—a tour that would be a whole lot bigger than our first.

The team at Slash Records was understandably excited about us getting the support slot on the U2 tour. They weren't open to giving us actual financial assistance to offset the lower fees that we were getting as an opening act, but instead they gave us the use of their corporate Union 76 credit card for tour support—hardly the stuff of tour buses and large road crews that would later be tossed our way, but still enough to make the trip possible. We ended up eating a lot of 'trucker's breakfasts' at Union 76 truck stops along the way.

We went out with a two-man crew—a guitar tuner/stage tech, and our tour manager, Pat, who doubled as sound engineer. Yes, two months after tossing us out of the van and onto the freezing New York City streets, Pat was still there with us. Despite the occasional temper flare-ups, he was a good guy, and he steered a tight ship as a tour manager. This time around, though, that ship would quickly drift off to some rocky shores.

We flew into JFK and drove our rented van to the first show in New Haven. We were all understandably awed when we stepped into a theater that held twenty-five hundred people. It was far bigger than any venue any of us had played before, and it was most certainly a leap for the headlining band as well, since only a few months earlier, U2 had been a one-hit band ('I Will Follow') with a poorly reviewed second album. But *War* was getting tons of play on MTV, and the impact they were having on these shores was palpable. They were rocketing into the big time, and the theaters they had booked on the tour had all sold out long before the first show began.

We were entering unchartered territories with big productions and venues, our presence reduced to near-negligible. There were more people and rules to navigate than we'd ever had before, and most of that pressure fell on Pat. Between the daunting gauntlet of our new environment and maybe the after-effects of too much speed, he was finished. Upon returning to our hotel in Manhattan after the first show (we had graduated to sleeping on the Gotham side of the Hudson River), Pat had barricaded himself in his room and wouldn't come out. He spoke to us only through the locked door. He did not want to come with us to our show in Passaic, New Jersey, that night but wanted to go home immediately, and we were suddenly on our own, without a tour manager, driver, or soundman.

My roommate back in LA, Joanna 'Spock' Dean, had worked in the music biz and knew how things operated on tour. She agreed to come out immediately to steer the ship. To be honest, I don't know how we paid for or arranged any of these things. Managers and labels just took care of things back then; the bands were oblivious. But by the time we rolled into Passaic, we were a fully functioning team once again, with Pat sent home on what must have been a long, sad flight, and Spock at the helm of our first big rock tour.

U2 were ready for their newfound limelight. They played an emotional and ambitious show, and their singer, Bono, was an outsized personality. I watched their set that first night in New Haven and felt the excitement that I had the first time I saw Bruce Springsteen a decade before. Like Springsteen, Bono had a way of connecting to the audience like he was speaking to each person directly, while at the same time expanding the scope and intensity of the theater to the point where it felt like a gospel rally in a giant stadium. It all seemed so real, so direct, and so spontaneous. At least, it felt that way until they played the exact same show and Bono said all the same things in the same way the next night. And the night after that. And the night after that. I stopped paying attention after the third show.

Even through the cockiness, arrogance, and obliviousness of youth, we could feel we were in the midst of something big happening, stars being born—not that we were always paying the closest of attention. One day at soundcheck, Dennis found himself in a conversation backstage with a member of U2's entourage. The two of them chatted and made small talk for a while, as musicians will do on the road: 'How was your drive today?' 'Any plans after the show'—stuff like that.

Finally, after a few minutes, Dennis, who couldn't figure out where or when he had met the guy, was bold enough to ask, 'Now what exactly is it that you do on the tour?'

'Uh, I'm the drummer,' his new pre-show buddy replied. 'Larry Mullen.'

I'm not sure what Dennis said next, but I can only imagine his embarrassment. 'Uh, yeah . . . uh, I know that but . . . uh, I mean what else do you do for fun on the tour?'

Karl, in the meantime, was letting paranoia get the better of him. He spotted The Edge in the theater, watching a few of our soundchecks, and grumbled after one show, 'He's stealing everything I do. Look at how much feedback he's using in the show.' It's true that there was some feedback coming out of The Edge's amp, but I'm also pretty sure that rock bands had been using feedback long before we did and long before The Edge introduced it into his sound. But Karl would not be convinced otherwise.

Bono? We didn't see him much apart from one night after our set when he came to visit us backstage. Nice guy. Hung out for a bit. Said he loved our set, all the things an opening band likes to hear. And then he said to Karl, 'You know, you should have a big hollow-body red, white, and blue guitar—something with the American flag on it.' Bono had barely left the backstage before Karl's placid and patient face turned to a smirk. Needless to say, it was an idea he never adopted.

Me, I was drinking my usual fifth of Jim Beam over the course of each night, much of it before our set. It was how I managed to buck up the courage to feel that I could play to several thousand people every night. And, generally, it worked pretty well—it made me fearless and ready to slay a dragon or two. It also made me an idiot on occasion, especially the time when I channeled my inner field-goal-kicking football star and felt it was a good idea to punt an empty glass beer bottle from the stage into the audience. Not smart. Somebody could have been badly hurt. Once the show was over, U2's tour manager took me aside with the warning, 'If you ever do something like that again, I'll break both of your fucking arms *and* legs.' Lesson learned. Buzz killed.

To be honest, we were raw, mercurial, and better some nights than others. And it was admirable and daring for a band like U2 to subject their audience to a weird, scruffy band like us. And if they didn't hang out with us all that much, who knows, maybe they thought *we* were standoffish. Either way, they generously gave us a full forty-five minutes onstage each night to do our thing.

It was exciting to play some beautiful and historical venues. I particularly loved performing at the Tower Theater in Philadelphia, where David Bowie had recorded his *David Live* album just a few years before. The Palladium in New York City was another in the growing list of legendary Manhattan venues that we were chalking up in a city that lately we had been playing more than Los Angeles. The U2 audience, for the most part, tolerated us, and we likely made at least a handful of new fans on the tour.

We traveled in a rented Ford Econoline van. U2 toured in a big, luxury bus. But when we got to Minneapolis, with the prospect of a two-thousand-mile drive to Vancouver for the next show, U2 and their management decided that they were doing well enough to blow off the drive and instead fly to the next city. The empty tour bus still had to make the journey, and they were kind enough to offer it up to us. Our van and gear still needed to make the trek too, and we felt a little sheepish asking our crew to drive to Vancouver without us, though they were probably happy to have us out of their hair for a few days. And the four of us? We got to live the rock star life for those forty-eight hours—our first ride in a tour bus, drinking and smoking weed, eating junk food, and watching cheesy porn and Cheech & Chong movies. It was heaven. We were truly grateful, though we may have had a strange way of showing our gratitude, accidentally leaving the remnants of a joint on the bus that was found when U2 made their way back across the Canadian border into the US the day after the Vancouver show.

And that was it. Our last show with U2 was in Seattle, and it was attended by, among others, my future bandmate in The Baseball Project, Scott McCaughey. After that, we were vaulted back into reality: tiny clubs, much smaller crowds, and most certainly no tour buses. Not for a little while, anyway. Our first show after leaving the U2 tour was a noontime gig at Stanford University. Karl and Dave ate some mushrooms, I downed a few drinks. We encored with a ramshackle 'I Will Follow,' and then moved on down the road.

———

PLAYING IN THE BIG LEAGUES

My relationship with music changed around this time. I was no longer the kid who had ridden his bike five miles back and forth, up and down, on steep, perilous mountain roads to buy a copy of the new Kinks album, or the college student who needed to know every single punk and new-wave single that was coming out in New York and London and would drive from Davis to Berkeley just to get the new Clash album on import.

Instead, I found myself listening to music to see how we fit in, how we might progress with or rebel against what was going on, for signposts of what could lie ahead for us. I listened to more and more commercial FM rock radio and obsessively watched videos on MTV to figure out the nuances of mainstream and classic rock and what was viewed as cutting edge by the kind of people who championed Haircut 100 and The Human League as the next big thing. I'd hear a song on the radio like 'Jack And Diane' by John Cougar Mellencamp or 'You Got Lucky' by Tom Petty and think, *Well, that's not too far from what we're doing. I bet we could do that.*

At the same time, I had separated myself from my lovingly assembled record collection. I moved out of the house on Crescent Heights, put my things in storage, and spent the next year couch surfing, mostly with Tom at his apartment in Van Nuys. I needed to save money now that I was on the road so much. The time at the Spock House in West Hollywood had been great—Vicki Peterson from The Bangs had replaced Wazmo Nariz as a roommate, and her enthusiasm and relative sobriety were a good counterbalance as I started to drink and drug more and more. She was also always up for an adventure. One night, we were sitting around listening to records sometime past midnight and I said, 'Hey, let's go to the ocean, dive in the water, and then drive right back,' and, despite the late hour and the thirty-minute drive, Vicki said, 'Sure.' We made our way across Santa Monica Boulevard to the beach, we submerged fully clothed, and then came immediately back in my Honda Civic—soaking wet, the car reeking of the Pacific.

I think staying in the house, especially with nurturing and honest roommates like Vicki and Spock, not to mention the grounding presence of my records and other things, might have kept me in check more than the vagabond life I would live for the next year. Instead, I gave up my room to The Bangles' new bass player, Michael Steele, and lived out of a suitcase for the next eighteen months.

The courtship of our band continued. Geffen president Eddie Rosenblatt invited us to his office and told us that we could have an unreleased Bob Dylan track if we signed with them. Carol Childs worked at the label and was dating Dylan at the time, allowing them to offer up that tasty perk. Gary Gersh at EMI wanted us as well. His pitch was very hands-on: 'We won't just sign you and put you in the studio, we'll work with you every step of the way from your songwriting to your playing.' Somehow that did not appeal to us at all.

We were most intrigued by A&M, feeling they were more of an artists' label, maybe because they were, in fact, founded by Herb Albert (who, along with Phil Spector and future Who and Kinks producer Shel Talmy, had been a classmate of my mother at Fairfax High School in West Hollywood). I liked a lot of the artists on their roster, and they were also the distributors for IRS Records. It felt like a place where we could remain the band we wanted to be without too much interference.

There was still the matter of our two-record deal with Slash. My initial plan was to honor our present contract with a second album and then begin fielding offers. It seemed like the honorable thing to do. But one day, our manager called me after he had spoken to Slash's head of business affairs, who reputedly told him, 'If your band doesn't sign a seven-record deal extension, we will put out the next record and bury it.' That was shocking and hurtful, and it gave us the defiance and permission we needed to let the dogs loose and give Tim the green light to see what he could work out. We ended up signing with A&M, who paid Slash $25,000 to let us go.

Now we had to choose a producer. I don't even remember who we discussed, as I was still unsure exactly what a producer did. Our only experience had been with Chris D, who wisely let us alone and made sure we got the job done and made a record that we liked, represented who we were, and satisfied the people who liked our band. We would need someone with more of a name and reputation this time around—or, at least, that's what our new label and manager were telling us.

Sandy Pearlman was a friend of our manager and had made a good impression on us when he stepped in hours after Pat had quit to mix our gig in New Jersey on the U2 tour. I liked that he had produced The Clash and The Dictators. Karl liked that he had produced Blue Öyster Cult. There was never any second choice. We chose Sandy and planned to make the record in October in San Francisco.

There was also the issue of new material. I hadn't been writing much, and Karl had kept to his one-a-year contribution with a new song called 'Bullet With My Name On It.' That song, along with 'Armed With An Empty Gun' and 'Merrittville,' had started out as blazing, speedy punk songs with a bluesy, country edge, presaging the cowpunk and eventually Americana movements that would follow in the years to come. Sandy convinced us to slow all three of them down—'Merrittville' most radically—to give the songs room to breathe and to allow for more epic, cinematic production. That decision was the first major step away from the band we had been toward the band we would become on our sophomore album.

We were given a recording budget of $150,000—fifty times what we had to work with on *The Days Of Wine And Roses*. A&M also paid for new equipment. I got a brand-new white Fender Stratocaster and a Mesa Boogie amplifier; Karl got a sunburst Les Paul and a Marshall stack. These were the tools of Rock Bands, and our Champ amps and persnickety, annoyingly difficult-to-tune Jazzmasters were left behind. At our last gig before going into the studio, Karl smashed his cheap Silvertone guitar into a post onstage at Berkeley Square, shattering it to bits. It was the death knell for our first wild eighteen months with an even wilder eighteen months to follow.

—

FIVE MONTHS, EIGHT SONGS—MAKING MEDICINE SHOW

There was no fixed timetable for the making of our new album. We knew we'd be spending longer making it than we had on our first, but we figured it might take a month or two instead of three nights—and taking even that amount of time to make an album was something we couldn't begin to imagine. Anything beyond making a studio document of our live show was unchartered territory. 'We're in the big leagues now,' Karl would often say. He'd say it with pride and joy. I'd hear it with trepidation and fear.

It didn't help that we were making the record in San Francisco, four hundred miles from home, friends, family, favorite record stores, our own records and books, and other touchstones that might have kept us grounded. We were put in a furnished apartment complex on the corner of Market and Van Ness called the Fox Plaza, a thirty-story building of lodging geared toward temporary residents, transitory workers, and travelers. The views were stunning, Twin Peaks visible through the morning fog from the balcony. Dennis and Dave shared one apartment and Karl and I shared another.

We had booked two weeks at a fancy, well-known San Francisco studio called the Automatt, where Sandy often worked. We came in with only eight songs, and that number would not increase in the months ahead. We had two weeks of twelve-hour sessions to record acceptable master takes of a handful of songs. How hard could that be? The life of Riley! What would we do with all those days and hours just to get good versions of eight songs down to tape? How many times could a band play the same songs over and over? We'd soon find out that the answer was *many, many times.*

But, yeah, the big leagues. That meant having a producer, Sandy, sitting behind the mixing desk, alongside an engineer, Paul Mandl, plus an additional person hired just to keep our guitars tuned, amps working, and mics moved where they needed to go, as well as a very attentive team of accommodating studio employees who brought us snacks and coffee throughout the day. All we had to do was play our songs and keep playing them until we were told to stop.

The two weeks set aside to get master takes could have easily allowed for well over a hundred takes of each song if we so desired. We were better musicians than we were when we made the first album, more seasoned from our months of touring. Sure, we had lost the irreplaceable chemistry that we'd had with Kendra, but Dave was unquestionably the better bass player and had much more studio experience. It should have been easy. But we had yet to begin to learn the mysteries and frustrations of working with Sandy Pearlman.

Sandy was one seriously smart dude. He heard and processed music on a cinematic and even scientific level, rather than the traditional metrics of just going for a rock-solid, grooving take. But he also never seemed to know or be able to communicate what he wanted. He would just know that what was happening was not what he wanted. We quickly went from defiantly and confidently doing the thing that came naturally—the thing that had brought us to the dance—to just trying to figure out what would make Sandy happy. We'd rock out, we'd slow down, we'd strut, we'd crawl, we'd get trippy, we'd go compact. And none of it landed.

There were big changes afoot in record-making and recording-studio methodology in the early 80s. Drums, more and more, were beginning to reign supreme and were expected to sound gigantic, in the forefront with metronomic precision. The larger-than-life gated snare sound first suggested by Peter Gabriel on his third solo album had been taken to new bombastic levels by his old bandmate Phil Collins, in particular on a new hit single by Frida of ABBA called 'I Know There's Something Going On,' which was seen as the future and even somewhat hip. I actually liked the song and dug the production of that single. But it was not a sound that was conducive to the music that we were making.

Dennis Duck is and has always been a fantastic drummer. We would not have been on a label like A&M or in a studio like the Automatt had it not been for Dennis. He had a rock-solid style, simple but muscular, not unlike Chris Frantz of the Talking Heads. He knew how to set a solid, simple beat that allowed the guitars to travel wild and untethered over the top. Aside from being a punky noise band, we were also very much a groove band, and those two things worked together in a way that made us unique.

But Dennis, much like the rest of us, relied on interplay and responding in the moment, much like a jazz musician, or like Charlie Watts, who was said to have followed the guitar of Keith Richards, rather than the other way around. Dennis held down the fort while constantly processing what was happening around him, keeping us in line but also allowing us to drag him along for a wild ride. That push and pull was an integral part of the music we loved and felt very natural to us.

Push and pull, however, does not work when you isolate a drum track and listen without the other elements. It sounds unsteady. On big-budget records in 1983, the drums were all that mattered, but we didn't know that was the game plan. We figured we'd play and play, get the magical take, and then throw some stuff on top and be done with it. Any other way of working was unstated and hard to follow, even as it was happening.

Sandy and Paul listened back from behind the mixing desk to out-of-context soloed drum tracks, suddenly wobbly in their nakedness. We didn't feel confident enough to say, 'You guys are missing the point here—we're a band, not a pace car for a robotic beat.' This miscommunication—and this new way of working, which would handcuff and vex other underground bands who managed to leapfrog to major labels in the next few years—set the tone for the next five months. We were chasing something that was never there because we had never intended it to be there.

We were not only the first of our LA paisley underground compatriots but also one of the first bands of the American underground scene to record for a major label. Bands we considered our peers at the time managed to stay within the comfortable fold of independent labels for much longer than we did. Our meteoric rise was also our curse. We never had the chance to develop at our own speed and in our own time. We were babies thrust into the belly of the beast, and we had no intestinal road map once we got there.

Sandy Pearlman kept an office at the Automatt, since he managed, ran, and most often worked out of one of the three rooms at the studio. It never occurred to me at the time, but years later I realized that he likely made more money the longer he was able to keep the studio occupied. It would be tempting to think that this unmentioned kickback might have been the reason for his legendary long recording sessions. Maybe it's true. His production company being called Time Enough World Enough was more of a clue to his way of working, as was the lone poster on his office wall: a framed promo poster for Francis Ford Coppola's similarly rudderless, budget-breaking epic, *Apocalypse Now*. We were indeed entering the heart of darkness.

After two weeks of basic tracks, recording the songs together as a band, Dennis was the first to return home to LA. Sandy and Paul shifted over to what they perceived as the need to strip away all the instruments and 'fix' Dennis's work, which meant editing together his drum parts from various takes to produce an unerring performance of each song. Dave put new bass parts on these edited tracks, and we found ourselves with very solid, muscular, and relatively flawless rhythm section performances. Had we known that was going to be the process, we would have just had Dennis and Dave perform similarly solid bass and drum parts on their own in a day or two, without the distractions of me and Karl slashing away. Dennis and Dave were locked into following something that was no longer in the mix, a reaction without the initial inspiration.

One song was not done in this fashion. We had introduced a free-form jam in the key of E built around a Television-inspired riff that we called 'It's Gonna Be Alright' when we played that 2am live radio show on KPFK a year earlier, and we felt it would be a cornerstone of the new album. We played the song once on each of the fourteen days of tracking, the resulting versions ranging from five minutes to almost a half hour. I wish all those versions were still around, but those tapes are long gone.

After two weeks of tracking, we chose our favorite take from the various versions of the song. It stretched to about twenty-five minutes. Over the course of the following months, we edited it down to a little under ten minutes for both the purpose of focus and the need to keep the album under the twenty-two minutes per side length that would allow the pressing to sound good and not skip when played on a turntable. I eventually changed the name of the song from its original generic title to 'John Coltrane Stereo Blues,' inspired by the lyrics, which I was still writing and changing throughout the session. It ended up being the one song on the album without any replaced, fixed, or overdubbed instruments. Aside from my vocal, it is the only track that was us playing together, and tellingly it became the track that got the most attention and praise upon release and in the years since.

A week after Dennis left, Dave was the next to go home, and after three weeks of recording, it was just me and Karl living in our one-bedroom apartment. Our personalities and desires from the record were diverging daily. Karl wanted to make a big classic rock record that would catapult us to new levels, and, to that end, labored to change his guitar style from the feedback-laden, assaultive noise-fest of the first album to something that would not have been out of place on a record by Sandy's protégées, Blue Öyster Cult, or one of Karl's favorites, UFO.

I was drinking more and more and spiraling into a depression over the lack of control over the record and where the band was heading. Maybe it was the need to be the steadying force during the parental divorces of my youth, or maybe it was all the time I spent alone when I was young, but I was averse to and not equipped for confrontation or even negotiating a compromise. Instead, I got more and more resentful, more and more isolated, as Karl and I saw our friendship collapse. One night in our apartment after the day's session, I was drunkenly ranting to Karl about my frustration with what was happening to our record while The Who's 'Substitute' was playing in the background. Karl was scribbling while I vented, and the next day I saw 'pacify, pacify' in his handwriting, a reference to both a lyric in the song and also his exasperation with my displeasure.

That's the way it went for six weeks—the time that it took for Karl to replace his parts and do the lion's share of the guitar work on the album. Six weeks. Seven days a week. Twelve hours a day. That's a lot of time for lead guitar overdubs, even during the most indulgent of recording sessions, and it drove me nuts. And the more it drove me nuts and the more I made my frustration apparent, the more Karl and Sandy made me feel unwelcome in the studio. I'd walk in while they were working and everything would stop, like a scene out of a western, when the bad guy walks into the bar. Every few days I would blow up and corner Sandy and try to figure out what the hell was going on, asking when we'd be able to move on from endless guitar solos. Sandy and Karl would just pacify, pacify.

Sandy and Karl were having a great time, each flattering the other's ego and sense of purpose. Karl was living the Big Rock Dream, and Sandy had a pupil who justified his process. Karl seemed to have no problem doing take after take, trying out different solos and being put through the wringer by Sandy's eternal seeking and indecision. But I found it even more aggravating when I would drop by the studio each day and find that nothing much had changed since the day before. My frustration was apparent but hardly welcome, and I felt like I had become somebody who had to be tolerated but not indulged.

The ship quickly sailed on my friendship with Karl, and, after a while, I just stopped coming by the studio. It felt weird, frustrating, and disheartening to feel the days ticking by and not seeing much progress or even being asked to come down and listen to anything. I ended up spending most of my time drinking at the apartment and wandering around the city. We were given $150 a week for expenses, which wouldn't go too far in restaurants or bars, but it covered my daily pint of Jim Beam, as well as burgers or tacos around town.

I had driven my Honda Civic to San Francisco and was given a parking space by the building, so I also spent a lot of time driving around town, often to the top of Twin Peaks, where I parked to crank *Fun House* by The Stooges at top volume while watching the city lights. I knew that my father had lived in that same neighborhood shortly after he left my mother, and I'm sure I felt some kind of nostalgic melancholic connection to the surroundings.

I also went to see some live shows. I was a big fan of John Cipollina of Quicksilver Messenger Service, and I saw that he was playing in the North Beach area, just off Broadway. He was booked to play four sets that night, and the cover charge was three dollars. I went in shortly before the first set, found my place in the small club among the handful of patrons, and watched all four sets. It was inspiring, and it would have been great if I'd had a way to channel that inspiration and excitement onto the record, but it was becoming clearer and clearer that my role was to be the second guitarist—very different from the balanced, twin-guitar attack and chemistry we'd shared on *The Days Of Wine And Roses*.

It made me sad. More than just a blow to my ego, it was also frustrating because I knew that my guitar had been so much a part of our sound up until we walked into the Automatt. My clanging rhythm was the louder of the two guitars on *The Days Of Wine And Roses*, allowing Karl's shards of noise and feedback to provide commentary and add tension underneath. It worked. But my guitar's presence on *Medicine Show* would be strictly as a rhythm part tucked into the mix.

The final blow came when we were working on 'Still Holding On To You,' a song built around a guitar riff I had written. But neither Sandy nor Karl liked the way I played it. I came into the studio one day to hear that Karl had replaced my riff with one of his own—similar, but most definitely different from the one I'd written to anchor the song.

My evenings remained mostly free during the six weeks that Sandy and Karl were toiling away and racking up studio bills. One night, a friend in town asked me if I wanted to go with him to see R.E.M., who were playing at the Kabuki Theater, with Let's Active and The Neats as support. What a lineup! I said yes.

As I've mentioned before, R.E.M. guitarist Peter Buck had come to see us a couple of times, including our KPFK radio broadcast, and there's a possibility I might have taken the band's first single on consignment at Rhino when Peter was going from store to store trying to get their first independent Hib-Tone single in stores. We also had a mutual friend in New York photographer Laura Levine, who had passed messages back and forth between us via cassette recordings made in her Soho loft. In other words, we were very much on each other's radar, and I really liked their first EP and album, *Murmur*.

The show was great, and, although I've never been that big on making my way backstage for other people's shows, I went back to say hi to the band that night. I've read since then that Andy Gill and Jon King of Gang Of Four were also there and that they ended up playing 'Sweet Jane' with the band for their encore. I don't remember. Along with Let's Active and The Neats, there were a whole lot of people hanging out in the dressing room. Peter and I immediately found each other and hit it off like long-lost brothers, talking about records and travel and books and many of the other things we still talk about today. We hightailed it out of the crowded backstage area and moved on to various bars around town, ending up with us sitting on the shoreline near Fisherman's Wharf as the sun came up, sipping from a bottle of whiskey and still going strong. It was the beginning of a lifelong friendship, one that would find us collaborating on songs and records and many more adventures in the years since.

Once the R.E.M. circus rolled out of town, I went back to my solitary life of drinking and wandering the city while dropping by the studio once a day, just to verify that things were continuing to move along at a glacial pace. Strangely enough, A&M Records kept paying the bills without bothering to check up on us at all or ask to hear what we were doing.

I was starting to feel homesick for LA, so I was very happy to see that Green On Red were in town for a show. My buddies! A connection from home! Of course, I went and had a great time. The band said they were driving back to LA immediately after the show to get back to their day jobs the next morning, a routine I knew well from our own twenty-four-hour San Francisco runs. On the spur of the moment, I asked if I could hitch a ride back to LA with them. It wasn't like I'd be missed in San Francisco. They had rented a cargo van with no seats or windows. I'm pretty sure that their drummer, Alex MacNichol, was driving, but the rest of the entourage, including Leaving Trains singer Falling James Moreland, had all variously prepared for the drive home with either booze or psychedelics. We drove through the night, the insanity of the henhouse hotbox of bad behavior seeming almost like some sense of normalcy and comfort to me at that point.

When I got back to LA, I got in touch with our manager, Tim, who told A&M that I was going to be in town and said they wanted to meet with me. I got together with Tim and our A&R man, Jordan Harris, who sensed an impasse in our sessions and wanted to know if I was interested in dumping Sandy and bringing in Chuck Plotkin, who had engineered *Born To Run*, among many other notable records, to finish the sessions.

I often think back and wonder what would have happened had I said yes—how much longer the record would have taken, how the final results might have been different. But whether it was a weird Stockholm Syndrome loyalty to Sandy or whether it was a fear of upsetting the apple cart even further, I politely declined. Even though things were moving more slowly than I wanted, I felt like it couldn't take all that much longer—that we had to be in some kind of home stretch.

I was wrong. We still had four months to go.

By Thanksgiving, Karl had wrapped up his guitar parts and moved back down to LA, leaving me as the last man standing, my lead vocals being the final task ahead. I had eight songs to sing, so I figured it might take a week or two at the most. I had sung all the songs live, and, aside from a few parts of 'John Coltrane Stereo Blues,' I had the lyrics all in place.

We moved from the main room, where we had done the basic tracks and where Karl had done his guitar work, over to Studio C, the smaller room that Sandy managed, and where he usually did most of his work. It was a cheaper room for us and a larger take for him. Nowadays, I would know every part of the budget and how and where to cut costs, but back then I didn't think about those things. We had a manager for that, and I just wanted to finish the record.

Up until that point, we had been recording on two-inch, twenty-four-track tape, as was the standard at the time and would remain so until digital recording became the norm a few decades later. But at some point, Sandy's hesitancy to make a decision and settle on any one thing meant that twenty-four tracks just wouldn't be enough so a second twenty-four-track machine was rolled into the control room, the two machines linked by what was called an SMPTE (pronounced simp-tea) track, allowing the machines to talk to each other and line up, making a horrendous sound much like creaky gears lining up on heavy machinery—appropriate for the heavy lifting ahead. It was a sound that would haunt me for years.

Sandy Pearlman. At the time, what I knew about him was his discography and that he always—and I mean always—wore a grey baseball cap. I assumed it was because of hair loss, but the one time in six months that he took it off in my presence, I was surprised to see that he had a healthy head of hair. Sandy had a heavy New York accent (specifically Long Island, I would later learn) and that when he listened to music he would close his eyes and move his fingers across an imaginary notepad, with a movement that suggested something between reading braille and playing tic tac toe. I came to know that he could not run a mixing board or do much of anything that resembled studio engineering, so he always worked with an engineer —Paul Mandl, in our case. In the early days of recording, producers had been adjunct A&R men whose main job was to philosophically shape the session and make sure everything got done. In more recent years, it's been more common for a producer to do double duty, turning knobs and pushing faders as well.

What I didn't know about Sandy was that, along with the likes of Paul Williams and Sandy's good friend Richard Meltzer, he had pretty much invented rock criticism. I was so focused on just getting the album done and getting home that I didn't bother to ask many questions, afraid I would somehow derail the process. I now realize that had I dug deeper into his history, I may have had more empathy and appreciation for Sandy's way of working, and very likely would not have seen him as the adversary.

But he most certainly became my nemesis once it was time to record my vocals. I'd roll into the studio around noon and find Sandy and Paul waiting for me with the song they had chosen for me to sing, the tape machines all set up and ready to go. I'd have a look to see what snacks the studio had brought in that day and then start singing. And singing. And singing. Every take was followed by Sandy saying to me in the headphones, 'Eh, not quite. Do it again.' I would sing the song around ten times, and then Sandy and Paul would give me a break while they chose the bits and pieces that they liked of each of the takes and bounced them over to a new track, a process known as 'comping.' I'd come back in and hear the comp; we'd all agree it was fine, and then we'd move on to a new song.

This would go on until around midnight, with maybe a quick dinner break. Otherwise, it was twelve hours solid of singing and comping and more singing and more comping. I'd usually head out around six to the local liquor store and buy a bottle and start hitting it hard. Naturally, the style and sound and level of inhibition changed in the second half of the day. Sandy seemed to like, or at least was entertained by, my drunken, unhinged performances, which encouraged me to drink even more. At the end of the day, I'd stumble back along Folsom Street and make my way along the mile-long walk to the Fox Plaza, passing the gauntlet of leather gay bars with names like the White Swallow, the End Up, and the Man Hole, to settle back into my studio apartment to drink some more and watch a TV evangelist named Gene Scott, whose rantings and ravings, if not his actual message, connected to me in those wee hours in my shaky and unsettled state.

When I'd come back to the studio around noon the next day, we'd listen to the assembled vocal, and Sandy would say, 'I don't think we have it yet. Go out and sing some more.' I would end up singing ten more takes of each song, which would then be comped with the comped vocal I had done the day before to make a brand-new comp. The process would repeat each day—comps comped against the old comp, over and over. This went on seven days a week, twelve hours a day, for six full weeks. It was maddening. I felt like I had been taken hostage and the process broke me down. I went from having some kind of idea of how I wanted to sing the songs to not having a clue and losing confidence entirely. Eventually, I would just try to figure out what Sandy wanted—he was never able to put it in words—and I wanted nothing more than to give it to him so that the process would all be over. Some days I felt like he wanted controlled, crooner-style baritone takes, so I gave him that. Some days I thought he wanted the wild prophet from atop the mountain, so I whipped that up. Some days I would emulate Jim Morrison and other days Gene Scott.

I got so frustrated at one point that I threw an empty whiskey bottle at Sandy. It was the only time I saw him lose control and get angry. 'Mick Jones never once threw a bottle at me,' he exclaimed, referring to the mercurial guitarist of The Clash. Yeah, but I bet he was tempted.

Around this time, an old friend from Davis, Suzy, paid me a visit. I'd always had a crush on her back in college, and I was glad to see her. She ended up spending the night at the Fox Plaza, and we began a relationship that would last the rest of the time I was in San Francisco making the record. She shared my enthusiasm for drinking, my growing unhinged behavior attracted rather than repelled her, and we enjoyed playacting our version of a Bukowski novel.

By Christmas, the vocals still weren't done, but Sandy and Paul planned to take a two-week break. A&M wasn't going to pay for my lodging during those two vacation weeks, but I chose not to go back to LA, preferring neither to curtail my behavior nor to unleash it on family and friends back home. I wanted to revel in the new character I was creating and to spend time with Suzy. I moved across the street into an SRO flophouse for two weeks over Christmas and New Year's Eve and then, after two solid weeks of heavy drinking, found myself in much worse shape once vocals resumed early in 1984.

Something happened once the new year began and I reunited with Sandy in the studio and started singing again. Maybe the time off had done us all well and given us perspective, but the vocals started coming more easily, and the album began to take shape. Up to that point, I think I was so distraught that we were no longer the band we had been—either in sound or mode of working—that I bristled every step of the way and alternated between anger and desolation, making the process difficult for everyone around me. Now, after I'd taken some time away, the record no longer bummed me out but instead began to feel like its own thing—a widescreen, dramatic, and cinematic experience that sounded unlike who we had been but also unlike anything I had heard before. I started really digging it, maybe because I started singing better, and that pleased Sandy. I was no longer singing every vocal like a giant fuck-you to the process but rather as a person who loved the music and wanted to add the right element.

By now I had fully abandoned who we were and what we represented, not only to ourselves but also to the indie-rock scene, and I just let things go where they were meant to go. Over the course of my life, I have often had a very specific agenda and stubborn idea about how things should sound and have often mistaken a potential collaborator for someone who was going to sabotage my vision. It's not an easy lesson to learn, and there are times when sticking to your guns can make for an uncompromised success. But, at the same time, compromise can make things better. It's tricky. Knowing how much to let in and how much to shut out is one of the toughest lessons to learn, whether you're in a band or a relationship or in any management situation.

Chalk it up to finally letting go of my ego or learning to embrace the process or even the much-needed two weeks apart, but Sandy and I were now on the same page, enthusiastically pursuing the sound and style that became *Medicine Show*. We both agreed that keyboards would really bring out the dramatic feel of the record, so Sandy suggested a New Jersey musician named Tommy Zvoncheck, who he had worked with on a Blue Öyster Cult spinoff project called Imaginos. Tommy had the very strange pedigree of having played with both Aldo Nova, who was a fixture on MTV at that moment, as well as Public Image Ltd on their recent tour and live record from Japan.

The vibe in the studio had improved, but the pace of work had certainly not quickened. With my vocals finally done, Tommy's keyboards took another two weeks. Once again, I found myself wondering how this could be possible. Tommy was an incredibly talented musician who immediately understood the vibe of the songs and instinctively knew what needed to be played. But, again, Sandy was looking for something that was there, wasn't there, and all points in between. The pattern of play, comp, play, comp continued—and so, miraculously, did the checks from A&M.

We had already surpassed our $150,000 budget and needed more money. For the first time in the process, the label decided it would be a good idea to send up the two people most involved with the project, Jeff Gold and Mark Williams—the two guys who had signed us based on a show they had seen at Joe's Star Lounge in Ann Arbor, Michigan not quite one year before. They came to the studio, and we cranked up rough mixes, complete with Tommy's keyboards, at top volume on the biggest speakers in the room. I'm not sure if they were impressed, dazzled, or simply decimated by the volume, but they were excited by what they heard. Jeff, Mark, and I went out for a fancy dinner and drinks on the company dime afterward, and the floodgates continued for another month of backing vocals and mixing until the record was finally done a month later.

We'd spent $250,000 over five months making the record, all in a vacuum away from the friends and fans and journalists who had supported and loved the music we'd made a year before. We'd come out the other side of the Rubicon a very different band with very different music, and there was no turning back. We had made a record that was markedly different from our first, and I was a very different person, having adopted a character to fit in with the songs, music, and alcohol that had shaped the five months in San Francisco. I was ultimately very happy with the record, but I was physically and mentally a mess.

The mastering session for the record was booked at the prestigious Sterling Sound in New York City. Normally, the artist does not need to attend this final part of the process, but I had no home, having put all my things into storage before going to San Francisco, and I was up for any excuse to spend time in a city that had become my favorite on Earth. I called a woman I had briefly dated who lived in Hoboken, New Jersey, just across the river from Manhattan, and asked if I could stay at her place while I was in town.

There may have been doubt on both of our parts as to what our relationship might resemble when she made the offer, but after a first fumbling, drunken night on my part, she banished me to the living room couch, where I ended up sleeping for the month I stayed at her pad. To her credit and to my amazement in retrospect, she was quite tolerant of her new, badly behaved roommate, and I was happy to have free lodging to live out my Gotham fantasy. I was a ghost, a phantom, and our paths rarely crossed. I went into Manhattan or over to the Maxwell's every night to watch a band, listen to a DJ, or just drink myself into a blackout state. Many of my Manhattan nights ended at an after-hours basement club called No Say No, where you paid five bucks to get in, listen to whatever band performed in single file atop the bar, and drink all the cans of Budweiser you wanted from a trash bin at the corner of the room. I'd stumble out as the sun was coming up, make my way back to Hoboken on the PATH train, stumble in as my host was going to work, and proceed to pass out until late afternoon.

This went on for a month as the May release of the record and the need to start planning tours began creeping up. I honestly felt like I was going to stay in New York, although I'm sure I had worn out my welcome as the house guest who wouldn't leave. My plans, or lack thereof, abruptly ended one day in April, when I got a call from my sister Samantha. Our grandmother had died, and I would have to come home for the funeral.

I was very close to my Grandma Anne, having eaten dinner at her West Hollywood apartment almost every week when I wasn't on tour. At eighty-six she showed no signs of slowing down. Her death was sudden, and the funeral was both sad but also a celebration of a family matriarch who had moved from Ukraine to New York City and, like many other immigrants, courageously and doggedly forged a new life in a new country.

Rather than giving me pause or the impetus to straighten out my ways, the homecoming and loss of my grandmother gave me more excuses to continue drinking heavily and continue with the unhinged dark character I had chosen to inhabit. I drifted around in LA, much as I had in San Francisco and New York, with cheap thrift-store suits, four-day stubble, and long, thick, wavy unkempt hair that rarely encountered a bottle of shampoo. I moved into the famous Tropicana Motel, which had been home to other denizens of bad behavior like Jim Morrison and Tom Waits. It was a well-known rock'n'roll party motel where touring bands stayed and would host gatherings until all hours. I had a little one-bedroom apartment that I remember being very inexpensive, and most of my money aside from my hotel bill went to bourbon and cans of soup to heat up on a hot plate that the motel provided.

By day, I often went to the A&M Records lot, the former Charlie Chaplin studios on La Brea and Sunset. The lot was set up to be more of a village than an office complex, with a series of bungalows each housing a different facet of the label, from executives to art department to publicity to artist relations. The head of artist relations was Bob Garcia, who had been a fixture at the label since its very beginning. He had no problem with me wandering into his office in various stages between hungover and drunk. He allowed me to hang out, chat, read his books, and cool my heels, all under the guise of planning and setting up our impending release. It was a good place to hang out.

Bob's secretary was a woman named Johnette Napolitano, and we hit it off immediately. We went on a date and ended up being a couple for the next three years. One night we were invited over to Bob's house for dinner, where Bob plied us with wine and conversation while a chicken slowly cooked in the oven. The three of us drank until midnight, at which point the chicken was charred beyond recognition. Bob had passed out snoring on the couch, so Johnette and I let ourselves out and returned to the Tropicana. In other words, my bad behavior was not seen as a cause for alarm; instead, it was part of what was considered normal at that time in the music business. As would be the case in years to come, the people who worked for the labels were often worse behaved than the musicians themselves. If I or a younger musician behaved now as I did back then, an intervention wouldn't be far behind. But back then, it was Rock. And. Roll!

Unlike the slow pace of the making of the record, things were moving forward quickly. I was still not spending much if any time hanging out with my bandmates, even though I was back in LA. One night, however, the label arranged for me and Karl to go over to mainstream rock station KLOS for an interview and call-in show. I showed up drunk, and I still remember the look of disgust on Karl's face. It's clear that everything I did at that time, to his mind, was sabotaging what he saw as a chance for our band to become more popular. On the other hand, inspired by beautiful losers and flameouts, I felt it was a badge of honor to behave like a train wreck in real time. These were two modes of how to handle a major-label record campaign, and those modes were incompatible, the chasm between me and Karl growing every day.

With the record release quickly approaching, we started to think about touring plans. R.E.M. had just released their second album, *Reckoning*, on A&M subsidiary IRS Records. It seemed like a natural combo for us to open for their upcoming US tour. But they had already offered the tour to Nashville cowpunk band Jason & The Scorchers. I was disappointed, but within a few weeks, for whatever reason, Jason & The Scorchers turned down the tour, and we were invited to be the opening band. The tour was booked for eight weeks across every major market in the US, so our next few months were in place. My chaotic life would now have some sense of focus and daily purpose.

But things weren't that simple. Dave's girlfriend insisted that he hold out for a larger salary. He seemed ambivalent about the hardball tactic, especially as he was making what the rest of us were making, but the girlfriend wasn't about to back down, leading to a parking-lot confrontation between the two of them and our management, which ended with Dave quitting the band with only a couple of weeks before the tour. Much as we were unfazed when Kendra quit the band right before our U2 tour—what *is* it with bass players and big break opening slots?—we unsentimentally and pragmatically went into action to find a replacement.

Through friends on the local scene, Karl knew and recommended a local guy named Mark Walton. Mark didn't have a notable pedigree, having not made an album or toured or even played much on the local scene before, but the tour was starting in two weeks. He seemed like a good guy and was a quick learner and a solid player. That was more than enough to pass the audition. He had only a handful of days to learn the songs and rehearse with us, but he was up to top speed well before the first show. No surprise there—as I have learned in the forty years we've since played together, Mark is one of the best bass players around.

We also decided to bring along Tommy Zvoncheck on keyboards, to better recreate the sound of our new album. To do the tour, Tommy would need us to supply the proper keyboards—a costly, heavy, and very large Hammond B3 organ, and an equally mammoth Yamaha digital grand piano. Once again, A&M rubber-stamped the request, wrote the check, and added the cost to our unrecouped tally of outstanding studio costs, apartment rentals, salaries, and the very pricy Marshall stacks, Mesa Boogie amplifiers, and Fender and Gibson guitars they had already bought for us. I'm amazed even as I write these words, but it was really that easy; their pockets were really that deep and ready to be opened for us.

But why *was* it that easy? Were the floodgates open that wide for every new band? Or were we an enigma—a weird band that didn't sound like other major label bands and who seemed to have had some kind of success of our own making, and thus the label figured we knew what we were doing, and that the critical success would continue? Good reviews were a big deal in those days.

As it turns out, the record was received with middling reviews in the US, mostly resembling giant shrugs of befuddlement, with critics asking, 'What happened to The Dream Syndicate I knew and loved?' The bulk of the reviews also acknowledged that it was a good record and that the songs were strong, but it just didn't fit the narrative of who the band had been a year before—unlike R.E.M., who had made a sophomore record that resembled their first album enough while also taking small, logical steps forward. The marathon experience in San Francisco served in our own minds to divide everything into what came before and what was happening now. It was only two years since our first show, but the band who made that first EP seemed like completely different people at this point, strangers as much to ourselves as we appeared to be to fans and critics.

—

3.5

OUR SIDE WON—ON TOUR WITH R.E.M.

The band's reinvention and ensuing audience confusion continued with the R.E.M. tour. We had very consciously made the decision to represent the new album and current sound of the band rather than to revisit the Paisley Underground combo we had been less than one year earlier. Those jangly, feedback-laden days seemed like another lifetime that happened to other people at that point, and, in fact, with Mark Walton and Tommy Zvoncheck, we really were a very different band. Compared to the spring of 1983 and our days of opening for U2 and our status as critic's darlings, we had changed in many ways. Our hair was longer, our A&M-purchased amplifiers were more expensive, Karl and I were barely speaking to each other, and the feedback and noise had been eschewed and replaced by a big-room bombast that seemed exciting and bold to us but couldn't have been more different than what we had sounded like before.

We had a few days of rehearsal in Los Angeles before the first show of the tour in Fresno to come up with new arrangements and setlists that put Tommy's keyboards front and center, much as they are on the album— the focal point of our new sound. We decided we would open the show each night with a thirty-second bit of solo piano by Tommy that would incorporate elements of twentieth-century classical music and free jazz and conclude with him playing the riff to 'Tell Me When It's Over,' at which we point we would kick in and start the show. We were excited by this dramatic presentation, but it would serve to confuse the college rock fans who felt like they were coming to see the shining lights of the underground rock music scene. (While we chose to draw a line between who we were pre-and-post San Francisco, R.E.M. would perhaps more wisely deliver on who they had been since they began and delight the uninitiated they had picked up along the way.)

Another big change was our mode of traveling and touring. We booked a tour bus and hired a four-man crew—tour manager, sound engineer, and two stage techs to better handle our new, bigger, and much heavier gear. I remembered the days when we were able to fit our guitar amps and entire entourage into my Honda Civic. Not anymore.

At the time, I did not know the concept of recoupable expenses. I just thought the label pays for stuff and we gratefully accept their generosity, free of charge. A&M did indeed agree to foot the considerable downfall of a budget that would include the tour bus, crew, and decent mid-level hotels for the tour. The rest of the band and crew would have to share rooms; I was the lone person given a single room, maybe because I was perceived as the star but more likely because I was perceived as a drunken, loose cannon with whom nobody would want to room. I had used the excuse that I needed time to myself to write songs after the show, and that was good enough justification for A&M.

A tour bus is considered a line of demarcation for bands—a sign that you've made it and have entered the fraternity of rock stars that have come before. It's a rolling party pad on wheels, refrigerators filled with beer and snacks, AV setups for music and movies, shared tables for games and socializing, and bunk beds a few steps behind for sleeping it all off when desired.

Personally, I've never been a fan of tour buses. Needing a larger level of solo time, I prefer vans where you mostly stare at the back of your traveling companions' heads rather than at their faces for hours upon end, creating the illusion that you're alone in your own world even though five or six bodies are within a few feet of each other. Also, in a touring van, you can stop for food or to stretch your legs anytime you want. The bus routine is usually dictated by the driver, especially as there are snacks and even a little room to roam on board. You're in a bubble, and often you don't even look out the window or have any idea of the scenery you're passing along the road.

In the back of most tour buses, there is usually a smaller lounge room that is often given to the star or leader of the band, and, once again, that private and socially distanced lounge was bequeathed upon me. Much like the single room, it was likely done under the justification that I might write a few songs and that the others might appreciate a break from me.

Or maybe it was the smell of my hair spray and increasingly odorous thrift-store suit jacket that wasn't cleaned a single time during the two-month tour.

Despite the baffled stateside press response, the record was doing quite well at radio, and 'John Coltrane Stereo Blues,' at almost ten minutes in length, managed to scale the top of the college radio chart for two straight months. The lyrically sinister yet traditionally rocking 'Daddy's Girl' was the song pushed at commercial stations and was getting more traditional FM rock airplay than anything we'd had before. If our critic's darling status had diminished a bit, our foray into the mainstream was being embraced in ways we hadn't seen before.

From the first show with R.E.M. in Fresno, it was apparent that this tour would be very different from the one with U2. The band knew and embraced us as friends, and it was apparent that we were invited to hang out with them as much as we'd like. We were also mutual fans and would check out each other's sets nightly. At some shows, they would invite me and Karl onstage for their encore. I remember one night at the Orpheum Theater in Boston, singing a duet of 'There She Goes Again' by The Velvet Underground with Michael Stipe, probably as close as we would come on the tour to evoking the band who had been our constant touchstone and comparative point only a year earlier.

The blurred edges between the bands also extended to my traveling choices. While the tension grew between me and Karl, Peter and I had become closer, and he would invite me to travel with them and hang out on their bus as much as I wanted. Michael had his own bus, and the parties on the R.E.M. bus with Peter, Mike Mills, and Bill Berry seemed more welcoming to me than the ones on ours.

There are a lot of great things that I like about being an opening act. Most of all, you have the chance to win over new fans, and that challenge has always kicked my performances into a higher gear, more intense and ambitious and wider in scope. It appeals to my sense of desire for inclusion and cohesion, as though I'm throwing a party and want all my guests to feel comfortable. I'm sure I do the same when I'm the headliner, playing to my own fans, but I also tend to feel more relaxed, knowing that they paid to see me do what I do and that I don't need to do more than whatever feels right that night. I throw myself on the line more when playing to the uninitiated and see it as a nightly crusade.

Both scenarios usually yield good results, but they can result in very different shows. Trying too hard in front of your own fans, much as it would be with your closest friends, can be unnerving and imposing. Being too diffident or lazy with newcomers can leave a bland and forgettable impression.

Being an opening act also means you have a shorter day. You can arrive later for soundcheck, and you're also done earlier. Rather than the eight hours you are on the job as a headliner, an opening act's time at the venue could be as brief as two or three hours. It can leave more time to see the city, visit friends, or get some rest. Or, if you're on tour with a band like R.E.M., whose company you enjoy and whose music you like, it means you're done early, usually before 9pm, and can shift over not only to being a fan but also to being a fan with an all-access pass, a spot saved for you right by the side of the stage, and all of the snacks and alcohol you could want only a few steps away in the dressing room.

I made a point to be well lubricated even before our own set so that I could channel whatever demons lay behind the character I had invented on *Medicine Show*—a character that I also felt worked on the big stages and theaters we were playing. Our manager, Tim, had instructed me on the U2 tour to *play to the back row*, something I had never even considered before. On this tour, I was playing to the back row and probably even somewhere deep into the parking lot. It was a big performance for a big widescreen record, and very different from the insular, internal approach that had gone along with the similarly tightly coiled *The Days Of Wine And Roses*.

Or maybe I just liked to drink whiskey and had become accustomed to drinking a lot of it every day, usually well more than a fifth of Beam by the time my night was done. And with my work night done and a very entertaining band to watch from the side of the stage, the drinking shifted up a gear for R.E.M.'s two-hour set. They were truly fantastic, Peter and

Mike athletically kinetic, covering every inch of the stage as well as a few feet above it, all vertical leaps and scissor kicks. Unlike our mostly static setlist, theirs changed from night to night, mixing up the choices from their two albums and new songs from the album that would follow, plus an exhaustive supply of cover songs, often learned that day. They even played our own 'Medicine Show' a handful of times, out of tribute and playful parody, Michael imitating the grandiose dead 'STOP' of the band that I had begun to employ on our live version of the title track from *The Days Of Wine And Roses*.

'I do a great Steve Wynn impression,' Michael said one night, 'and he does a great one of me.'

For the most part, my alcohol consumption made for more fun and extended the evenings. I had a greater capacity for high quantities of booze, and rather than today, where that kind of drinking would simply leave me catatonic and fuzzy, it worked mostly as a stimulant and made it easy to keep the party going into the night, whether that meant listening to music with Peter on the bus, going out to more bars once the show was over at 11pm, or venturing out to flirt and hopefully make a connection for the evening. But alcohol is also a depressant, and I would find myself spiraling from what I rightly perceived as Karl's growing disgust at my drunken prophet persona, at odds once again with his desire to put himself across as the arena-rock lead guitarist he dreamed of becoming.

With his Marshall Stack amplifier and bare chest covered by a black vest, Karl was as different from the scruffy art-rocker he was two years earlier as I was from the shy record store clerk I had been at the same time. The two characters we had since adopted were not built to coexist. If I may have put off a few fans by what could veer into pomposity at times, Karl left himself open to shouts of 'Nigel Tufnel!'—a reference to Christopher Guest's rock-star parody character from *This Is Spinal Tap*, which had come out a few months before the tour.

Mark Walton and I were interviewed recently to promote a new record, and we started talking about 1984 and the touring behind *Medicine Show*. I was recalling tense, fraught times filled with angst and bad behavior, tearing a giant hole into a band that had previously been fraying at the edges.

'I don't know,' Mark said. 'I just remember having a good time.'

And perhaps he's right. Despite my personal narrative of that year being the beginning of the end of a very good and improbably meteoric rise, it was also a blast. It was easily the biggest, most high-profile tour of the new wave of the US indie-rock movement that had begun a few years earlier. What had previously played out in tiny, sweaty clubs and at new-wave nights across the country was now on display during nightly sold-out shows to a few thousand excited fans who knew and loved the music they had come to see. Our side had won, we all knew it, and it felt great.

R.E.M. had begun the ascension that would lead them to multi-platinum success. If, a handful of months earlier, we had been peers of equal standing, we were now as big as we would ever get, while they were just getting started and pulling away rapidly. Yet for me, there was no jealousy or frustration. I was proud of our new friends from Georgia, and it didn't matter that I wasn't reaping the biggest benefits of the victory. The music that had been restricted to stores like my own alumnus, Rhino Records, and late-night specialty radio shows was now edging toward the mainstream, and as a music fan and someone being collaterally picked up in the wave, I was pleased.

Not that R.E.M. were above letting their contrarian and rebellious indie-rock roots shine from time to time. A bit weary and frazzled and restless at the mid-tour point in Buffalo, they chose to play a set of mostly covers, including gems by ABBA, ZZ Top, Fleetwood Mac, our own 'Medicine Show,' and more. We, of course, were delighted. It almost felt like a private show; an inside joke for us all to share. The fans did not agree. I went out into the parking lot after the show and was collared by more than a few who said, 'Do you know those guys? Please tell them we're pissed off—we came to hear their songs, not a bunch of covers.'

The tour was a crowning success for R.E.M. in most cities, but a select few had yet to get the message, particularly Boise, Idaho, a place we had never played before. It was a city not commonly part of the underground rock circuit at the time, and the isolation showed when I picked up the local paper the morning of the show and saw an article about the show with the ludicrous headline 'New Wave Comes To Boise,' as though it was still 1977 and we were going to come onstage wearing safety pins and start spitting at the fans. As it turns out, the audience at the venue (half the size of those on the rest on the tour) was lifeless and stared at us dispassionately like we were zoo creatures. Peter, in particular, was so frustrated that he tossed his beloved Rickenbacker guitar against the low ceiling, smashing it into several pieces. I remember his very sad and disconsolate face after the show, once the reality sunk in. Amazingly enough, the guitar was quickly mended, and it remains in his current six-string arsenal.

Chicago, on the other hand, felt like a coronation. We played the historic Aragon Ballroom, where my maternal grandfather Harry Robbins told me that he used to go to dance events when he was a young man, growing up in the Roaring Twenties. We had played there on the U2 tour as well, and I remembered being roundly booed—thankfully a rarity on that tour. This time around, it was one of the tour highlights, sold out weeks ahead of the show, and both bands gave tour-highlight performances. The sets were broadcast live on local radio station WXRT, and both ended up being commercially released in the ensuing months and years.

After the Chicago show, the conquering heroes made their way quickly over to the Cubby Bear club near Wrigley Field, where The Replacements and Del Fuegos were playing, as did many of the fans who had seen our show. It was quite a night for our little scene, which was rapidly becoming not so little. The Del Fuegos were one of the best live bands in the country at that time, and while The Replacements could be notoriously revelatory or shambolic, they were all aces that night. The members of our band and R.E.M. stood by and watched it all like underground royalty, not unlike Brian Jones at Monterrey. As Mark said in retrospect, it really was a lot of fun.

Most of my time on the tour was spent with Peter and Mike, both of whom were always up for a party, and both of whom would later become my bandmates in The Baseball Project, as well as two of my best friends—friendships forged on that heady tour. I rarely spoke to Bill or to Michael, who seemed impossibly shy. On the rare times we spoke at length, he spoke so quietly as to almost be impossible for me to understand. One of the times that we did connect, however, was after a Sunday night show in Salt Lake City, when Michael finished the set and immediately grabbed me and suggested we go out of the stage exit to the parking lot and watch the fans leave for their cars. It was dark and we were never spotted, but we enjoyed the voyeuristic thrill of being so close to everyone who had only minutes earlier been watching us from across the chasm between the stage and beyond—a chasm that didn't exist when we were playing smaller venues a year earlier.

The tour ended up in R.E.M.'s home state of Georgia, at the Fox Theater in Atlanta, where they had sold out two nights at the nearly five-thousand-capacity venue. It was a heroic finale to a great eight weeks, and we were simultaneously exhausted but also sad that it was over. Luckily, we were able to begin the decompression and emotional withdrawal from the lofty life and big crowds with four days in Athens, cooling our heels before the start of a week-long run of headlining shows in the South, beginning in Atlanta with a show at the 688 club to an audience ten percent of the size of the one we had played to a week earlier.

We had a good time with our new friends in Athens. All the members of both bands went on a field trip to a strip-mall movie theater to see the movie *Purple Rain*, which had opened a few days earlier. Another day, Peter called me at my hotel and said that the local Uptown Lounge had a last-minute cancellation that evening and had asked if he could come up with something involving members of the two bands to fill the night. They said they could offer each of us $25 credit at the thrift shop next door and all we could drink at the show. Peter was up for it, and he wondered if The Dream Syndicate would want to play a bunch of covers and some of our own songs with him on guitar. We said yes, and the one-evening legendary band Adolph & The Casuals Featuring Raoul (named by Peter) was born.

I remember some things about that night, but others have had to be recounted for me. I do know that my $25 was spent on a pair of suspenders, as well as a red smoking jacket that I wore onstage for the rest of the year and also ended up wearing the one time I was on the David Letterman show years later. I also know I made the most of the modest pay for the gig by taking the 'all you can drink' offer quite literally. Peter tells me the club owner had to cut me off at some point, but not before I had cajoled our makeshift combo to play the current hit movie theme to *Ghostbusters*, not once but three times during our set. It wasn't an ironic gesture. We all liked the song, and that night we reduced it to a distant cousin of Van Morrison's 'Gloria,' which it resembled in chords and cadence. I think the third rendition came with Tommy on drums and most of the handful of fans who had come to the show long since gone. The night ended with me asleep on the sidewalk outside our tour bus and the driver jostling me to get me back into my bunk. It's a very resilient jacket.

3.6

AN EASY CHOICE TO MAKE

'You have a choice. We will finance either a big-budget, professional video clip or a European tour.'

I was sitting at a large, luxurious wooden desk across from Jordan Harris, the head of A&R for our label. For the uninitiated, A&R stands for 'artists and repertoire,' and it's the department that dictates which bands will be signed and dropped, and (for the former) how much money will be spent on recording and promotion. Our manager, Tim, had begun to pull away from our band, maybe sensing our inner turmoil and the middling response to the album, or maybe he just had his sights set on higher things. He would eventually become the president of Capitol Records, where he was responsible for the revival and great success of Bonnie Raitt in the early 90s.

Jordan seemed very happy to deal with me and take me seriously as proxy manager of The Dream Syndicate. I had run my own label, after all, and had logged time at record stores, studying music mags and the scene in general. And now I was being presented with a big choice. MTV had in a matter of a couple of years become immensely important in launching careers, and a video could dramatically change our visibility. On the other hand, I had never been to Europe, and I really wanted to go.

'We'll take the European tour,' I answered, without hesitation. It was that simple. I don't even remember talking to the rest of the band about it.

There were other factors at play in this decision. While *Medicine Show* had received mixed reviews in the States, it was beginning to get full-on hosannas in the very influential British press. The burgeoning American independent music scene was the hot new thing over there, and, along with R.E.M., we were seen as being at the forefront of that reverse British Invasion. *Medicine Show* got rave reviews in *Melody Maker*, *Sounds*, and *NME*, as well as other mags on the continent. The music press was particularly influential on those shores, and reviews like the ones we were getting pretty much assured a good tour.

And I just wanted to go to Europe. Karl and Mark and Dennis felt the same. We agreed to do the tour as a four-piece, sans keyboards. I don't even think we discussed it with Tommy, who was probably happy to be done with an underground scene that he viewed with some confusion and a touch of condescension. We were ready to return to being a down-and-dirty four-piece guitar rock band.

Even though I was taking some of the decision-making, I was still completely out of the loop on how a tour would be put together, where we would go, and things like crew and vehicles. But somebody was obviously at the helm because it all came together quickly. Within a month, shows and flights were booked, a crew was hired, and a four-week tour was in place. We were going to Europe!

For all the sold-out theaters, large venues, tour buses, and extended crews and budgets of the R.E.M. tour, nothing about the experience seemed out of the ordinary to us. We had already been on tour with U2, and even our club tours worked along the same routines—drive all day, show up, unload gear, rock out, have a few drinks, hunt for a late-night slice of pizza, go to bed, and then do it all again. It didn't matter if it was

CBGB's or the Beacon Theater, touring the US had become comfortably familiar to us over the course of eighteen months. Europe would be a very different experience.

We landed at Heathrow Airport and were immediately shuttled in a no-frills, rickety passenger van to our first gig at the venerable and legendary Dingwalls in London. The show had sold out shortly after it was announced. We knew that. But we hadn't been told much more about what to expect. As we pulled up to the club in the Camden neighborhood, we saw a giant eighteen-wheeler truck parked outside.

'That must be ours,' I joked.

It was.

On a club tour of the US, a band would normally travel with drums and guitars and amplifiers, knowing that every club would have its own PA and monitor system. This was apparently not the case in many of the European venues we would be playing. Or maybe somebody at the label decided it would be more professional to bring our own PA system. I don't know. What I do know is that the giant truck was ours, and the crew was in the process of loading our theater-sized sound system into the humble punk-rock club.

The label had hired a five-man crew: tour manager, sound engineer, monitor engineer, lighting director, and a stage tech who would oversee setting up our equipment and making sure guitars had all of the necessary strings and were hopefully in tune as well. As hard as it is to believe now, at a time when I meticulously plan every one of my tours down to the letter, we did not know any of this until we showed up.

The money lavishly spent on crew did not extend to travel comfort, however. The rickety van would indeed be our home for the entire tour. Goodbye, tour bus. This van was several steps in comfort below the Ford Econoline vans we had rented back on our earliest twenty-four-hour runs to San Francisco. And niceties like a day to sleep off the jet lag, or even time for a first soundcheck, or the chance to get to know our new rented gear, were not considered. We were rolling up to the sold-out show with fans already waiting outside and stage time a few hours away.

We had become accustomed on the R.E.M. tour to everything being handled, to not worrying about a thing, and just getting up and playing. We assumed things would be the same this time until about ten minutes before the show, when Mark noticed that the guitars we had brought from the US were still in their cases backstage, strings completely loosened from the flight and far from ready to be played onstage. It's hard to say what the gentleman who had been hired to look after our guitars had been thinking, but there was no time to ponder such things. Mark, Karl, and I quickly tightened the strings, tuned up the guitars the best we could, and hit the stage.

Unfamiliar amplifiers and drums, a new and seemingly absent crew, jet lag, a first day on a new continent, and a return to being a four-piece band—none of these things seemed to faze us. In fact, maybe they lit a fire beneath us, as we played a ferocious set to an enthusiastic crowd. We were on the top of our game, loud and proud, and, for a moment, united in the excitement that something brand new was happening.

Granted, we were a ragged, jet-lagged, questionably tuned band who chose to end the set with our Adolph & The Casuals rendition of 'Ghostbusters,' an inside joke bordering on a meta wink at the current pop culture. Ironic or defiantly reverent, a sloppy mess or an untamed beast; it didn't matter. The UK music scene was waking from a hypnotic haze of icy cold synthesizer bands, a future that already seemed stale and mired in the past. We offered something raw and real, and that seemed to be what the doctor ordered at that moment. We were the first of many American bands to follow, raised and reared in garages and sweaty bars rather than producer's lairs and pricy studios, and it must have felt like a revolution. Our casual, laissez-faire attitude was our badge of honor and part of the lure of this new, unvarnished music scene from the US.

In other words, we were, once again, the Hot New Thing . . . and it felt great.

———

Shortly after the London show, and well over twenty-four hours since the last time we had laid down our heads to sleep, we were off into the night.

With the four members of the band and our tour manager in one van, the rest of the crew in another, and the big truck driving through the night up the motorway to Newcastle, we caught a morning ferry to the west coast of Norway. I honestly could not have found Norway on a map a few days prior, nor had I ever been on a ferry, so the parade of novel adventures continued to unfold.

Rather than attempting to sleep, I instead found myself at the bar on the ferry with a handful of Newcastle truckers, gamely trying to learn to speak their local Geordie dialect while matching them beer for beer, shot for shot. I was a little worse for wear by the time we approached land, but I was glad to be awake and on deck to witness the sight of the approaching shores of Bergen. There are few cities more beautiful, and it was a picturesque welcome to the European continent.

We got off the boat and drove directly to Sweden. Obviously, the last-minute booking of the tour had made for some circuitous routing, and we needed something to revive our flagging energy by the time we made our way to Stockholm. That revival came in the form of a surprise visit from some friends from LA: Green On Red, who were also on tour in Europe and had played Copenhagen the night before. They had decided that since they were 'in the neighborhood' (an eight-hour drive), they would surprise us with a visit. I was thrilled. These were my buddies from back home, and I ended up spending the evening with them at their budget hotel on the outskirts of Stockholm, skipping sleep once again and dragging myself back on a commuter train to meet my band and crew in the morning.

'Where have you been?' asked our tour manager. 'We've been waiting for you. There's a bit of a problem.'

It turned out that our monitor engineer had gone for a drunken joyride in one of our vans after the show, had an accident on a bridge, and was taken to jail. Both the van and crew member were quickly replaced. I never heard what happened to him, but I know that Swedish drunk driving laws are severe, so I imagine he didn't get back home anytime soon.

Alcohol, lack of sleep, and a seemingly disinterested crew were enough to bring back the tensions in the band, particularly between me and Karl. I was becoming increasingly miffed by his defiant, arena-rock posturing; vest over bare chest, foot on monitors, cliched and unimaginative posing that bugged me no end. The more he posed, the more I sabotaged. The more I sabotaged, the more he posed. The simmering reached a full boil at soundcheck in Oslo, and I took the stage for our set in a full state of seething hatred for the bandmate who was once my closest ally.

By the end of the show, I had left the stage completely certain that we had played the worst set of our lives. *Well*, I thought, *I guess that's the last time I'll ever play a show in Norway.* I've since been told by promoters, friends, and rock critics who saw the show that night that it was one of the best they've ever seen, and Norway has become a mainstay on my touring schedule ever since. It just goes to show how wrong you can be.

Despite the growing animosity between me and Karl, we were playing solid shows to packed clubs and theaters. We played the prestigious Pandora's Box festival in Rotterdam, arriving well after midnight for our scheduled 2:30am set. We were far less interested in the four pork chop dinners that were brought backstage well after midnight than we were in the case of beer and bottle of whiskey that was already there. We ignored the former and consumed much of the latter, and, following a blistering set, were greeted by the sight of Jeff Conolly (aka Mono Man) of Boston combo The Lyres, in the process of polishing off every single pork chop dinner we had left behind. He looked sheepish.

'Were you guys going to eat those?'

'Uh no, pal, have at 'em,' we replied—which he did, before hitting the stage for his own 4am set.

In Münster, we played a popular German TV show called *Rock Convoy*. It was held in a town square and hosted by a well-known media figure and DJ named Alan Bangs. The lineup was deliciously improbable—us, Pete Shelley of the Buzzcocks, The Gun Club, and Jethro Tull, each of whom would lip-sync and play along to a backing track of a song from their newest album. We had never done anything like that before, and I wasn't too happy to be in the position of faking a performance, so instead I made my way to The Gun Club's dressing room and introduced myself to lead singer Jeffrey Lee Pierce.

Jeffrey and I had many friends in common, and our bands had both made records in the same East Hollywood studio, produced by Chris D for Ruby Records. His first two albums, *Fire Of Love* and *Miami*, were among my favorites, and I had seen them play many times. But we had never met before. We hit it off right away and, knowing that our responsibilities for the evening did not extend beyond faking one of our songs, decided to decamp to a local bar after rehearsals and proceed to compress a lifetime of catching up into a few hours and many drinks.

By the time it came to 'performing,' we were both well in our cups. I've seen a recording of the show—Jeffrey's eyes are glazed over, somewhere far away from his band and the Münster stage, while, later in the show, I'm clowning it up, playing the back of my guitar for most of the song. Well, it seemed funny at the time. I don't think my bandmates, crew, or label representatives were impressed or amused, but I had endeared myself to the top dog, Alan Bangs, who invited me back to his apartment for an evening of more drinking and listening to his vast record collection. It was the first time I heard Bob Dylan's unreleased 'Blind Willie McTell,' a song we later recorded.

In other words, the good times, the new experiences, the enthusiastic reception to the 'new band' we thought we'd never have the chance to be again had been shaken and stirred with the weariness of friction and increasing exhaustion, hastened by misbehavior. A triumphant return to London and the Marquee Club, a venue that loomed large in my 60s rock fandom, was preceded by a visit to Paris by a journalist from *Melody Maker* for an interview and a cover placement that we eventually and frustratingly lost to Heaven 17. Chalk one up for the synthesizer brigade.

The tour finally ended with a last-minute booking to fly to Madrid and play on Spain's most influential TV show, *La Edad De Oro*. We would be given the show's entire hour, broken into three twenty-minute segments. This was not the most ideal format for a singer who was excited to be reunited with the bottle of whiskey backstage after each mini set. The clip from the show that can be found online remains our most viewed video. I could personally account for a few of those views, watching my younger self with a touch of amusement and a dollop of mortification. You can feel the chasm between me and Karl in that flashy, high-production stage presentation, and it's no surprise that the end of that period of the band was coming quickly.

3.7
BACK HOME

All my worldly belongings had been in storage for almost eighteen months, ever since we left for the U2 tour in early 1983. I had lived out of suitcases in San Francisco, on the road, at the Tropicana Motel, and on friends' couches. But while on tour in Europe, Johnette had moved into an apartment on the eastern fringes of Hollywood on Raleigh Avenue, just down the road from Paramount Studio. I moved in with my records and books and ragged thrift-store clothes and began my first stab at cohabitation in a bungalow courtyard apartment we would call home for the next year and a half.

It was a stability that I needed after the exciting, gratifying, but also careening European tour. I felt the period of inhabiting the guise of a dangerous, off-the-rails alcoholic poet—something between Jim Morrison, Charles Bukowski, and my grandfather—begin to melt away, and I took quickly to this version of settling down. Even in my darkest period of the year before, I never had a death wish, and my mind and body were ready for a turnaround that would prevent that self-immolation from reaching its sad and pathetic conclusion.

Karl and I got together in my new apartment one day to attempt for the first time to write a song together, resulting in 'Witness,' which we would play a few weeks later in San Francisco. When A&M told us that they had arranged a week of shows and promotion in Tokyo to take place just before

Christmas, I found myself excited about the prospect and looked forward to the trip. It was another new frontier for which we would be joined by our friends in Rain Parade and my friend Jeff Gold, who would double as label representative and tour manager.

With this newfound stability in my home life, my touring life also felt moored, and I made a point to enjoy the city as a tourist. The label had booked two shows a week apart, and even with interviews and meetings and dinners with local label representatives scheduled, we still had plenty of free time on our hands to wander the city and do some shopping. The latter was greatly aided by a dollar that was particularly strong that year. I remember Mark buying a Yamaha DX7 synthesizer—at the time the hottest new sound on the block—and carrying it home on the plane. I bought several dozen LPs, mostly jazz albums, neatly packaged in that 'Japanese Import' format that we felt was the ultimate mark of quality in packaging and pressing in those days.

Our hotel was outside of the center of the city. There were no restaurants or shops nearby, and we were at the mercy of our label and promoter representatives for most of our activity. One morning, Dennis and I woke up famished and decided to wander beyond the hotel to find some food. We had no luck. The few restaurants we found had yet to open for the day, and as our wandering path extended, so did the level of our hunger.

We finally found a restaurant that was open. It was around 11am, and we didn't really care what we ate, as long as it got rid of our hunger. Unfortunately, there was no menu in English or anyone there who could communicate with us, and unlike at the other restaurants we had encountered in the city, there were no plastic models of menu items in the front window to which we could point.

We agreed to walk up to the counter and just point randomly to an item in Japanese on the menu and take whatever we got. Dennis went first. The cashier nodded, took Dennis's money, and came back a few minutes later with . . . a bowl of curried rice. Not bad! Emboldened, I tried the same. A similar nod, a similar handful of minutes, and the gentleman came back and plopped a sizable glass in front of me, containing what I discovered was a gin and tonic. Oh well. Sometimes you must drink your breakfast.

It was a fun trip, and it was nice to have the Rain Parade guys with us for a taste of home and to stave off whatever animosity and tensions we may have carried over from the previous year. But it wasn't enough. I found myself getting more and more annoyed with Karl. Silly little things set me off—mostly that he seemed to be barricading himself in his hotel room and not venturing out into the city except for shows and interviews.

That should hardly have been a point of contention, but it just added to the gnawing feeling that Karl and I should no longer be in a band together. Joe Strummer fired Mick Jones from The Clash for similar reasons—for having taken on the trappings of being a rock star and turning into the antithesis of what he felt was the proper attitude and behavior of The Clash. Like Joe's, my views about Karl were most likely a naive overreaction and the result of exhaustion, frustration, burnout, and just too much time together on the road with the same people. Mostly, it was just the impatience, intolerance, and impulsiveness of being young. We were still babies, albeit babies who had been through quite a bit in just a few years.

I came back from the ten days in Tokyo with the feeling that we could no longer go on. I didn't want to play another show with Karl, and in my mind that meant the band was done, despite the successful tours and a label that was most definitely eager for our next record.

I called each of the members on December 27—intentionally the three-year anniversary of that first rehearsal with Dennis—and said that I was breaking up the band. I was sad, slightly fearful of killing an unlikely and impossible dream, and uncertain about what would come next, but I had a strong feeling of liberation from the negative feelings I'd had since we decamped for San Francisco a little over a year before. It was the conclusion of the darkest, most ill-behaved period of my life, and I just didn't want to be that person anymore. Something had to die so that I could move on.

The rest of the band were all surprised by my decision but offered very little pushback or effort to change my mind. Mark was the most disappointed, having been in the fold for only a handful of months and having made the most of his first, brief time in the world of high-level rock touring. He wanted more. Dennis, on the other hand, had been there from the start, and he shared some of my frustration and sadness over how things had changed as well as the stifling tension. Karl had very little to say. Just a simple 'okay' and the call was done. We were both young and didn't have the skills to talk things out, to address and maybe resolve our grievances. Walking away was far easier.

A three-year arc was complete. I had somehow and against all odds gone from being a music-obsessed record-store clerk making songs in his father's basement to being an underground sensation navigating a major-label bidding war, theater tours with the coolest bands on a similar but loftier ascension, and then descending to a contentious flameout and the ultimate crash and burn, all within those three short years. The party was over. Now it was time to get to work.

PART FOUR
SPIT OUT THE POISON AND GET ON WITH IT

4.1
ONE SMALL BLOCK

Raleigh Street stretches exactly one block between Van Ness and Wilton Avenues on the outskirts of Hollywood, just east of the far tonier Larchmont district. It was once largely populated by actors and other figures in the film industry who worked at the nearby Raleigh and Paramount studios. A one-time showbiz meeting spot called Nickodell was around the corner, as were a coterie of burrito stands and convenience stores. The tiny street makes an appearance in an early novel by James Ellroy. I liked that. Most of the homes were bungalows built around a common courtyard, the kind you may have seen in *The Big Lebowski*—so many things typical to Los Angeles compressed in one small block.

Johnette and I got an apartment on Raleigh Street late in 1984. Our landlord said that the actor George Raft had once lived in our humble one-bedroom flat back in the 40s, and I had no reason to doubt him. It was my first home in well over a year, the first time my belongings were out of storage, and the first time I had ever lived with a romantic partner. After a period of turmoil and off-the-rails behavior, everything suddenly felt calm and clear, almost as if the previous year had been a hazy and unsettling dream, barely remembered the following morning.

I had no band. I had no upcoming shows. There were no plans. I was a few months shy of my twenty-fifth birthday with no idea of what I would do next—a weird feeling after a full year of big-budget recording sessions, a tour with R.E.M., and jaunts across Europe and Japan. Johnette would go to work each day at her day job for a film company across town, occasionally rehearsing or gigging at night with her band, Dream 6 (another Dream band!).

I would take long walks during the day, often ending up at the nearby apartment of my friend Dan Stuart. During the *Medicine Show* sessions a year earlier, I had taken a brief trip from San Francisco to LA to record a song with Dan for a compilation his girlfriend, Susie, was putting together to showcase the growing cowpunk scene in LA—a scene that found local punk and indie-rockers discovering and embracing the country songs they had been hearing in bars and on vinyl and finding it an exciting new fit. Dan and I had quickly knocked off a song called 'Bend In The Road' and recruited a collection of friends—Dennis from our combo, Chris Cacavas from Green On Red, and three members of The Long Ryders, Stephen McCarthy, Sid Griffin, and Tom Stevens—for a one-day session that was fun, smooth, and easy. The exact opposite of what I had been experiencing up in San Francisco with Sandy Pearlman.

Now, a year after writing and recording that song, Dan and I found ourselves with some free time on our hands. We'd get together at his apartment in the seedier shadows of Hollywood and Highland and drink cheap beer, watch football on TV, trade stories, and pass an acoustic guitar between us, casually and easily spitting out boozy tales of characters we would see or imagine or maybe occasionally inhabit in our time spent in local bars. I'd strum and he'd sing an outlandish verse to make me laugh, and then I'd volley back with one to top what he had just sung. I'd return to my apartment later in the evening to find an even wilder verse that Dan had written and sung into my answering machine while I was on my way home.

Before long we had come up with a half dozen songs and decided to get the same gang together for a three-day recording session at Control

Center, a very affordable eight-track studio just a few blocks from the apartment where we had recorded 'Bend In The Road' the year before. I asked Paul B. Cutler, who had engineered the first Dream Syndicate session three years before, to come in and help us get the songs onto tape.

Paul, like Dan and the other guys in Green On Red, heralded from Arizona. Pretty much everyone I've met from Arizona over the years has had a bit of an eccentric, contrarian, freaky bent to his personality, and Paul was no exception. With his frizzy afro and laconic and acerbic voice and delivery, Paul was a self-described anarchist—a stirrer of the pot who had also become a frequently employed producer while continuing to lead his own popular goth-punk bands, 45 Grave and Vox Pop. An anarchist with a strong work ethic that also extended to a mastery of guitar beyond anyone else I knew at the time. Paul knew how to get things done and shake things up at the same time.

We arrived at the studio on Friday morning with our guitars, amplifiers, a ragtag collection of songs, several cases of beer, and a few bottles of bourbon. Sometime after midnight on Saturday, we had an album. The record was later appropriately named *The Lost Weekend* although, in fact, we were done on Sunday. With Dan and Chris winging their way to Europe to start a Green On Red tour, the rest of us were left to nurse our hangovers while listening proudly to the songs we had recorded.

It was, above all, a fun session, and fun was something that all of us needed after a year of trying to figure out what to do with the various spotlights that had been gratifyingly and yet jarringly shone in our direction. This was just friends playing outlandish songs about lowlifes and outsiders, making each other laugh while tossing back drinks. We were doing it 'just for fun,' and it's not a coincidence that many of my favorite and best-received records have been made with that spirit. Also, it didn't hurt that we had such a good band, fired and fueled with a bit of the cockiness of having had a touch of success in the previous year.

We had to come up with a name for the project. Dan had taken to calling me 'Dusty' during our times hanging out together. I don't know why. Maybe he just liked the sound of it. Maybe it's because I regularly wore cheap thrift-store sports coats that never saw the inside of a dry-cleaning establishment. Who knows. But I was Dusty, so I started calling him Danny, and it stuck. Danny & Dusty was a fun name that had enough echoes of Waylon and Willie or Moe and Joe to suit the roots-oriented, ramshackle, convivial style of our music.

I knew we had recorded something good that warranted being released and heard, but contractually I was tied to A&M, and I knew that I'd have to get their permission to release the music elsewhere, maybe on my own Down There label. I set up a meeting with Jordan Harris, who despite having much bigger fish to fry and much bigger artists on the roster had been regularly checking in with me to see what I was doing next. I played a few of the songs for Jordan and waited for him to give his blessing for me to shop it to another label.

'Why don't you just let us put it out?' he asked.

I hadn't expected that response. After spending five months and a quarter of a million dollars making *Medicine Show*, our label—the home of The Carpenters, Cat Stevens, The Police, and Joe Cocker—wanted to put out our $1,000 souvenir of a drunken near-weekend. The funny thing is that a label the size and profile of A&M is required to pay union fees to be able to release a record, which meant that $20,000 was immediately added to our paltry budget—an amount that was divvied up seven ways and paid everyone's rent and groceries for a little while.

At a speed that remains shocking to me, the album was released just a few months later, adorned by a lovely cover photo taken at one of our favorite watering holes, Bob's Frolic Room on Hollywood & Vine. Bar manager Bob Brieden is right there on the cover with the look of bemusement bordering on annoyance that we had seen many times at many bars. He was a good sport, though, and he was delighted when we brought in the finished product at the record-release party that A&M held and catered at the bar in May of that year. The label put a lot of effort into promotion, the album got great reviews, and suddenly everything felt easy and fun, just like it had a few years earlier. We were only able to play a few local shows as both Green On Red and The Long Ryders had already made touring plans for most of that year, but it was just the tonic I needed to remember why I liked making music.

Fueled by the excitement and joyousness of the Danny & Dusty sessions, I started thinking more about what I was going to do next. I had written a few new songs, so I called up Dennis and Mark to get together and try them out at Uncle Studios, a rehearsal studio in the San Fernando Valley that Mark co-owned with his brother, Scott. It felt great to be playing with Mark and Dennis again. I had missed them, our natural camaraderie and the musical chemistry we had built together having been obscured by the bad vibes of the previous tours. The new songs came to life, and the music felt like a natural extension of what The Dream Syndicate had been.

We were excited and we wanted more. We knew we'd need another guitarist to achieve the full potential of the sound and songs, so we made the rounds of players we knew and admired from our immediate circle. Given that we were still signed to a major label and were not that far removed from our own days of wine and roses, all those players were happy to see if they could fit into our band. There was Mark's roommate Stevie Fryette, soon to launch a successful amplifier company of his own. There was Eddie Muñoz, fresh from The Plimsouls, who had been left in the wake when lead singer Peter Case had chosen to start a solo career. There was my old Rhino Records workmate Nels Cline, still on the jazz scene but starting to make waves locally in a trajectory that would take him to being one of the world's most respected guitarists with Wilco and other combos.

All of them were great, all of them were eager, all of them were friendly and good company. And yet somehow none of them seemed like the right fit to bridge the weird, raw, ragtag collection of inspired amateurs we had been with whatever would come next. At some point, one or all of us hit on the idea—what about Paul Cutler? He was very much in our circle and our history, having recorded our first studio session and my most recent session with Danny & Dusty. He was also an incredible guitarist who was not afraid to go off the rails with noise and dissonance. He was more than a good fit—he had his own strong personality and would challenge and inspire us and take us in a new direction. We got together, and it immediately felt like a band, familiar and new at the same time. There was never any doubt.

I don't remember when or how we decided to continue to just call it The Dream Syndicate. Was it a pragmatic decision, knowing we were a signed band with what at the time felt like a lengthy history? Did we even think about it all that much? I don't remember, but we very quickly started booking local shows and then a US tour. With the excitement of a new sound and a new collaborator, I started writing songs at a far quicker pace than I had at any point since we began.

There was never a thought of what Karl would think of the whole thing. In fact, I had not thought much about Karl since Tokyo. But, looking back, I can't imagine he was thrilled to so quickly see a band called The Dream Syndicate playing local shows without having been consulted. Even though we hadn't been getting along, he liked being in the band, he liked being on a major label, he liked the trappings and lofty treatment of being in the spotlight, and it must have stung to have seemingly been kicked out rather than having had the band just dissolve into the ether. I'll never fully know since he and I have barely spoken since.

These days, tours get booked way in advance—sometimes a year, sometimes more. There are so many more bands out there, since seemingly every band that ever existed is still out there playing music along with every new group that comes along every day. The once-imposing barrier back in the 70s of needing an established agent to even have a chance of cracking the major clubs across the country was eventually replaced by the scrappy DIY approach that began with the indie-rock scene of the 80s of personally calling clubs on the phone and sliding in for the new wave Tuesday or third bill on a tour that was coming through town. Eventually, most clubs were easily able to fill any night of the week long in advance, even getting bands to 'pay to play' by buying up their own tickets with the onus on them to sell those tickets to the fans.

Back in 1985, it was easier, especially if you had the visibility, history, and critical support like The Dream Syndicate. Paul joined in late March, and we were already playing local gigs by May and out on a national tour by July. We were a ferocious band right away, as recordings from that period make clear. Each of the lineups with Karl after Kendra left felt like putting a patch on a bald tire, trying to get some more miles on an old car without the desired performance or speed, resembling the vehicle from the glory days but with every deficiency reminding us of what once was.

With Karl, for example, Mark's bass playing felt like a replacement—a quickly procured part fitting into an old slot. But with Paul, everything felt new. His assured and provocative playing was an immediate focus to our new sound and brought out the best in Mark, whose studied chops of his own were never best suited for a ragtag indie band but instead gained strength when he was required to rise to the musicianship of an accomplished bandmate. Mark's finding his own way, in turn, served as a perfect anchor for Dennis, and the two of them became a muscular section with a groove and solid swagger that they still have together—an unmistakable sound all their own.

And my rhythm guitar fit with Paul's high wire act better than it had with anything since the earliest days with Karl. My raw clang-and-jangle had its own space, a cranky loose cannon commentary against the more rock-solid surroundings. I quickly began to write songs for this new sound, inspired by the chemistry I was feeling in rehearsals and onstage. And the old songs, in turn, felt like standards, fleshed out each night but never playing it safe. Paul made sure of that. His playing drew attention and turned heads consistently, night to night. And, unlike the previous lineup, where I would be foolishly jealous of any positive attention Karl might receive, I was now one hundred percent proud to be playing with such a dynamic and unique musician. As a band, we had become both professional and dangerous.

There was also a positivity in the lyrics I was writing for the new songs, maybe reflecting my newfound happiness and optimism, as well as the calm that came from having a stable home life. Sure, I was writing about desperate characters in songs like 'Boston' and 'Now I Ride Alone,' but I was also writing near-religious tales of rising from the ashes in songs like 'Out Of The Grey' and especially 'Dying Embers,' a song about romantic salvation in face of life and career annihilation. To be sure, there was still plenty of drinking, speed was still the drug of choice (albeit to a lesser extent), and there were domestic squabbles, but that there was a domicile at all was a positive step in the right direction.

The tour across the US was successful. Fans came out to the shows and seemed to have no problem with the lineup change once we delivered the goods, which we consistently did each night. And we had a great time. The four of us got along well, and there was a spirit of fun and united purpose that the band hadn't had in some time. Paul had a great sense of humor and a willingness to go beyond the pale, whether onstage or off, and that loosened me up as well. We had a new tour manager, Nicholas Hill, who we had met on an earlier tour, and, while being fully professional and resourceful, he was also more of a friend than a hired hand, so we felt like a family out on the road. At a club called Scorgie's in Rochester that summer, Pat Thomas, the drummer for our opening act, Absolute Grey, recorded the show. It ended up being released thirty-five years later, offering proof even after all the passing years that this was a band to be reckoned with.

4.2

DEMOS AND DEMOS AND DEMOS

With all this confidence in our new lineup and songs freely flowing, we were hot to trot, ready to dive into the studio, make a new record, and continue the revival and reframing of our story. We did not want to wait, and we most certainly did not want to repeat the arduous, endless process that was *Medicine Show*. We wanted a record that would be quick and raw and reflect what we were hearing and playing every night. We felt very confident about our new lineup and sound and were eager to get the music out to the fans and into the stores.

A&M was not so quick to agree. The 80s were in full swing, and that meant it was the era of the producer. Squeakily polished, rhythmically quantized records ruled supreme. The drum machine and click track were the guide, rather than a band's push-and-pull; magic and vibe had been replaced by an errant estimation of perfection; snare drums were isolated and pushed in their own hermetically sealed world by noise gates and digital reverb to sit atop the mix, the star of the show. A record like *Exile On Main St.* could not have existed in this era. But we were a band that— even in our current, more rock-solid state—relied on vibe, surprise, and improvisation to take us where we needed to go.

There were several recording studios on the A&M lot, a charming five-acre collection of one-and two-story buildings that had been built by Charlie Chaplin, taken over by Red Skelton, and would eventually house Jim Henson's empire. It was an easy place to hang out, wander around, and casually run into employees and executives, as well as fellow artists on both A&M and IRS. I spent a lot of time there and never felt out of place, always welcomed by a company that seemed happy to have us as part of the family.

The mood began to shift once we started availing ourselves of the in-house studios, however. It did indeed seem to be a godsend to have a professional studio at our disposal, free of charge, in which to work out ideas, and we did several series of recordings on the lot with the new songs I had been writing. The demos felt solid if not release-ready but were at least an indication that we were ready to get into a proper studio with a producer to quickly knock out the real thing. After all, hadn't A&M just happily put out a $1,000 one-weekend record I had made with my local buddies?

It wouldn't be that simple. In the dreaded statement that every band fears, the label 'didn't hear a single.' I don't know what they wanted to hear, but it wasn't what we were delivering. Years later, I would find out from Jeff Gold, who had signed us to the label, that they were very much looking forward to another record but had also viewed me and Karl as a team and were dismayed once he wasn't in the band, never to fully embrace our new sound and lineup.

We soldiered through, only mildly perturbed. We had tours and shows to distract us at the time. We had one demo session in April, then another in August, fortified by the tour we had just finished. No dice. They needed to hear more.

Around that time, John Mellencamp reached out to us via a mutual crew member, A.J., who had worked with us on the R.E.M. tour. In one of my caustic loose cannon interviews with *Creem* magazine in 1983, I had said this about John Cougar, in the days before he had added his birthright last name:

> I think John Cougar is the best spokesman of our time. The guy's not fucking around. He says, 'Well, I'm an idiot, but I know what I like, and where I come from, people want to hear rock'n'roll.' John Cougar's a better spokesman for our time than any art critic's band. I mean, what has Gang Of Four done for the heartlands of America that John Cougar hasn't done? Maybe '*Oh, yeah, life goes on long after the thrill of living is gone*' is kind of a stupid thing to say, but it made a lot of people probably feel like, *OK, I've got some ground to stand on*. Of course, if you want to play for a cult following and just be a cult band for critics . . . but I think the point is to move as many people as possible.

To which Cougar/Mellencamp responded:

> That's great because it's exactly how I feel. What's the sense of making records if people aren't going to listen to them? Let's face it: in the beginning John Cougar was the biggest joke in the music business. It's not like I don't know that. I understand that completely, but I think it's worked for my strength. To start out with such stupid, ignorant, ridiculous beginnings as I started with, and then to be able to still make records ten years later. Here it is 1983, and a lot of the same critics have turned around and said, 'Well, John's changed his style, he's better now.' It's not true. I'm

still doing the same old shit I've always done. It's just that people are willing to listen to the shit I'm putting out now. People are more open to what I do because—like Wynn said—be it however silly or stupid it may have sounded when I said it, I think a lot of people did connect to it.

A connection was made, and John must have kept tabs on us, because he put out the word through his people that he wanted us to come to Indiana to make a record in his home studio. At the time, I thought his records were the best-sounding on the radio, the closest to the loose rock'n'roll sound we all loved: traditional, natural, largely unadorned, and not afraid to turn the guitars up in the mix. But we had already been touring a lot and, with a new relationship, I didn't want to take even more time from home. I may not have even brought it up with Johnette, nor even the label or my bandmates. I just dismissed it out of hand, thinking we didn't need to leave town to make a record.

Was it truly because of Johnette or was it the fear of repeating the rootless experience of making *Medicine Show* so far from home? I can't say, but it's a decision I've regretted ever since. I think John and his producer, Don Gehman, might have been the right fit for us at the time, and it would have been fun and inspiring to work with them. A connection with a current hitmaker might have brought the label enthusiastically on board. You can't change the past, but you can wonder about it sometimes. One year later, Don Gehman would produce *Life's Rich Pageant*, a record that set R.E.M. on the multi-platinum path that followed.

Instead, we looked at the credits of Mellencamp's records and saw that they had been engineered by a guy named Greg Edwards. He lived in LA, and we figured that it would be a way to make our record at home and still get the sound we were hearing on those albums. A&M liked the idea and hired Greg and a fancy studio in the valley to make what would become a $25,000 three-song demo—not quite the excesses of *Medicine Show*, but enough of a reminder of that episode to make me squeamish.

Greg did not like us. He thought we were uncooperative. He wanted

Dennis to play to a click track, but that was not something that Dennis had ever done, and it would not have worked for the songs we were recording. 'Blood Money,' 'Out Of The Grey,' and 'Now I Ride Alone' were driven more by mood and interplay than they were by pop construction.

Could we have been a little more cooperative? Could we have just said, 'Yes, Mr. Edwards, modern hitmaker, whatever you say?' Yes, of course we could have. But our initial attempt to hew to the instructions just didn't work—it felt stiff rather than assured, sucking out all the life that we had rediscovered and embraced in the previous months. We bristled in frustration, as did Greg, a guy not much older than us and someone who was far more interested in getting within the good graces of A&M than he was in being on our team. He went back to the label with an admittedly flaccid demo and told them we were impossible to work with, effectively throwing us under the studio bus.

That was the beginning of the end with A&M. Shortly after that, I went into Jordan Harris's office with what I thought was a simple proposal.

'Jordan,' I said. 'We're a touring band with a good following. We can go into the studio, make an album for a modest budget, get out there and tour our asses off, and sell fifty thousand copies, which means everyone would turn a profit. How does that work for you?'

'We're not in the business of selling fifty thousand records,' Jordan replied.

Yes, that's what he said. Of course, selling fifty thousand physical records would put you high on the charts. But in that mid-80s period, in the midst of the sugar high of MTV and fluffy, shiny productions, Ronald Reagan's hollow, winner-take-all 'Morning in America' translated grotesquely to art and culture, and turning a modest profit just wasn't enough.

'Then we'd like to be dropped,' I boldly and impulsively stated, and Jordan quickly agreed.

Here's the funny thing. Our contract had a buy-out clause. Despite being almost $500,000 in the hole from *Medicine Show* and the tours that followed, the label still had to give us $15,000 to go away. That would be enough to make our next album just a few months later.

That modest buyout from A&M wouldn't have gone very far when we were making *Medicine Show*, but it would easily be enough to make our new album. We decided that bringing in an outside producer would be unnecessary, since we had a skilled and experienced one in-house: Paul B. Cutler had recorded our first EP four years before, and it would be a nice bit of symmetry, as well as an efficient cost-cutting measure, to have him oversee the sessions.

We booked a few weeks at Eldorado Studios on Vine Street, just north of Hollywood Boulevard, in the shadows of the Palace Theater, around the corner from Bob's Frolic Room, and across the street from the Capitol Records building. It doesn't get much more Hollywood than that!

We brought in Jim Hill to engineer the sessions. He had been on my radar because of the great work he had done recording albums for Rain Parade.

As opposed to the grueling and seemingly endless *Medicine Show* sessions, these were a breeze. We were knocking out song after song with the same confidence and swagger that we had developed in our previous years jelling as a band on tour. But even with the tightest of bands, this kind of ease and chemistry in the studio isn't always guaranteed. Once headphones are in place and soundproofing baffles are situated between each of the musicians, that red RECORD button can suddenly bring on a bit of overthinking and panic. Not in our case. I mostly remember laughing, goofing around, having a ball. In fact, we started amusing ourselves between takes by attempting incongruous covers of the day, as well as some from our childhood, and asked Jim to record us whenever we started playing. These half-baked, sometimes silly, sometimes inspired stabs at being a warped party combo helped keep things light, and they ended up on the record's reissue, decades later.

We wrapped up the sessions on my twenty-sixth birthday. Dennis's wife, Amy, came in with a guitar-shaped birthday cake she had baked for me. We had a party and felt very good about what we had recorded, the nightmares of endless demos and arduous recording sessions left on the scrap heap of history, cautionary tales rather than fearful patterns.

Our tour manager, Nicholas Hill, had been so great on the road—organized, eager, and, maybe best of all, amiable enough to make friends wherever we traveled. He seemed the perfect candidate to step in as manager and help us find a label to put out this new record. And he quickly succeeded.

Big Time Records had been started in Australia by Fred Bestall, who had made some money and a name for himself as the manager of the easy-listening hitmakers Air Supply before starting his new label with fellow Aussies The Hoodoo Gurus, who were very popular in their native land and were beginning to make a name for themselves with their hooky garage rock in the US as well. The label was quickly being populated with a roster of like-minded groups like Dumptruck and my old pal Alex Chilton. They were also hiring a staff of savvy young employees, many of whom would move on to influential posts at major labels in the indie and grunge-rock scenes of the following decade. It felt like a good new home, and we quickly signed with them to release our new recordings.

The good-vibes lovefest from the recording session continued with our new label, which was housed conveniently enough in the same building, just a few floors down from my publishing company, Bug Music, over on the corner of Hollywood and Highland. It all felt like the kind of kismet we had earned, and which had been so elusive. The rough mixes from the Eldorado sessions were on heavy play in the Big Time offices, and the staff were excited to get the record out and begin promoting it to the outside world.

We still had to mix the album, but that seemed a mere formality. A June release date was scheduled, and an extensive tour of Europe was being booked to time with the release. Paul once again was the perfect choice to mix the album since he was part of the session and had solid skills behind a mixing board. We had enough money left in our budget to book a handful of days, and Paul found a reasonably priced mixing studio just a few blocks up in the base of the Hollywood Hills.

And then—inexplicably, and without warning—things changed. Paul had booked a somewhat state-of-the-art studio with a new mixing board and technology called SSL (short for Solid State Logic). This book not being a guidebook for recording technology, I'll spare you the deep dive details, but the upshot of this new board was that, rather than the tangible, hands-on, traditional form of mixing, this new setup allowed for information to be saved and automated on computers and displayed on a screen that, compared to even the most rudimentary of home recording systems today, would feel analogous to equating an ancient video game like Pong to flying a modern 757 jumbo jet. The computer display looked and felt cheesy and silly even back then. And, like many forms of technology, it served to alienate and exclude those not privy to its methodology.

Whether Paul was equally intimidated by its unfamiliarity or merely felt more pressure due to our new label and our love of the rough mixes is hard to say. But after a year of having nothing but fun together, he isolated himself in the mixing studio with the studio owner, who guided him through the new technology while the rest of the band, myself included, were left to feel like intrusive outsiders whenever we dropped by to see how things were going. It's common during mixing for the artist to leave the studio and return when a final mix is ready to be presented, to be able to listen and judge and make suggestions on fresh ears. But our presence in even that selective attendance felt strained and unwelcome.

I would drop by a couple of times a day to hear how things were going, and I was alarmed to hear the modern sonic trappings we had been so eager to avoid. There was the icy digital reverb, so ubiquitous at the time, adding a shrink-wrapped shine to what had previously been very natural and organic sounds. There was the unnatural thwack of the gated snare drum, pushed muscularly to the front of the mix. What we had recorded at Eldorado felt like the band we had become onstage together in the previous year, and we liked what we heard, as did our label. What was taking shape in mixing, even with those same performances, felt like an artificial reproduction, one step removed from who we were. It might have felt like the sound of the day, but not the sound of our band.

Had it not been a member of our band who was doing the mixing, I may have bristled more, and, having learned the lessons I had learned during the making of *Medicine Show*, I may have put on the brakes immediately. But this was Paul—our friend, our bandmate, and a guy whose work we liked and admired. I was afraid to bum his high, and my attempts to steer the mix and sound back on track were met by annoyance and a request to trust the process and wait for the final results.

I've said over the years that *Out Of The Grey* is my least favorite of the albums I have made in my life, only to have fans tell me it's their favorite. To be sure, the album contains many fan favorites, like 'Boston,' 'Now I Ride Alone,' 'Slide Away,' 'Forest For The Trees,' and the title track. I still play those songs today, with The Dream Syndicate and at my solo shows. But the album also contains songs I now see as filler, as exercises, and as signs of growing pains as I was trying to figure out where my writing might be going. If I never hear or play 'Dancing Blind' again, that would be fine by me.

And then there was the sound. Dennis, Mark, and I were severely disheartened when we heard the final mixes, and I suspect that deep down Paul may have felt the same. I often feel that it's a big mistake to try to sound cutting-edge, current, or 'of your time.' Using the most modern, state-of-the-art sounds and styles means you're also guaranteed to have that same work sound quickly and forever 'of another time' in a very dated way. It was clear the label felt similarly let down, but we all had to put on a brave face and promote and tour behind the record.

Listening back now, my criticism has softened, largely due to a reissue that was made with modern remastering technology that was miraculously able to soften and reduce the dated production elements of its time. The newly restored version brought back the sound of a confident, strong group playing at full tilt. If the record lacks the intensity and danger of the other three albums we made in the 80s, it does have in its place an enjoyable, breezy listenability and instant friendliness. At the time, I may have seen that as lightweight and 'copping out,' but now I can enjoy it as a non-jarring, pleasant listen. Funny how these perceptions can change over time.

On the other hand, back then we also learned a lesson about critical response that I always make sure to remember. In the US, where *Medicine Show* had received lukewarm reviews, *Out Of The Grey* was seen as a strident, strong return to form. The video for the title track received regular play on MTV while the album climbed up the college radio charts. But in the UK, where *Medicine Show* had garnered nothing but over-the-top glowing reviews, this new album was received with the kind of disappointed, 'what happened to the band we loved?' response we had heard two years before on our own home turf with the previous album. We were simultaneously experiencing a rousing comeback and a woeful slump, depending upon the side of the Atlantic where we were standing. To paraphrase Ernest Hemingway on critics, 'If you believe them when they tell you that you're good, you'll have to believe them when they tell you that you're bad.'

All of that was forgotten once we hit the road, and a year of lofty thrills began. We expanded our European touring circuit with more shows in Scandinavia and Spain. We also played our first shows in Italy, where we were greeted with the fervor and feeling of being the hot new band we had been in previous years in countries we were visiting for the first time. We were invited to the prestigious Glastonbury Festival in the UK, where we played in the rain for ten thousand enthusiastic fans. I remember hearing echoes of The Cure on the nearby stage as we packed up our gear and quickly left the festival to make our way to our next show down the road.

Glastonbury was our only scheduled festival, but within a few weeks it wouldn't even be our biggest festival experience of the summer. Ten days later, we were driving through the middle of Italy and stopped at a payphone (pre-cell-phone times, kiddies!) to check in with our agent back in the UK.

'Oh, I'm so glad you called,' he said to our tour manager. 'We just got a call from the Roskilde Festival in Denmark. The Cult was scheduled to headline the main stage on Saturday and had to cancel. They want to know if you could take their place. I know it's only two days from now, but would you be willing to cancel your next few shows and fly up to take their place? We can arrange the flights out of Italy on Saturday, get you into Copenhagen on time, and smooth things over with the venues where you'd have to cancel. This is a once-in-a-lifetime opportunity.'

We didn't hesitate. Of course, we said yes. Once in a lifetime? This was a once-in-many-lifetimes opportunity. These days, a band like us even being invited to Roskilde would never happen—it's one of the biggest music festivals in the world. Even back then, it was a freakish anomaly. I can't imagine how they came up with the idea of an underground band like us filling the void of the headliner on the main stage, but I'm glad that somebody had that crazy and most likely desperate idea.

On Saturday, the morning of our appearance, we flew out of Milan to Copenhagen, where we were picked up at the airport by a festival runner and driven one hour in a van to the festival site, directly to our backstage trailer. We had less than an hour to tune up our strings, make a setlist, have a beer or two, and then walk up the steps just after sunset to the stage where fifty thousand fans were ready to see The Cult.

The festival host bounded onstage with purpose and fervor and told the crowd, 'We are sorry to say that The Cult had to cancel. But this band came all the way up from their tour in Italy on two days' notice to be here today and entertain you instead.' Rather than boo or gasp in disappointment and disperse the field, the crowd responded with huge cheers for a group that, I'm sure, was mostly unknown to them. Bearing in mind that Denmark is usually listed as the happiest country on earth, it may be that we were beneficiaries of that sunny disposition.

'Ladies and gentlemen, The Dream Syndicate.'

The crowd was immediately on our side. Despite the lack of a soundcheck or even any chance to have a look at the stage, our monitors and equipment were perfect—as though we had fine-tuned and tested everything for hours during the day. We were in mid-tour form, and we played what I'm sure was one of the best shows we ever played. Rather than being conservative and cautious, we played as though we were playing a small club to our most devoted fans. From start to finish, we were playing at full throttle, moving across and owning the stage as though we were headliners from the start. It was one of those levitating, out-of-body perfect experiences that translated to seemingly every one of those fifty thousand fans who ate it up and gave us a hero's welcome from start to finish. We walked offstage sweaty and stunned, knowing something special had just happened.

We had to fly back to Italy the next day, but that Saturday night was one for celebrating. Our set was followed by a band booked to close out the evening in somewhat of a mop-up roll for fans getting ready to call it a night. Not helping their cause were the skies, which turned dark and started pouring down rain shortly after our set. That band was Giant Sand from Tucson, mutual friends of our Green On Red pals and fronted by Howe Gelb, who I had met briefly when he dropped by during the Danny & Dusty sessions. We partied with them late into the evening and began what would become a lasting friendship.

Over the years since, I have had a strong career in Scandinavia, particularly in Norway, where my records often scale the upper reaches of the mainstream charts in versions of my own or by other artists, and where I have had the chance to create the soundtrack for a few of the country's all-time biggest TV shows. I trace all that goodwill and success back to that one hour in Denmark.

In one other particularly memorable and consequential show on that tour, we made our first visit to Greece, playing to five thousand people at the Theatro Alsos, an outdoor venue in Pedion Tou Areos Park in the center of Athens. We were told we were the first American band to play in Greece since Talking Heads about five years before. There was a feeling of excitement as we hit the stage, only to be dampened when the PA suddenly went silent. We heard later that the precariously placed cables from the stage to the speakers had been cut somehow. Our own monitor speakers were working perfectly well, however, and we quickly and industriously got on our knees and proceeded to turn our own speakers toward the audience so that the show could go on. This instinctive move was seen as selflessly brave, and the already excited crowd went nuts and embraced us as conquering heroes. Much like in Scandinavia, this began a long love affair between me and the audience of Greece, which I have visited for shows countless times over the years. I like to say that I've played Greece more times than any non-Greek artist, and I defy anyone to claim otherwise.

Europe was suddenly our reliable home turf. Back in the States, our touring was solid, if not quite as frenzied and eventful. We made the rounds of all of our favorite cities and made our case every night, the brief *Out Of The Grey* recording session misstep long forgotten, and the nightly joys of inhabiting our studio recordings and taking them to new places in a live setting. If touring the US didn't bring the heady highs that we had experienced in Europe, it at least showed that we still had a steady and loyal following on our home turf.

Our record-release homecoming show in Los Angeles was at the Roxy. As always, we put a lot of importance on who we chose to open the shows, preferring to shine a spotlight on local, up-and-coming acts whose music we particularly enjoyed. For this particular show, we had The Leaving Trains on the bill. Their most recent album, *Well Down Blue Highway*, and their first self-released independent single, 'Bringing Down The House,' were big favorites of mine, and lead singer Falling James Moreland had been a friend since my record store days.

We felt confident we could sell the show out with just the two bands. So, imagine my surprise when I heard some noise from a daytime barbecue party in the courtyard outside my bedroom window one day and went out to check out the action. A young, skinny, dreadlocked kid bounded up to me and said, 'Steve Wynn! My band is opening for you guys at the Roxy next month!'

I called Nicholas on the phone to see what the hell was going on and he said, 'Yeah, the Roxy wanted us to put this new band on the bill and I agreed. They're called Jane's Addiction, and they're starting to get a little bit of a following.'

A few weeks later, I was watching my bounding backyard buddy Perry Farrell and his band at soundcheck, playing a cool, droning two-chord song about a mountain, thinking, *Hey, these new guys are pretty good*. There was a wave of new groups on the rise, and only four years after our first record, we had quickly gone from being young upstarts to road and life-tested veterans.

The year closed out with a handful of shows in Australia and New Zealand. As in 1984, we ended a long record-release year with shows on a new continent, but this time it was a gratifying experience—packed shows, enthusiastic fans, and the members of our band soaking up new terrain and sunny beaches in the middle of the December summer Down Under and reveling in what, despite the brief mixing hiccup, had been a very joyous year.

My old friend Mikal Gilmore wrote a great book called *Night Beat: A Shadow History Of Rock And Roll* in which he calls *Out Of The Grey* 'a bracing work of redemption. In particular, it seemed to be a record about what it means to lose one's way and to summon the will to find a new direction and start again,' adding that I 'conjured bitter, dark remembrances of blown chances and bad choices.' Mikal continues:

> While he clearly cared a great deal about the people who get swallowed up in such dissolution, he refused to surrender to the romance of it all. 'Spit out the poison and get on with it,' he sang at one point, even though he was singing about somebody whom he knew could never let go of his own decline or broken past. Maybe Dream Syndicate lost their crack at the big time, but they still had music to make, and Wynn sounded as if he intended to make it as honestly and compassionately as he knew how. . . . Wynn went on to make two fine solo albums, *Kerosene Man* and *Dazzling Display*. But *Out Of The Grey* was the best music Dream Syndicate ever made.

Now, who am I to argue with that? Thank you, Mikal.

—

HOLLYWOOD SWINGING

Shortly before leaving for Australia, Johnette and I decided to move out of our Raleigh Street apartment and put all of our things in storage. It made sense. I had spent most of the year on the road, while her band, Dream 6, had changed their name to Concrete Blonde and signed to IRS Records, with a debut album and a lot of touring on the books for the beginning of 1987.

From the first time I saw Johnette perform with Dream 6 at the Music Machine in 1984 and heard their EP around the same time, I was blown away by her strong, skilled, and soulful voice. I would go and see her shows and listen to and give encouragement to the new songs she was continually writing. But I also made a point to keep our careers separate, never inviting her band to share a bill with us or asking her to sing onstage with us.

In retrospect, it's hard to say why I kept that professional distance, but I think it was an attempt to avoid having Dream 6 be tagged as 'Steve Wynn's girlfriend's band.' Or maybe it was because, despite honestly liking her music, I may have also felt that their more professional, mainstream sound was at odds with the underground indie band I still wanted to believe that we were.

Either way, I know that it rankled with her. One night she saw a video from a Danny & Dusty show I had played in LA early in 1986, where Kendra got onstage to sing backing vocals with us, and she was livid. She was offended that another woman—albeit one who had started The Dream Syndicate with me—was onstage singing backing vocals with the band when she had never been asked to do the same thing. She had a very good point. Nonetheless, we had a lot of fun together and having a home and a relationship provided some much-needed stability after the rootless, careening years that had come before. But it was nonetheless a tempestuous relationship, hardly helped by plenty of drinking. Before she quit her job with the film company, Johnette had been asked to stock the bar for a release party. Rather than fill it up with the three or four favorite types of liquor, she instead bought one of everything in the store, and at the end there were plenty of leftover bottles of root beer, apple, pear, and other schnapps, along with crème de menthe and other unpopular varieties that kept our liquor cabinet stocked with syrupy sustenance for a good portion of 1986.

Upon hearing the final mixes of what would become Concrete Blonde's debut album, I knew that change was afoot—that soon they would become very popular, and that Johnette would have a big year ahead. Both of those things quickly proved to be true. The record took off on radio and MTV, and the band was immediately booked solid for the first part of the coming year, beginning a very successful career for Johnette.

In the years to come, I would open many shows and tours for Concrete Blonde and Johnette's other projects, and we would remain friends. In 1990, Concrete Blonde would record a version of 'When You Smile' with Paul Thompson of Roxy Music on drums, which was quite a thrill. But as 1987 began, things between us had become far chillier.

I found a studio basement apartment on Ivar Street in the lower reaches of the Hollywood Hills, just a short walk from the Hollywood & Vine crossroads where we had made our previous record. I paid the first and last month's rent by myself and felt certain that my sole inhabitance would not be changing. It would be the first and the only time in my life that I lived on my own.

A few weeks after I moved into the apartment, Johnette and her band were coming back from their first US tour. I knew from her manager when the flight would be landing, so I decided to surprise her by meeting her at the airport. She saw me and her eyes flashed with anger. Much as I had taken unnecessarily strong steps to keep our musical endeavors separate in the previous years, she was now flying high on her own and resented any indication that I might be imposing myself onto her space. She stormed past me without a word, got into a taxi, and left me behind. If there had been any doubt before, this was the final punctuation. I would be starting out 1987 flying solo.

There were a lot of conflicting feelings at play. I enjoyed having my own pad so close to all of the Hollywood action, and my little studio apartment was crammed to the gills with my thousands of vinyl records and the Marantz receiver and Garrard turntable leftover from my high school days, along with stacks of books, guitars, amplifier, and a fold-up futon couch. There was a tiny kitchen and bathroom and a big window behind my bed that faced onto stairs that would lead me up one small flight to street level and an exciting world just down the hill. It was a small apartment, but it was all mine.

On the other hand, this was my first major breakup, and many of the wounds from a childhood of divorces and moves and the comings and goings of family members were being brought to the surface. Sadness and desolation would unexpectedly wash over me one moment and then quickly be replaced by the lure and escape of the bars and clubs that were just a ten-minute walk from my front door.

During one of those bleaker moments, I went to visit Dennis and Amy, who lived just a few blocks away. They were good enough friends to be able to withstand at least a little bit of my whining, fortified by whatever beer or wine they might be serving. When I arrived, it turned out that they had invited a friend for dinner. I knew Brigid Pearson a bit from when we both attended UCLA. She was studying art, and we had many friends in common among the music fans and the new-wave contingent who would hang out on what was known as North Campus—a gathering place for the cool kids. She had dated our first producer, Chris D, for a bit before he worked with us, and I would often see her at shows. We had never spoken much, but I always found her attractive and mysterious, dressed in black with touches of goth makeup.

I was happy to see her there and quickly shifted from mopey to lively and chatty. We hit it off and started dating within a week, beginning a relationship that would last the next ten years. It had been only a couple of weeks since that tempestuous airport encounter with Johnette, who nonetheless felt we were still a couple. She resented what she perceived as a sudden encroachment, and thus began a confusing and often stressful six months where I continued to live in my Ivar basement hideaway, unable to fully commit to either one.

Truth be told, my main relationship for that first half of 1987 was with the Hollywood nightlife; music, drinking, and friends who could connect the dots. It was my version of the John Lennon years with Harry Nilsson, a dozen years before in the same city. My main partner in crime was Bob Forrest, the singer of Thelonious Monster. He would call me almost daily to see what I was up to, and we would meet up, have several drinks, and then head down most often to Raji's, a new club that had opened on Hollywood and Argyle.

Bob was the perfect companion for those times—scraggly-haired, bespectacled, easygoing, chatty, and fun. Thelonious Monster were just getting started and I loved their music, which had a touch of the shambolic Replacements-influenced sound of the day but focused on his naked commentary on his life and the world around him. We both loved listening to and talking about music. And we drank. A lot. Bob eventually sobered up and became a well-known drug counselor and wrote a great book about his life.

I was writing at a rapid pace. The songs were pouring out of me, fueled by the heady brew of a recent breakup, a new relationship, an exciting new music scene, a stronger connection to the LA nightlife than I'd had in years, new friends, and alcohol. There was plenty of stimulus and input, and I wrote songs that would appear on not only the next Dream Syndicate album but also on my first three solo albums. Most of the songs reflected the mix of melancholy, anger, remorse, and doubt that came in the wake of the breakup—a separation anxiety put to music.

Many of these songs did not fit the sound and style of The Dream Syndicate. They were more folky and gentle, without room for guitar solos. Fortunately, I had been doing more and more solo acoustic shows, starting with a few 'play for beer money' gigs in Hoboken and Boston back in 1984, and then continuing in 1985 and 1986 on the new folk scene that was rising out of the indie-rock scene at venues like the Lhasa Club in LA, as well as the well-known folk mainstay McCabe's, where I had bought my first acoustic guitar back in 1974.

I was never afraid or nervous about playing solo shows with nothing more than an acoustic guitar, and over the years it has become one of my favorite ways to deliver my music to an audience. The way I like to explain it is that when I play with a band, we're interacting and connecting with each other, shifting from moment to moment, depending upon what we hear and how we respond, and the audience is there to watch us like fish in a fishbowl and see us doing our thing. But when I play solo, I'm jamming with the audience. I'm feeling them every second I'm onstage, and there's a push and pull in what I'm doing and how I sing and play that feeds off what I perceive they're feeling. If with a band, I'm back in school and learning to play with others; when I'm playing on my own, I'm once again the only child, alone and figuring out how I fit into the world outside my own head. It feels natural.

With new songs coming quickly and The Dream Syndicate relatively quiet in the first half of 1987, as well as playing solo acoustic shows I also put together a small acoustic combo with Chris Cacavas from Green on Red on accordion and my friend Robert Lloyd on mandolin and piano (or accordion when Chris wasn't around). Robert was a well-known local rock critic and one of The Dream Syndicate's earliest supporters, but I really got to know him when I produced a record for his band The Romans in 1986 and was floored by his talent and versatility. I found him instantly to be a kindred spirit. We've played together ever since in my solo groups or in more stripped-down acoustic settings. He remains one of my closest friends, as well as a very successful TV critic for the *Los Angeles Times*.

The Romans record was the fourth release on my Down There Records label, following records by The Dream Syndicate, Green On Red, and Tucson's Naked Prey. Each of those records had done well, especially considering my label was always just me with no promotion staff. Whatever work I could put behind the release fell in line way behind whatever I was doing with The Dream Syndicate, but they were good records that ended up getting attention and, in all three cases, launching careers that lasted through the rest of the decade.

My only reason to put out these records was that I liked them and felt that they wouldn't be released unless I did it myself. Putting out records on my label was, to me, no different than when in previous years I had played a song on my radio show or talked someone into buying a record from behind the counter at a record store. I liked the music, and I wanted people to hear it. My pitch to bands was, 'If you can't find anyone else to put out your record, I'll do it.' I would front the money to press up the records and then split all profits 50/50 with the band. It was a nice little deal for everyone.

Local scenester and musician Phast Phreddie Patterson had been to Boston early in 1987 and called me on the phone when he came back. 'I just saw this great band play their first two shows,' he told me. 'They're fans of The Dream Syndicate and the music you've put out on Down There. They'd be great for your label.' He brought back a demo tape of their tunes, and he was right. It was killer stuff and most definitely a good fit. They even reminded me a little bit of Green On Red.

I got in touch with their lawyer, who said the band was into it but needed $2,000 to recoup their recording expenses. I explained that the way I ran the label was to put out but not pay for a group's recorded material. I could have paid the two grand, but I didn't want to change the format. The lawyer said fine, no hard feelings, but we're going to look elsewhere. The band was The Pixies. I often wonder about the possible trajectory of the label, had I put out the record, but I usually figure that rather than having vaulted me into the record-mogul stratosphere, more likely it would have meant they would have never become as famous as they did.

Down There had taken on a bit of local awareness, however, and I ended up being approached by Bill Hein, the head of Enigma Records, to see if I'd want to do a P&D (pressing and distribution) deal with his label, where I would bring him six records a year for which I'd get a signing advance and guaranteed release for whatever I wanted to put out. The signing advance allowed me to hire my old Davis pal and former Suspects bandmate Russ Tolman to run the label. Russ had just gotten his business degree, so he was up to the task. We put out a handful of records in the following years, including Russ's debut solo album (which I produced), and the one of which I'm proudest, the only recorded document by the legendary Top Jimmy & The Rhythm Pigs, whose shows I had often DJed in the early 80s.

Unfortunately, the good vibes of the label then began to change. A member of one of the bands began making threatening phone calls to Russ at all hours. And there was also a cover story in the *LA Weekly* about me and the label, which meant that more and more people around town were beginning to see me as a music business executive rather than as a musician, which did not make me happy. By the end of the year, I had abandoned the label, and I now only use it as a logo on some of my self-released tour and mail-order music.

Adding to the mix of solo shows, record label adventures, romantic indecision, clubbing, and drinking, I was getting very little sleep because my upstairs neighbor, a woman with a couple of dogs, was up at all hours and had her own imaginary twenty-four-hour puppy-centric universe that crept through her floorboards and haunted my waking hours. I'd find empty gallon-sized vodka bottles in the trash regularly, and judging from her sleeping habits, I pegged her as an amphetamine enthusiast, much as I had been in recent years. I knew the signs. What's more, she had a crush on me. She would leave half-cooked plates of grey food on my doorstep at all hours, often knocking on my window to show me a lizard she had found, or making rude, inappropriate comments about whichever girlfriend had most recently come to visit.

All of this added up and, after a half-year, I knew it was time to step back from my six-month Hollywood adventure and dive back into whatever would come next to propel things with The Dream Syndicate. We had barely played together in the first half of the year, but a European tour was booked for July. We had been invited back to the Roskilde Festival for the second year in a row, most likely out of gratitude for our last-minute gig the summer before. The summer run concluded with a festive two-night run at an outdoor amphitheater atop a hill in Athens, with The Fleshtones and The Hoodoo Gurus—a residency of guitars, garage music, and late nights fueled by the celebration of the realization that the music our three bands had been cultivating for so long was being enthusiastically embraced in lands far from home. By that point, we had all been around long enough and had experienced enough ups and downs to know how special that was.

I got home from the tour, packed up my belongings, and moved back into my father's basement on Sunset Boulevard. My time in Hollywood had been wild and exhausting but also very productive. My little breakup bender was over. I had a bunch of new songs, and it was time to start thinking about getting back into the studio to make a new Dream Syndicate record.

4.5
BACK IN THE BASEMENT

It had been five years since I moved out of my father's basement. Back then, in 1982, I was twenty-two years old, working in a record store, DJing at night, playing in an up-and-coming rock band, and doing my best to keep afloat in my college studies. Living at home at that age and in that state of flux made sense and seemed like a necessary part of growing up and finding my way in the world.

Since then, I had been featured in nearly every music magazine; signed to and been dropped by a major label; toured the US, Europe, and Japan; and been the support act for a few of the biggest bands around. I had been in my first serious, grown-up relationship and then seen it crash and burn. If living in my father's basement five years before had felt like a workshop where I was building the master plan for my life, this felt more like a retreat, tail tucked neatly between legs; a need for retrenchment and reinvention.

My father, meanwhile, had plenty on his hands. A woman that he and my stepmother had invited into their polyamorous relationship had stayed on longer than the scheduled night or two and was now living upstairs in the main bedroom with my father as his new girlfriend. Meanwhile, my stepmother had fallen for the third wheel in a similar fling and was now living upstairs in the second bedroom with her new girlfriend. It all worked surprisingly smoothly for a bit, but it also meant that their hands were quite full. I was left fully to my own devices and comings and goings downstairs.

On the other hand, my romantic life had simplified greatly. Johnette and I were now strictly friends; Brigid and I continued to date while she was living just down the 405 freeway with her parents over in Marina Del Rey. We were both twenty-seven and felt similarly sheepish about living at home, but it sure saved money at a time when that definitely came in handy.

Johnette offered to sing backing vocals on a version of 'Let It Rain' that The Dream Syndicate had recorded in an eight-track garage studio owned by a friend of Mark's after a day of knocking out demos for our next album. The song had been a hit for Eric Clapton in 1970 and had been a regular part of our set back in our earliest days, when our cover choices would blur the line between irony and tribute. In this current lineup, the choice instead felt more like a punk powerhouse—a giddy expression of joy and transcendence—and Johnette's backing vocals allowed it to soar almost to the level of gospel exuberance. We gave a cassette of the recording to Big Time, and within weeks it was pressed up as a twelve-inch single and sent to college and alternative radio. It got more airplay than anything we had ever recorded before.

Despite the success of this new single, our relationship with Big Time was beginning to fray at the edges. There were murmurings among the staff that the owner was misappropriating money, and that less attention was being paid to the daily management of the label's business, causing several key members of the staff and a portion of the roster to peel away from the fold.

We had parted ways with our manager, Nicholas Hill, mostly because he had never truly aspired to be so closely tied to the music business, or to a group's daily minutiae or drama. The split was amicable; Nicholas went on to found the Singles Only Label with Bob Mould and become a fixture on the New York City music scene.

It became increasingly clear, though, that we needed a new label and a new manager. Johnette spoke highly of Dave Lumian, who managed Concrete Blonde as well as the local ska band The Untouchables and was also involved in nonprofit community organizations. He was open to working with us and seemed competent and easygoing, and that was good enough for us. We had our fourth manager in as many years and were now on the hunt for our fourth label during that same period as well.

Looking back on The Dream Syndicate's run back in the 80s, my only regret is that we changed labels, managers, producers, and lineups so often, and that, due to that instability, we didn't release more records or ever fully gain traction with the band we could have become. We were continually trying to patch newfound holes. But each of those changes seemed necessary and unavoidable at the time. Perhaps not coincidentally, it also seemed like a reflection and parallel of my own childhood—of stepparents and siblings and homes regularly shifting and changing, leaving me to either adapt to or to sometimes ignore and operate independently from those seismic shifts in my life.

Nonetheless, the changes continued to occur. Each one necessitated action; choices were sometimes made and acted upon very quickly, without any thoughts of where it was all going. We were a working band with a path forward, and we didn't want to end the ride.

Earlier in the year, while I was still living on Ivar Street, I had been introduced to Elliot Mazer, who was best known for producing Neil Young's *Harvest*, along with early hits for Linda Ronstadt and Big Brother & The Holding Company. He was a friendly, enthusiastic guy with thick furrowed brows, and he very much liked our music. He and I hit it off right away, and we ended up getting together regularly throughout 1987. I would give him demos of the songs I had been writing, and he made comments, chose favorites, and before too long became the logical choice to produce our next album. I think Paul was relieved to not have to do double duty this time around.

Dave Lumian was able to quickly extricate us from Big Time Records and get us signed to Enigma—a natural choice, as label president Bill Hein and I had already worked together. Along with our choice of producer and new manager, our choice of label was quick, logical, and a path of least resistance. Things were going quite smoothly for a band that had endured a lot of bumps in the road in the not-too-distant past.

After the European shows, we didn't play much during the final months of the year, but we never went too long without getting together. We would rehearse regularly, and I made a point of showing up with a new song or two every time. We also had a way to publicly test out the songs in the form of Deirdre O'Donoghue, whose *SNAP!* radio show on local station KCRW (long before the station became the international presence it is today) had been a steady and loving incubator for the local jangle, post-punk pop scene and like-minded musicians from around the world. Deirdre's boundless enthusiasm created its own universe where bands of all sizes, whether local and unsigned acts and breakthrough groups like 10,000 Maniacs and R.E.M. could exist on a similar plane, as though their import and influence were completely the same.

Deirdre was particularly supportive of the music that I was making with and without The Dream Syndicate, and both my solo combo with Chris Cacavas and Robert Lloyd and my more established 'day job' band would appear regularly on her show. The station had a top-notch recording setup, and it was exciting to go on a live radio show and play songs that were written that week or perform cover choices that I'd thought up on the drive to the station. It was a luxury to have such a well-appointed sandbox of sound at our disposal, while simultaneously getting our music out to the local fans via Deirdre's shows.

Around the same time, our new manager was also working with the National Committee For A Sane Nuclear Policy, also known as SANE. He and other members of the group organized an anti-nukes benefit at the Variety Arts Center on Figueroa Avenue in the heart of Downtown LA. We were asked to be a part of the show, along with fIREHOSE, Peter Case, Divine Horsemen, and other locals. The planners also had the idea of putting together a supergroup covers band to close out the show, and I was recruited along with Ray Manzarek of The Doors, Randy California of

Spirit, Mike Watt of The Minutemen and fIREHOSE, and Dallas Taylor, the drummer for Crosby Stills Nash & Young.

We booked one day of rehearsal to decide what we would play. I was excited to be able to back Randy on his biggest hit, Spirit's 'I Got A Line On You.' I was also chosen to be the evening's Jim Morrison (in song choice, not, as I might have been a few years earlier, in stage behavior), so I got the chance to sing 'Riders On The Storm,' and 'Roadhouse Blues' backed by Those Keyboards. It was a surreal kick to hear Manzarek's signature sound while I was singing some of The Doors' most well-known songs. In the thirty-five years since, I have tried to find any photographic evidence or an audio recording of the night, but to no avail. But it looms large in my memory.

If 1987 had begun with the emotional devastation of a romantic breakup and a period of besotted behavior, it ended with creativity, stability, and clarity. I had a new girlfriend, a new home, a whole lot of new songs, and two great combos—one with a new label, producer, and manager. I hadn't entered a new year as optimistically in quite some time, and I couldn't wait to get started.

4.6
ONE EYE ON THE EXIT

Uncle Rehearsal Studios in Van Nuys was opened by our bass guitarist Mark Walton and his brother Scott and has hosted countless bands as they plot and plan their way to the big time or hone their craft so that they can remain there once they've arrived. Hang out in the office and you can generally hear several bands playing at once from each of the four rooms—a cacophony of hope and desire and pride and fear.

Ever since Mark joined The Dream Syndicate in 1984, Uncle had been the obvious place for us to work up new tunes and rehearse old ones between tours and recording sessions. Mark, a solid businessman ever considerate of his brother's fifty percent stake in the business, never gave his own band a discount, but he did allow us to keep our gear permanently in one of the space's lockers, making things easier each time we had a rehearsal.

Sadly, our regular routine of rehearsing and working out new songs hit a snag when Paul discovered one day that his beloved red Gibson SG guitar and Marshall amplifier had been stolen from the rehearsal space. Paul had played the same guitar-and-amp combo since he first joined up with us. It was his sound, an extension of himself, and he was devastated, not only for sentimental reasons but also because, with few gigs booked over the final months of the year, we weren't making any money.

We decided to do a benefit show at Raji's to raise money for Paul to get a new guitar and amp. Raji's had become my main hangout throughout 1987, and the club's owner, Dobbs, who had also hired me as a DJ at the Cathay De Grande years earlier, was happy to have The Dream Syndicate play an intimate show at his club. It was a good deal for everyone.

I was spending a lot of time with Elliot Mazer at that point, and when I told him about the gig, he asked, 'Do you mind if I record it?' Elliot had long been particularly interested in the documenting of live events. Two of his most famous records, Neil Young's *Time Fades Away* and Big Brother & The Holding Company's *Cheap Thrills*, were live albums.

Elliot had the idea to record the show directly to a DAT machine. DAT was the hot recording format at the time—a digital recording process that would capture sound onto a storage device that looked like a shrunken-down VHS tape that could fit in your pocket. They had the pristine and clinical sound of CDs, which were also just starting to take hold at that time. Digital was the way of the future, we all thought, and Elliot was intrigued. His plan was to perch himself in a small room above the stage and have a feed out from the PA to a mixing board so that he could mix the show in real time. When the show was done, the recording would be done as well.

We didn't think much about it, and we weren't in the least bit nervous. *Hey, Elliot,* we thought, *if this is what you want to do, then knock yourself out!* Mostly, we just wanted to play a show, have some fun, and make some much-needed money. Elliot had us over to his pad nearby between soundcheck and the gig for some spaghetti and red wine, and we were in great spirits when we got back to the club.

It's typical for bands to be more cautious and concentrate harder when the red RECORD button is pressed, but not that night—we were in a great mood, we had been rehearsing and playing regularly, and we came busting out of the gate. Aside from a version of Blind Lemon Jefferson's 'See That My Grave Is Kept Clean,' we didn't play any of the songs that we had been rehearsing for our next album. It was our greatest hits and our proven winners, played live with full volume and abandon. Everything about the show was free and loose and performed without any semblance of holding back—we even asked Peter Case to play harmonica with us on 'John Coltrane Stereo Blues' without rehearsal or any idea what he would play. He went wild and let his freak flag fly in the spirit of the evening.

When the show was over, the bar was closed, and all our friends had left, we went upstairs to listen to the recording. We were blown away. Elliot had done an impeccable job of recording and mixing on the fly. It was one of the best shows we ever played, and it was all committed to tape. One year later, it would be released as *Live At Raji's*, and it's considered by many of our fans to be among the top live albums of all time. I might put The Who's *Live At Leeds* a little higher, but otherwise, I'd find it hard to refute that claim.

The Dream Syndicate were at peak power, we were all getting along, and even if we were no longer the hot new thing, we had a well-delineated future with an excited new label and manager, a passel of new songs, and a coterie of dedicated followers around the world who could fill clubs and small theaters wherever we chose to go. Sure, it was becoming apparent that we were not destined to reach the commercial heights of our friends in R.E.M., for example, but our level of success would have seemed like winning the lottery to the kid I had been just six years earlier. It still does.

Creatively, however, I was more engaged in my solo shows. I was feeling more and more frustrated by the limiting constraints and the maximizing volume of the standard two guitars/bass/drums rock band.

As good and tight as we had become, I often felt that both the band and audience would be left sonically and physically exhausted, wrung dry, dazed, and battered at the end of every show we'd play. Rather than see that as a badge of honor, I felt it was more of an albatross. When people's comments about our shows became 'YOU GUYS WERE SO LOUD!' or 'YOU REALLY KILLED IT UP THERE,' I felt sheepishness rather than pride. At that point in my life, I found myself wanting to soothe and entertain, to leave them smiling and laughing rather than devastated. Even at our earliest, noisiest, most dissonant shows, we were still seductive and sexy. This current version of the band was a test of will and endurance—a charm of its own, but a charm that mostly appealed to a certain audience—and we did find that our audience was skewing more and more male as time went on.

On the contrary, the variety of dynamics and the soothing and yet loose and ragged mix of my acoustic guitar with Robert's mandolin and Chris's accordion felt like a new, exciting world, allowing me to connect to a wider range of fans. It was a fun show that nonetheless had a punk spirit in its spontaneity, raggedness, and quiet intensity. Paul liked what we were doing, and eventually, he joined our combo on nylon-string acoustic guitar for our live shows and radio broadcasts. The two entities were rapidly blurring, and it became less and less clear which of the new songs I was writing would be designated for which band.

Playing under my own name, though, meant smaller venues and audiences and less money, and it most definitely still felt like a side project to the more established Dream Syndicate. But that was fine by me. I enjoyed both combos, and I got very different pleasures from each. They fed off each other. The ease and relaxed charm of the solo folk quartet would eventually leave me hungry for the power and danger—and, yes, higher fees and bigger audience and venue sizes—of The Dream Syndicate. I was happy to keep doing both.

Our manager, Dave Lumian, did not agree. We went out for a bike ride one day near where he lived in the Venice Beach area. At some point during the ride, I brought up the idea of maintaining tandem careers with both the band and my solo shows and making very different-sounding records with each. 'I don't think that's a good idea,' he said. 'There's a limited audience out there, and to get the best results, it's important to maintain focus. You have a good thing with The Dream Syndicate, and I think you shouldn't make the mistake of dividing your time or your fans.'

I was crushed. I felt like I could have been very happy doing both. These days, I juggle several groups with different lineups and sounds and styles, as well as my solo shows, and it works. But Dave may have had a point. Back in the mid-to-late 80s, side projects were less common; record releases and touring options were more limited, and musical acts were encouraged to do less, release fewer records, and have a focused strategy to get the most out of that one shot you might have to maintain and build a career. And, despite feeling like I was already a veteran at that young age of twenty-seven, I had also at the time made fewer records than I could count on one hand, and I felt no guarantee that the life I had lived for the past six years could continue indefinitely. For the time being, it had become my job, and I liked my job and didn't want it to end. The choice had to be made, and for the rest of 1988, I would focus on The Dream Syndicate.

I often wonder what would have happened if I had defied Dave and instead kept both projects going at full throttle. Such musings are never definitive, but most likely The Dream Syndicate would not have broken up a year later. We may have been able to ride the wave of the indie-rock and grunge movement that came along in the early 90s since we were a building block, soldiers on the front for the sound that led to the return of guitars in the mainstream. But we may also have just slogged it out to diminishing returns.

On the other hand, I've had so many great and life-changing experiences since then that may not have happened if The Dream Syndicate had been at the center of my life, including, as it turns out, a focused, purposeful, and joyous return of the band twenty-five years later. So, even at my most melancholy and nostalgic moments, I always come to the conclusion that I made the right choice.

But it was too early for reflection. There was still a year to go.

GHOST STORIES, YESTERDAY'S NEWS

We returned to Eldorado Studios in Hollywood in March, with Elliot, to start recording our fourth album. Still displeased by the overly slick mix of the previous album, and with confidence fortified from the exciting results of the live documentation at Raji's just a few weeks earlier, we were primed to record something raw, rough, and ready. Those qualities were right in Elliot's wheelhouse. He was decidedly old-school, aiming for vibe and excitement over everything. His ways of achieving that vibe, however, were a little unconventional.

Typically, the producer will sit with the recording engineer in the isolated crow's nest of the control room, peering at his laboratory rats as they perform behind glass, ready to make clinical suggestions before returning to a series of multiple takes until one finally meets a level of satisfaction. This wasn't Elliot's method. Instead, he was right there in the studio with us, wearing his own headphones, dancing and moving and grooving and gesticulating right in our faces, shifting from band member to band member like some cross between a symphony conductor and a shaman faith healer.

I was amused, inspired, and, most of all, happily distracted by the sight of this middle-aged Jewish gentleman positively losing his shit. It kept me from thinking too much about the songs or the chords or what we were aiming to achieve, and instead, I just lost myself in the surreal moment.

Paul didn't feel the same. He thought it was utter bullshit. It was not the way he preferred to work, coming from more of a no-nonsense punk-rock background. He responded with occasional annoyance or, at best, quiet compliance. It didn't affect his playing, however. Paul was too good a player and too disciplined to deliver anything less than high-level, accurate renditions of what he intended to play. Dennis and Mark played like the symbiotic, tight rhythm section they had become, and the takes came quickly and easily.

This fourth album, for me, was going to be the one where we took it all back from the studio frustrations that had encompassed the two previous records. If *Medicine Show* had been sidetracked by Sandy's endless indecision and mismanagement of time, and if *Out Of The Grey* had been marred by yielding to the temptation of shiny, modern sounds, this one was going to be the one that, like our first album, was going to sound exactly like who we were—a documentation rather than a studio construct. And we succeeded in that goal. The sound was unencumbered by trickery, and the performances were never intimidated or careful.

Choosing from the collection of songs I had written in the past year was also natural and effortless. Sure, we went for the most direct rockers—'The Side I'll Never Show,' 'Loving The Sinner, Hating The Sin,' 'Weathered And Torn'—but there was also room for more hushed, offbeat numbers like 'Whatever You Please' and 'When The Curtain Falls,' neither of which seemed out of place with the muscular machine we had become onstage.

Although I had temporarily abandoned my solo shows and ambitions, plenty of elements from those shows crept into our new record. Chris was gradually becoming a fifth member, adding keyboards to live shows and to about half of the album. And there was one song, 'Someplace Better Than This'—a regular in my solo sets—that was just my vocal backed by Robert on piano. I wasn't yet planning a solo career, but this record pointed in that direction, nonetheless.

There would be one more outside collaborator on the album, for a pop song that was earmarked from the start to be the first single. 'I Have Faith' was one of many songs I have written over the years with a repetitive, hypnotic guitar riff in the key of D. Set against an album with the recurring lyrical theme of emotional devastation, romantic heartbreak, and musings on the end of life or even the world in general and reflections of my messy six months living in the Hollywood basement, this song was about hopefulness—a path out after the darkest times.

I was having trouble getting inside such a positive statement, and I couldn't write the second verse. Johnette came through with those lyrics and added her signature layers of backing vocals. This made the label happy, of course, since Concrete Blonde were continuing their ascension to radio and chart success at the time.

Ghost Stories was a dark, raw record, but it was a positive experience. We mixed it up in Berkeley at Fantasy Studios—which, true to its name, was a fantasy experience for me, due to the connection to Creedence Clearwater Revival. Robert made the trip up the I-5 with me for the adventure, to record his track at Fantasy and check out some of the mixing as well. We stayed at a very cheap, rough-and-tumble motel along Telegraph Avenue. At night, after a day of mixing, we were treated to a whole different mix of sirens, helicopters, fights, and even, on one occasion, a police bust in the room next door.

I first met Pat Thomas a few years earlier, when his band, Absolute Grey, opened for us in Rochester. He was living in the Bay Area at the time, and he dropped by the motel and the studio a few times to check out the sessions and hear some mixes. Pat, who as I've learned over the years can be brutally but instructively honest with his opinions, really liked what he heard. I was happy. Elliot was happy. It was going to be the first record since *The Days Of Wine And Roses* that would reflect the power of our live shows with a collection of top-notch songs. In a decade where the recording process could become so easily derailed, this particular project fell neatly into place.

Things were smooth and effortless, in fact, to the point where there really wasn't much to say about the record. Merely saying 'a good band recorded some good songs in a good working environment' hardly makes for good copy in the musical press. When I was interviewed by the person hired by Enigma to write our bio, I casually mentioned that I had been battling a cold for much of the first weeks of the session, and that made it to the bio and became the thing most asked about in subsequent interviews. I got tired of recalling and expanding upon this decidedly non-story. Journalists can be so lazy sometimes. In the years since, I've generally written my own bios so that I can dictate the story I want to tell, knowing that very often the bio will be simply printed as is or slightly rewritten for publication. Keep that under your hat. It will be our little secret.

Shortly after the recording session, Brigid and I decided it was time to flee the familial coop, grow up, and stop living with our parents. We got a one-bedroom apartment together in Silverlake, a part of town that was showing the earliest signs of gentrifying into a hip neighborhood. There were cool coffeehouses a short walk from home, more conducive to a cleaner lifestyle than the enticing row of bars close to my previous pad in Hollywood. Brigid went off to work each day, and I continued to crank out songs on a regular basis, singing melodies and improvised words as I walked to and from the Tropical Bakery on Sunset each day.

Compared to the previous six years of drama, contention, and upheaval, things were starting to feel very settled and secure, and that extended to relations with the band. We all liked the new record, and we were all getting along great. The release was set for June, and tours of Europe and the US were set up for the fall.

Two years earlier, we had made our first music video, for the song 'Out Of The Grey.' It was played at least once a day in regular rotation on MTV over the course of two months. That may be hard to believe today, now that the station rarely shows music videos, but at that time we were still in the wild, wild west phase of music videos. The station was hungry for new content, and we had made a bit of a name for ourselves. It was also a decent video—a simple lip-sync performance of the song in front of a white screen, and even though we were far from being confused for pretty-boy male-model types like Duran Duran, we looked good. Against all odds, we had become an MTV video band.

This time around, the obvious choice for a video was 'I Have Faith.' This one ended up being a little more stylized: sheets of reflective mylar on the floor and scattered all around gave us a trippy house of mirrors effect that in some ways suited our music and history. On the other hand, the video was far slicker than we wanted it to be, making the band seem like almost an afterthought in some director's visual fancy. What's more, after years of steadfastly resisting the ubiquitous makeup and poofy hairstyles of the decade, we finally and lazily relented on the day of the video shoot, which also doubled as our press photo shoot. For the next six months, then, we were constantly reminded of that one day's ill-advised use of excessive eyeliner, giving us the appearance of a tired old goth group or housewives at the end of a night on the town. It was not a good look for us, and we cringed every time we picked up a newspaper or saw ourselves on TV.

Then again, for better or for worse, seeing ourselves on TV or in print would become less of a problem in the coming months than we might have expected.

We had been press darlings since our earliest shows in 1982. We had been written about extensively by nearly every music publication during our years together. Full-length features, extensive reviews, think-piece essays, and inclusion in articles about what was going on in the American music scene; articles in English and in the language of every European country became commonplace and almost expected. We definitely garnered press far out of proportion to the actual number of records we were selling, creating a house-of-mirrors illusion that made it appear we were more successful than we actually were.

The press, I'd like to believe, were partial to us because we were actually a good band, but also, I'm sure, because we checked all of the boxes of what critics of the time loved and hadn't been hearing in other records at the time. Velvet Underground? Check. Stooges, Neil Young, Television? Check, check, check. Wild noise countered by pop hooks and lyrics with literary allusions to flatter the intelligence of those in on the game? Check and checkmate. What we did when we started in 1982 eventually wouldn't be that unique, but in the years following our debut, we filled a missing contemporary gap in a good record collection with enough audacity and a compellingly messy story to keep the press assignments coming.

There had been unanimous critical love early on, followed by raves and pans, comebacks and backlashes in response to our second and third albums and the lineup changes during that time. But in those years we remained consistently worthy of comment and study by the music press. And fans came out to shows to see how that analysis would translate to flesh and blood, to the stage, to a moment to be lived and never repeated.

That all changed in 1988. Suddenly the formerly lengthy lead reviews turned into single-paragraph 'roundups' of records worth mentioning, but only barely, and the hyperbolic tones of 'this is the greatest' or 'this is a great disappointment' had been replaced by middling, generic, C+ reviews, mostly saying things along the line of 'nice job, boys. You really worked up a sweat out there.' We were just another band filling out the column inches, fattening up the back bins in record stores.

Simply put, we had been replaced as the interesting shiny new object, as eventually happens to every band or musical act, big or small. It's happened at various times to bands as big as The Rolling Stones or Bob Dylan or U2. It didn't happen to The Beatles because they broke up before it could, but it most certainly happened to the groups whose success never lived up to the promise of the earliest reviews and hype. Eventually, the critics want to be where the action is, not where it was.

And there was new action, some new underground mules kicking in our stall. What we had begun as messy, somewhat unique contrarians had been adapted, made consistent and more palatable by a new wave of interesting bands. The Pixies were on the radio with their distorted, noisy guitars and jarring dynamic shifts—a style we had mostly to ourselves in the years before. The Replacements had taken the notion of a shambolic, confrontational live show to larger venues than the ones we had been playing. Hüsker Dü had married buzzy punk and pop songcraft all the way to a Warner Bros contract (in his book, Bob Mould surmises that his rejection of bandmate Grant Hart's lovely '2541' as a rip-off of our own 'Tell Me When It's Over' was the beginning of their end.).

Far from being jealous, I was a big fan of all of those bands. But I felt the greatest melancholy gut punch that our time might be done one day after a visit to Enigma's offices in Los Angeles. I was filling my bag with the label's latest releases to listen to at home and on tour, which included some fun, perfectly enjoyable records by Social Distortion, The Smithereens, The Dead Milkmen, and Mojo Nixon. Perfectly listenable, one and all. But then I was stopped in my tracks by a new album by Sonic Youth called *Daydream Nation*. Sonic Youth had actually released their first record the same year as we did, but their rise had been more gradual, more organic, and less tainted by the promise of the mainstream, and this new ambitious and expertly accomplished album not only fulfilled the promise of their entire career but also showed what our career could have been. My hat was off to them, but my heart sunk nonetheless. I knew our time was nearly done, and we were indeed yesterday's news.

Nonetheless, tours were booked, plans had been made, and we were eager to get back on the road in support of the record. It had been a full year since our brief summer tour of Europe, and we hadn't toured the US since the release of *Out Of The Grey* two years earlier. We knew we were at our best in a live setting, and we could still get good bookings everywhere at good enough fees to allow the tour to break even. We said yes to everything that came our way and found ourselves with a seven-week tour of Europe, followed immediately by another six weeks in the US in place for the fall. The two legs would be separated by a mere twenty-four hours, a travel day between shows in London on November 9 and Syracuse, New York, on November 11.

Mike Watt famously said, 'If you're not playing, you're paying,' and he was right. A day off on the road means you still need to pay for van rental, hotel rooms, and crew salaries and meals. It's incredibly tempting to take a gig to fill a day off. We like playing music. We're out there on the road to play our music and spread the word. What good is sitting alone in your room? Come hear the music play!

These decisions are made at home, before the tour, calendar in hand, the distance between shows measured in inches on a map rather than hours of travel. It's doable, so let's do it. I still operate that way, often to the chagrin of my various bandmates. But how hard could a thirteen-week tour be? Most of us were still in our twenties (Paul a little bit older), and we had primarily been cooling our heels at home for the previous year.

Ahead of the tour, our label arranged for us to play at the New Music Seminar in New York City in July. At the time, in the years before the ascendence of South By Southwest in Austin, that convention and the connected series of shows across the city was an important lightning rod for music-business movers and shakers. We were booked at the Cat

Club with Pere Ubu, who had also begun as a confrontational, weird underground band, and then, like us, had moved toward the center with a rockier sound, better production, and evolving musical chops.

The show was fantastic. Pere Ubu played before us and were absolutely on fire. Actually, everything seemed like it was on fire since the stifling summer Gotham heat was magnified inside the jam-packed club. I remember glancing down the neck of my Telecaster and seeing rivulets of sweat continually flowing from my right hand to my left, a full-on tributary that rolled from pickups to tuning pegs and onto the floor below. It was quite a sight. The audience response was great, and we felt like we had made a good case for people to continue to pay attention to the grizzled veterans onstage.

Brigid came to meet me after the New Music Seminar showcase and the two of us enjoyed a vacation in New York City. Despite the sweltering summer heat, we covered some ground, and I had a chance to show off many of my favorite spots around town, having spent quite a bit of time there on tour in the years since I first visited the city and stayed at the 34th Street YMCA back in 1981. It's always fun to take someone around a city that you love, and I particularly felt like a big shot one day when a security guard at the Whitney Museum saw and recognized me at the back of a long line waiting to get in and promptly ushered Brigid and me to the front of the line and got us into the museum for free. I found out a few years later that the kindly Whitney employee was none other than Stephen Malkmus, still a few years away from releasing his first album as the leader of Pavement, a band who would draw a few Dream Syndicate comparisons in their earliest days.

A month later, we were playing for the first time in Finland, at the Ruisrock Festival. We were on a bill with The Stranglers, who were playing with a new lead singer after the departure of frontman Hugh Cornwell. They were actually quite good, and the new singer fit in well. But after the show with Pere Ubu, I began to see a pattern, and I wondered if we had already begun to shift over to a kind of oldies circuit of punk rock, new wave, and the early post-punk indie scene that followed. Were The

Dream Syndicate, The Stranglers, and Pere Ubu already our own scene's equivalent of The Coasters and The Drifters?

We certainly didn't play like a good-time oldies combo. We were ferocious, on top of our game, a band with a mission, and the audience responded in kind—no mean feat for an industry-oriented gig. Confident about our new record, despite the response, we were determined to take our mission from town to town to make a case for ourselves, justifying our continued existence, night to night, and picking up more fans along the way.

4.8

THE CRACKS START TO SHOW

The disappointment of the lukewarm response to the album was quickly dissipated by a European tour that would be our best yet on those shores. We found ourselves playing bigger venues to more people in cities we had played on previous tours, and to sold-out crowds in cities and countries where we hadn't been before. If our extended history had knocked us off the Hot New Band pedestal, it allowed us to settle into the comfy confines of being established veterans. Unlike on our earliest tours, we now had an actual catalogue of songs from which to choose each night, and our fans embraced the familiar tunes they had come to hear.

We had never been to Belgium, aside from a festival appearance in 1984, but when we were getting ready to take the stage at our first show in Brussels, we were asked to hold back our starting time because fans were scaling the two-story building exterior to shimmy into open windows at the back of the club. The show had been sold out for months, and the venue needed to deal with the situation. There you go! Keep finding new countries to play in and you'll always be a new band.

We played the main room at Amsterdam's historical Paradiso, one of the most beautiful venues on the planet. A few moments before we went onstage, a woman came backstage with a very large python draped around her neck like an exotic stole. She asked if any of us would like to hold the snake, and after we all began to decline—we were about to go onstage to a thousand people, after all—Mark said, 'Sure, I'll do it.' He wrapped the snake around his neck, and within a minute, the reptile let loose with what seemed to be a full year's worth of piss. The floor and our bass player were soaked. Time to hit the stage! I made a point of not getting too close to Mark's side of the stage that night.

In Paris, it was the equally historic Elysees Montmartre for one of only three shows we would ever play in that city. France can be a tough nut to crack. To its credit, the country is very supportive of its own musical scene and heritage, but often to the exclusion of outsiders. There are notable exceptions, of course (my friends in The Fleshtones do great over there), but that hasn't been the case for me. I've played France over the years far less than most other European countries, not for lack of trying. But on this night, with the great Australian band The Go-Betweens opening, we were fully embraced by the locals.

Italy was great once again; Norway, Denmark, and Sweden were equally fantastic, benefiting from the bump of playing the Roskilde Festival two years running. We returned to Greece as conquering heroes after our gig-saving monitor maneuver in the park. In other words, the seven weeks spent touring Europe was an unqualified success. The sense that we were spinning our wheels and no longer mattered had fallen by the wayside. We were playing powerful, assured shows and feeling more confident in ourselves and our place in the humble settings of our place in the music world with every show.

We had all gone back to drinking more and more. Mostly that excess resulted in madcap fun. One night, for example, roommates Mark and Paul were frustrated by a Florence hotel room that, rather than being in the center of the city, turned out to be in the suburbs overlooking a construction site. In their boredom and disappointment, they ended up dangling the frame of one of their beds outside the window of their hotel room. Two of the legs kept the bed from falling from the fifth floor to the rubble below, and they made themselves laugh by rolling items from the room—ashtrays and TV remotes, for example—along the top of the bed and into the empty construction zone. (It was well past midnight and there was no danger of hitting anyone below.) Finally, after running out of things to roll off the bed, they just threw the whole bed out the window, initially falling into hysterics before shifting to a sense of *what have we done?* remorse and fear of repercussions. The fear was not necessary. Upon waking up the next morning, the hotel staff had kindly and officiously brought the bed frame back up to the fifth floor and laid it next to their door. No comment was made when we checked out.

Sometimes, such hijinks—ill-advised as they might be—end up being hilarious, great stories to tell over the years. But the weariness of touring and the abundance of booze were also taking effect, even in the midst of a successful run. On our way to Italy, we took a night off in Monte Carlo—a tony stopover for such a scruffy bunch, but none of us had been there and we wanted to check it out. I chose to sit at an outdoor bar and catch up on postcard writing while having a few drinks. Paul wanted to gamble in the casino, the only hitch being that one was only allowed onto the casino floor while wearing a proper jacket. I wore the same sports coat every night onstage, and I happily lent it to Paul for the evening. I guess he'd had a few drinks at the blackjack table because he was stumbling and slurring by the time he found me at the same outdoor café, weaving up in my direction, and then proceeded to vomit all over himself and the coat. I was not amused. He was not amused by my lack of amusement. All was forgotten and forgiven by the morning. A dry cleaner was found, and on we went. But the cracks were beginning to show.

The tour ended with a triumphant show in London at the Town & Country, a venue now called the O2 Forum Kentish Town. The room holds over two thousand people, and the promoters hedged their bets with strong support from popular local acts The Weather Prophets and Biff Bang Pow. The latter band's leader, Alan McGee, couldn't do the show due to the increased demands of his rapidly rising Creation Records label. He was replaced onstage by a cardboard cutout of himself with a dedicated mic stand. This time, I was amused.

As was usually the case with that final lineup, we rose to the occasion, playing what was likely our best show of the tour, and the audience responded in kind. We were road-worn, tired, and weary, but we also felt on top of the world at the end of a successful European tour.

We probably should have gone home at that point, but home wasn't in the cards. We had a flight back to JFK the next morning, and a show in Syracuse booked the following night. If you're not playing, you're paying, right?

There's a song on *Ghost Stories* called 'Weathered And Torn,' and that's exactly how we were feeling as we boarded our flights to JFK, emboldened by a successful tour but physically worn down by seven weeks with lots of drinking, late nights, and very few days off. We were happy but we were beat, and we had another full tour to go back on our home turf.

4.9
TELL ME WHEN IT'S OVER

Since our first tour in 1983, our US shows had been booked by Frank Riley and Bob Singerman at Singer Management. Their roster was filled with bands who had come up in the independent music scene around the same time as us, many of them friends of ours. We were handled mostly by Frank, who had always done right by us. He knew us, knew our music, and knew the circuit of clubs and promoters most suited and welcoming for our music. There had never been much of a problem; we could always get dates when we wanted them, and Frank was showing the early signs of a career ascendancy that would eventually place him in the following years as a top agent, booking the likes of Wilco, Los Lobos, Drive-By Truckers, and more.

So, it's hard to imagine why we could have possibly thought it was a good idea to change agencies and move over to Premier Talent when they offered to book our US tour for *Ghost Stories*. Our manager must have made a solid case—'They'll take you to the next level,' 'they're big fans of the band,' 'you'll play better venues and make more money'—and we must have taken the bait. We all should have known better by then, even though it's hard to say no when one of the biggest, most powerful, and most respected agencies asks for your hand at the dance.

Because of the heavier hand that was now pulling our strings, our US tour for the fall of 1988 was dotted with larger fees and some larger venues in some cities where we had no right to be playing anyplace bigger than the cool, underground bars where we might have played in the past. These larger venues took us on and gave us bigger guarantees, not out of a certainty that we could pack the joint but rather as some kind of trade-off with our behemoth new agency. *If you want U2 or Tom Petty on their next tour, you had better take care of our smaller acts like The Dream Syndicate, know what I mean?*

None of this mattered much in cities where we were already popular and had a dedicated following. But it also meant our tour was filled with dates in cities where we were merely connecting the dots on the map and padding the tour budget. The itinerary and venues smacked more of a major-label band on the way up (or down) than an independent band trying to hang on to credibility and maintain or build upon a long-earned following. On paper, the dates looked fine, but we wouldn't be touring on paper.

We had that one scheduled day off after London to recharge for the US tour, then a four-hour drive upstate to Syracuse, where we would start the tour the next day. It would have made good sense to have a few days to catch our breath but, hey, good sense wasn't a big part of our touring life in those days. Weariness be damned—we had a show to play and a tour to begin!

We were met at that first show in Syracuse by a couple of young filmmakers hoping to make a documentary about their favorite band. Peter Cooper had approached me after a show a few years earlier with a screenplay he had written based on my song 'Merrittville.' It was a well-written, gritty mix of Southern gothic and film noir that was true to the tone of my song while expanding on the story and characters. He never ended up turning it into an actual film, but I was flattered that he had made the effort, so when Peter asked earlier in the year if he could shadow us on tour with his friend Jon Baskin and document our life on the road, I said yes.

I'm not sure what Peter was expecting when he met up with us at that first show in Syracuse. I'd imagine he was hoping to capture the power and majesty of a band he loved, much as Elliot Mazer had done at Raji's earlier in the year. And, along with documenting our live shows, he probably figured he could capture some fun adventures backstage, in hotel rooms, and along the I-95 corridor—a cinema verité portrait of a group on tour.

It's fortunate that Peter and Jon met up with us at the start of the tour. We were weary, to be sure, but we were also still hopeful about the tour that lay ahead. The two cameramen followed us down to shows in Providence, Northampton, Asbury Park, Philadelphia, Washington DC, Virginia Beach, and Baltimore. The resulting film, *Weathered And Torn*, has some fun moments. Paul and Mark go out for a round of golf in Baltimore. Dennis is joined in Philadelphia by his wife, Amy, and their two-year-old daughter, Elizabeth, who dances joyfully backstage before the show. And the live excerpts give good proof that no matter how weathered, how torn we were during the day, we had plenty of gas in the tank when we hit the stage.

The movie in some ways was our *Let It Be* (as opposed to the more recent optimistic redux, *Get Back*). It was a pretty accurate portrait of a band in its final days, the cracks showing and widening with each frame. The live concert material is solid—we were probably playing as well and with as much ferocity as we ever had, wringing ourselves dry each night onstage and leaving nothing behind. But all of the offstage footage shows a very weary Dream Syndicate, disheartened and ready to go home. We were all pulling in different directions, and, for differing reasons, had our eyes wandering towards the exit.

Paul, a self-professed anarchist with roots in punk rock, was increasingly annoyed by the rules and rigors of professional touring life, as well as the increasing exhaustion. He still enjoyed playing and the challenge and gratification of bringing his estimable talents to the stage each night, but the rest was a drag.

Dennis was equally conflicted, but for very different reasons. Inspired by, among other things, a copy of *Mere Christianity* by C.S. Lewis that I had lent him during the making of *Medicine Show*, our drummer had come to fully embrace the Christianity to which he had been born. He was born again, and he would spend most evenings after the show in bed reading the Bible while I, his roommate, would read Jim Thompson or Raymond Chandler from across the room. He was never judgmental of his heathen bandmates, but obviously, some of the touring behavior and chatter were in conflict with the life he felt he should be living.

I was feeling my bandmates' disenfranchisement and overall misery. It sparked memories of the unhappy and splintering home of my adolescence. Along with my need and desire to make music that felt new and not just a repetition of a past, I was feeling more and more out of step with what we were doing each day. I began hankering more and more to return to doing my solo shows and make music that didn't sound like The Dream Syndicate.

Mark just wanted to have fun, bless his soul. But we didn't always make it easy.

Our documentarians left the tour just before our show at the prestigious Manhattan showcase club the Bottom Line. It was my first time there, and I knew the venue's legend well as a place where the likes of Neil Young and Bruce Springsteen had played often. It was also the place where one of my favorite albums, *Take No Prisoners* by Lou Reed, had been recorded. I was excited.

To avoid exorbitant New York City hotel prices, bands who play in Gotham will often pack up and drive a few hours after the show to save a few bucks and cut down on the next day's drive. With that plan in place for our Bottom Line show, we got one large hotel room in the city where we could leave our bags, nap, and rest up during the day, then drive off after the show. It would be easy and efficient to play our show, get back to our room to grab our bags, and get out of town.

The show was great. The Bottom Line was sold out, and even with the restricted movement and formalities of the all-seated venue, with tables and chairs packed together, we still managed to build a sense of excitement and abandonment and that translated to the patrons even in that constricted environment. Our manager, Dave, had made the trip out from LA and invited various representatives from our label and booking agency. We wanted to pack up and hit the road as quickly as possible, but we also knew we'd have to hang out after the show to shake a few hands before taking off.

Paul had an old friend at the show, a fellow guitarist and producer named Rudy Guess, who he knew from his younger days in his hometown of Phoenix. Mark knew him as well from the rehearsal studio in LA, and when Rudy and his entourage suggested to Mark and Paul that they grab a drink nearby, they heartily agreed and were on their way out the door. I saw Mark leaving and said, 'Hey, we should probably all stick around to hang out with the people from our label and agency and then get on the road as soon as we can.'

'Fuck that,' Mark said. 'We're going out. We'll be back after one drink and then we can all take off together.'

Midnight came, the schmoozing was done, and the club had emptied out. Mark and Paul were nowhere to be found. The staff at the Bottom Line were ready to close up shop. Dennis and I found ourselves sitting in front of the club in our loaded van with the crew, ready to go but still missing half of our band. We waited. And we waited some more.

After an hour of sitting in the van in front of the club, I finally said, 'This is ridiculous. Let's just get in the van and drive around and see if we can find them,' an idea that in retrospect sounds far more ridiculous than it did at the time. After about thirty minutes of futility, driving up and down the nearby streets and avenues of Greenwich Village, we decided it would be best to just return to our one shared hotel room, park the van, and try to get an hour of sleep while waiting for Paul and Mark to hopefully remember where we all had been staying earlier in the day.

It was 5am. We were all fast asleep when suddenly we were woken by the sounds of the sloppy struggle of a key trying to get into the door lock, followed by Mark and Paul, inebriated as I had ever seen them—and that's saying something!—stumbling and falling into the room, babbling incoherently. They seemed to be excited and wanted to tell us a story, but the words didn't make any sense. We were in no mood for much of anything except shoving the two stumblers in the direction of the van and finally taking off for the hotel, which we hit a few hours after daybreak.

When we met up in the lobby the next day, Paul and Mark were quite hung over but more coherent at least than they had been a few hours earlier. Mark was bubbling with the tale he was dying to tell.

'It was amazing. We all ended up barhopping with Carole King. Rudy's producing her new album. We ended up at a karaoke bar.'

My fuming of twelve hours earlier returned and stepped into overdrive. I have always been a very big Carole King fan, not just because I had entered my record-buying days around when *Tapestry* came out (and saw her play a great show at the Greek Theater around that time) but even more so for the incredible songs she wrote with her ex-husband, Gerry Goffin. I would have loved to have been able to meet and sing karaoke with her, rather than playing Cinderella at the club while my band sisters were at the ball.

'It was so cool! She and I got up and sang a Beatles song,' Mark gushed. 'That one called "Chains."'

'Carole King WROTE that song, you fucking idiot.'

'Oh. Anyway, it was fun. I wish you could have been there.'

I was seething. As is so often the case, in retrospect it makes a good story, but at the time I was incensed, and it was just one more pulling of the unraveling thread. Much like when Paul threw up on my coat in Monte Carlo, I was once again unamused, and my failure to laugh it all off only added fuel to the fire.

Things went downhill from there. As we moved further away from the Northeast, we started encountering smaller crowds. A show at the glitzy, thousand-capacity Masquerade in Atlanta was canceled after pre-sales barely made it into double figures. We had always done pretty well at the smaller, sweatier 688 Club, and it's likely that our crowd didn't want to go to the fancier digs across town. We got paid in full and avoided traveling out of our way down south, but it still stung, and it added a few more lines of writing on the wall.

Similarly, we played a show in Minneapolis at the Caboose, another venue with a corresponding fee too large for us but obviously railroaded through by our big new agency. The club owner took me aside after we had played a solid show to about seventy-five attendees in a room that was built to hold many more.

'We really took a bath tonight,' the owner said to me. 'Would you consider taking a reduced fee?'

'Sorry, no can do,' I countered. We had expenses to cover and, anyway, I was increasingly unconcerned about burning bridges. With our entire operation in flames, what were a few more burnt bridges? The owner made some comment about us not being welcome back at the club, and that was fine by me.

This trail of disappointments reached a head after a show in Cleveland at Peabody's Down Under, where we played to an audience about half the size of the one who had come to see us the year before. We left after the show for an overnight drive to Toronto. Overnight drives in a fifteen-seat passenger van are never easy. It's tough to fall asleep sitting up or leaning against the window, and even if you do catch a few zs, you end up feeling ragged once the sun begins shining through the window. But it's what you must do sometimes to get to the next show, and in those days our solution, as it was to any nocturnal challenge, was to drink more to make it, if not palatable, at least a little more interesting.

And interesting it was. Sometime after crossing the Canadian border around 4am, Mark and Paul caught their second wind, fueled by a few shots of vodka, and began having a pillow fight in the back seat of the van. As they got louder and rowdier, the rest of us started getting more and more annoyed. Finally, our tour manager violently slammed on the brakes, throwing us all out of our seats, and told them to shut up.

Paul was having none of it. He'd had enough. He opened the sliding side door of the van, climbed out onto the shoulder of the desolate Canadian highway, and disappeared into the night. We all thought he was joking around, so we laughed and waited for him to climb back into the van.

After a few minutes of wondering where Paul was, Mark got out with a flashlight, but Paul was nowhere to be found. He did leave a trail of garbage he had dragged with him from the van. Mark followed the trail about fifty feet, calling Paul's name, but to no avail. He had gone AWOL.

We were in the middle of nowhere. It was pitch black, and we weren't sure what to do next, so, much like we had in New York City after that Bottom Line show, we just started driving and hoping for the best. Paul was gone. We drove ahead a few miles. Nothing. Finally, we turned around we went back in the direction from where we had come, and after a few miles, we found Paul in our headlights, hitchhiking back toward the US. We pulled over, and when he realized it was us, he started running away. Finally, he sullenly got back into the van, speaking to none of us, and he remained silent for the next few days. He still played the show in Toronto, but he went immediately to his hotel room the moment it was over.

Paul's sullen silent treatment didn't last long. Within a few days, he got over whatever had caused him to break down, most likely exhaustion and being disheartened by one too many disappointing shows. It made sense. Dennis and I increasingly felt the disappointment of the tour, only a half-decade after the giddy highs of our early artistic, critical, and label-bidding-war successes. It hurt when we thought about it, so we tried not to think about it.

'Doctor, it hurts when I do this.'

'Well, then, I recommend that you stop doing that!'

Even with the disappointments and the occasional flash of tension, we remained friends through it all, and there were plenty of laughs. Even on the nights when we faced the smallest crowds or the greatest indifference, we still locked in musically with tightness and intensity each night, maybe even more driven by defiance and the need to obliterate everything else we were feeling during the rest of the day and immediately before and after the show. My reaction was just to try to find that kernel of transcendence that a great show could bring—a kind of blissful obliteration that would allow me to remember those days of wine and roses, and why all of it still mattered.

There were some well-attended shows along the way, not surprisingly in cities where we had always done well: the Metro in Chicago, a pair of shows in LA, Liberty Lunch in Austin. Those nights stood out. And we were delighted to find out that our next-to-last show of the tour in San Francisco, at the I-Beam, was sold out a few weeks before we arrived. Aside from Los Angeles and maybe New York City, we had played more shows in San Francisco than anywhere else over the years, and we knew that plenty of hardcore fans and good friends would be in the room.

The night lived up to our expectations, and we lived up to our need for a bit of a lift after thirteen weeks on the road. For that one night, all of the frustrations of the last six weeks across America were swept away, and we were returned to the joys and exhilaration of not only the European tour but also the best nights of the years before. I finished the last song of the encore by ripping every string, one at a time, from my guitar. I don't know why. It just felt like an exclamation point on the evening. It also hurt like hell, wire ripping against flesh. I don't recommend doing it. I left the stage with some nasty indentations on my fingers and the knowledge that I'd have to string my guitar up again at soundcheck the next day before our last show at the Catalyst in Santa Cruz.

There would be no soundcheck or last show the next day, however. We made the short one-hour drive, rolled up to the Catalyst around 4pm, and were greeted by a sign on the locked front door of the venue.

'The Dream Syndicate show tonight has been CANCELED.'

Nobody had bothered to tell us. We called our agent at Premier Talent, who confirmed that, yes indeed, the promoter had canceled the show because of low advance ticket sales. It was all quite fitting, somehow. Our thirteen-week tour was over, that last successful show in San Francisco being the grand finale.

It would also be the last show the band would play, at least for the immediate decades to come. Like The Beatles, The Band, and Sex Pistols before us, our last gig was in San Francisco.

Earlier in the tour, just before our soundcheck in Asbury Park, I had asked Dennis to go out to the van with me. There was something I wanted to talk to him about and wanted to discuss on our own, away from the camera crew that had been following us in that first week of the US tour.

'I'm thinking about breaking up the band,' I said. 'What do you think?'

I can't remember what Dennis said at the time, but years later he said, 'I don't think we had previously discussed it or that you had brought up the subject before, but I wasn't surprised. It did feel inevitable at that point. I remember feeling happy that you were asking for my blessing. We both agreed it was time. We had hit a wall.'

Having told Dennis and having not been countered with any resistance, I spent the rest of the tour feeling certain that our days were numbered. And every disappointing crowd, every bit of weariness, every journalist who seemed to be talking to us merely out of obligation, every ensuing bit of tension within the band, only served to convince me that the decision was the right one.

We got home on December 21. In my own perverse logic and appreciation of round figures and anniversaries, I decided to call each member individually on December 27, the seventh anniversary of our first rehearsal, as well as the fourth anniversary of when we had broken up the first time. I've always been drawn to repetition.

As opposed to the surprise and disappointment and maybe even a touch of anger that I encountered four years before, this time my decision was met by a sense almost of relief. Paul was in no mood to go through anything like the thirteen-week tour we had just finished ever again—and, in fact, he never did. Dennis already knew my intentions. And Mark knew it was time as well. We were tired, we were indeed weathered and torn. But we were still friends, and it would be nice to be able to remain that way.

I remember my former bandmate Sid Griffin telling me, 'That's a really bad idea. You shouldn't make a decision like that right after finishing a tour. Give it a few weeks.' He was right, and since that time it has been my rule to never make any big decisions right after a tour is done. You're just not thinking straight, and you're seeing the world through deep-fried colored glasses. But we all knew. It was time.

Mark had met the comedian Rich Hall at the Bottom Line. Rich was flying high as a popular standup and cast member of *Saturday Night Live* at the time, and he approached Mark after the show to let him know how much he loved and had always loved The Dream Syndicate. The two of them stayed in touch in the weeks after, and when Mark told Rich after the tour that we were calling it a day, Rich said, 'I want to throw a party for you guys at the Comedy Club in LA. You'll have a VIP table and an open tab for the evening, and I'll join you after my set.' It was very kind of him, and it gave us all a sense of closure—a chance to hang out together, raise a few toasts, have some laughs, and remember what a special ride we all had been through together. The hard times were over, and a period of nostalgia had begun. It was the end of seven years and an incredible ride that I could never have predicted when we first rehearsed in the basement that evening in 1981, let alone when I was playing music with my neighbors as a nine-year-old kid.

I had no idea what would lie ahead. But as both Van Morrison and the title of one of our bootlegs had stated, it was certainly too late to stop now.

Tell me when it's over? Maybe yes, maybe no. But it wasn't over. Not by a long shot.

EPILOGUE
WHAT COMES AFTER

Paul, Mark, Dennis, and I remained friends. Not every band that breaks up can claim that. In fact, we even reunited a couple of times for short sets, without fanfare, in the early 90s. The first was a three-song performance at the Palace in Hollywood, at a benefit for our friend and LA rock critic mainstay Craig Lee, who was suffering from AIDS and needed funds to cover medical care. It was a great night and a who's who of our 80s LA scene.

We did it again at Raji's in 1992, at one of the weekly gigs by Mark's new band, The Continental Drifters. It was Dennis's birthday, and Mark, Paul, and I encouraged him to come to the show so that we could celebrate together. What Dennis didn't know was that we had agreed to play a surprise set during the evening, and at some point after the Drifters had finished their set, we handed Dennis a pair of drumsticks and said, 'Let's go.' We played a full set without rehearsal or even a setlist.

Both of those surprise sets went off without a hitch. We hadn't lost a step and, even with a layoff of a couple of years, we were quickly up to speed and able to play as well as we had before we broke up. We had done so many shows together that it was ingrained into our very beings at that point. We were tight, the unsuspecting fans loved it, and we had a great time.

Was there a temptation to continue beyond those two little returns to form? Not at all. I had already started a solo career, and my debut album and the following tours in support of those albums were both well received. I was exploring new sounds and instrumentation with new players, although I would tour with both Mark and Dennis in my solo band at various points in the 90s. I often missed my old bandmates, but they were never more than a phone call or a short drive away. We continued to see each other while never even broaching the subject of a reunion at any point.

We were done. It was a nice ride, but now there were new things to do. In the following years, there would be solo albums, side projects, stylistic detours and returns, zigs and zags, ebbs and flows, and many great adventures along the way—notably meeting, falling in love, playing with, and eventually marrying a very fetching, sweet, and talented drummer from Minneapolis named Linda Pitmon. That's first and foremost on the list of events and experiences I may have missed, had The Dream Syndicate not disbanded when it did.

My first two solo albums, *Kerosene Man* and *Dazzling Display*, brought me closer to the mainstream than I had ever been before or would ever be again. I was on the cover of *Billboard*, ironically listed among other 'best new artists of 1990.' There was mainstream radio play, especially for the song 'Carolyn,' whose video was directed by up-and-coming and soon to be massively influential video auteur Mark Romanek and was in regular rotation for several weeks on MTV. The albums and singles made the Top 40 charts across Europe.

But this brush with the 'next level' also left me frustrated, as many of the choices I wanted to make creatively were met with caution from management and my record label worrying that it wasn't the right move at the right time or that more care had to be taken to wait until I had written potential hit songs to take advantage of the momentum. I bristled against these restraints and instead followed up with a pair of quickly released albums, a solo record (*Fluorescent*) and a side project (*Gutterball*), both of which were recorded in a matter of days.

It felt liberating. I found that I preferred to fly below the radar, do things on my own terms, and keep active, both in the studio and on tour. In short, I reaffirmed my long-felt desire to be a creative artist rather than a rock star courting mainstream success. I just wanted to keep working and following wherever my enthusiasm lay at any given moment. I chose to build, nurture, and reward my cult audience rather than to reach for a bigger one that would very likely never materialize.

That decision, and the giddy freedom that followed, bore fruit in the form of a burst of creativity coinciding with moving in 1994 from Los Angeles to New York, a city whose energy and speed and street life matched the pace at which I longed to work. In the following decade, I wrote more songs, released more records, and toured more than ever before in my life, and it felt great. I was still popular enough to tour as often as and wherever I wanted, and able to get good labels to put out the music I was making. I increasingly realized that while I may never headline Madison Square Garden, I would be able to continue the improbable tale of surviving and making a life from music. That was enough for me.

Nonetheless, there were moments when it was hard not to indulge in the what-if game. When the grunge and indie-rock wave broke through to the mainstream around 1992, I was suddenly hearing the music we felt that we were alone in making in the early 80s not only be embraced but actually hit the top of the charts and become catnip for major labels and the power players in the music business. When we formed in 1982, it was largely because we wanted to make the kind of music we weren't hearing anywhere else at the time. We were filling a gap for ourselves, if for nobody else—and we quickly found that we were also filling a gap for a select group of other music fans, hence our quick ascendence.

But in the mid-90s? You couldn't swing a bat without hitting a Pavement or a Luna or others who were drinking from the same wells where we had dipped our cup back when we started. Other groups from the 80s—Yo La Tengo, Meat Puppets, Sonic Youth, and Flaming Lips among them—who had stuck it out were now rewarded in a scene where they felt at home, as elder statesmen rather than outsider freaks, with sales and audience attendance to reward their patience. Could that have happened to us? There's no point in wondering. It didn't.

We did eventually reunite many years later, in 2012, with Jason Victor on guitar in place of Paul, who made it clear that he was up for hanging out any time we wanted but did not want to reunite as The Dream Syndicate. Paul was never much for nostalgia. Jason had played with me in my solo band for the previous decade and had performed almost all of the Dream

Syndicate songs at one point or another onstage. He also was a fan and became our conscience when Mark, Dennis, and I would veer off from the ethos of what the band meant to our fans. 'The Dream Syndicate wouldn't do that,' he would often say, and he was usually right.

On the other hand, we would rapidly develop from a few successful and busy years on the nostalgic reunion circuit to becoming a very different band, embracing, focusing upon, and rediscovering some of our earliest influences, many of which had been abandoned after our first year. This new Dream Syndicate Mk II would end up drawing upon elements of Krautrock—the German movement of the 70s centered around Can, Neu!, and other groups that delved into the beauty of repetition and hypnotic grooves—along with bits of free jazz, psychedelia, and punk rock. We became the band we might have dreamt of being at the start, but now we had the experience and chops to pull it off. We were, in fact, a band that probably would have been our favorite band, back in 1982.

The reunion would not have worked had I not had other projects to offset and augment the music we were making, allowing us to be focused and not try to be all things to all people. If the Dream Syndicate had become an intense, trippy 'head' band, I also had The Baseball Project, for lighter fare. In this improbable combo with Linda, plus my old R.E.M. pals Mike Mills and Peter Buck and new friend Scott McCaughey, I have made four albums about, well, about nothing but baseball, while extensively touring the US over the past fifteen years. It's never easy to quantify anything in music as the best this or that—unlike the cold, hard statistics of sports, music is almost entirely subjective. But it's a stone-cold fact that no band in the history of music has released as many songs or albums about baseball.

I continue to tour regularly on my own as a solo acoustic performer, reinventing and revisiting my catalogue of over four hundred songs night to night. It's like a public workshop mixed with a town hall that I bring from city to city, and it remains one of my favorite ways to connect with an audience. My old manager was wrong—I actually *can* balance all of these projects. And, in fact, I am a happier and, I think, better artist because of it. The busier I am, the more I get done. The more I get done, the more I can relax and let each thing be its own, not trying to do or say too much with each thing I do.

At the end of the day, I can look back at the thousands of shows I've played, the several dozen records I've made, the friends I've met along the way, the meals I've eaten, the stories I've learned, experienced, and repeated, and I wouldn't change a thing or trade a single moment. All I know is that when I am filling out a form and see a blank space for 'Occupation,' I can honestly and proudly write 'Musician.' And that's good enough for me.

ACKNOWLEDGMENTS
BEFORE THE BAND PLAYS ME OFF

I'd always wanted to write a book. Check that, I always wanted to have written a book. There's a slight but important difference between the two. The actual writing part seemed a little more challenging. I came up with many of my most popular songs in thirty minutes or less, the amount of time promised by Domino's for delivering a pizza. Finishing a book would surely take longer.

And then the pandemic hit. I was off the road for the first time in decades. My wife Linda was spending a lot of time away from our apartment in Queens apartment with her parents up in Vermont. I was left with time on my hands and no touring plans, and it seemed like the opportunity to give it a shot.

I had heard some variety of the prescription of getting up every day and writing, for example, five hundred words. Sounded good, sounded doable. I'm a very fast typist thanks to my sportswriting days. Fortified by a bunch of coffee and Red Bull, I blew through that five hundred mark each day in no time. The book came together steadily and quickly.

But time and stimulants were certainly not enough. I had a lot of help along the way, and, much like an actor holding an Oscar in his hand at the Academy Awards, I'm going to take the time to thank everyone who helped make this book a reality, right until the band plays me off the stage.

There was Alex Abramovich, the journalist, editor, and author who had asked me to come up with a paragraph or two for a *New Yorker* piece he was writing about The Velvet Underground back in 2015. I gave him several pages. He responded, 'You know, you're a pretty good writer. You should do a book,' and proceeded to regularly encourage me, even before

I started writing this thing. His book *Bullies* is a wild ride and worth tracking down.

Linda's bandmate in Zuzu's Petals, Laurie Lindeen, had written a compelling and entertaining book called *Petal Pusher* about her life and her experiences with the band. She teaches a memoir writing class and was helpful not only with guidance and expert editing along the way but also indispensable with tips and instruction on putting together a proposal to get the book published. It worked. Laurie, I can't thank you enough.

The book passed through a lot of editorial hands—friends and bandmates who were there and/or had a solid grasp of grammar, spelling, and rock history. Rob Roberge was one of the first. His novels are adrenaline-packed thrill rides that will leave you drained. Dennis Duck is not only a solid drummer and a big part of the reason why this book even exists but is also a diligent proofreader. Thanks as well to Brigid Pearson, Pat Thomas, and Vicki Peterson, who previewed the book and caught things I had missed. And finally, I went to Ira Kaplan of Yo La Tengo for a back-cover testimonial quote well after I thought the book was done, and he made me aware of many mistakes which would have haunted me for life. Thanks to all of you for taking the time to read the work in progress along the way.

I also want to thank every musician with whom I've shared a van, bus, backstage, recording studio, or practice room. We've all had experiences together that we'll remember forever. We're compatriots in the foxholes of rock and have the war stories and battle scars and purple hearts to prove it. When the pandemic hit, I found that most of my contact, aside from flesh and blood family members, was with my bandmates. Most of you are contained somewhere in these pages.

Thanks to Pat Thomas, once again, and to John Kruth, who led me to my first and only book publisher, Jawbone Press. Pat is not only a stellar musician and author of fabulous and immersive books about the Black Panthers, Jerry Rubin, and Allen Ginsberg, but also, as he likes to be known, 'the facilitator' in many of my current musical endeavors. John Kruth has written a wealth of fine books about music including his latest, an incisive study of *Dark Side Of The Moon*, for which I wrote the foreword.

A big thanks to Tom Seabrook at Jawbone Press for taking me on and adding me to his very impressive catalogue. I blush a little bit when I see the company I keep on their roster. Thanks as well to all of my managers, lawyers, road crew, agents and record labels along the way, including my current home of Fire Records—kudos to James Nichols and everyone on the very impressive staff over there.

My father, Earl Wynn, passed away in 2012, but he gave me a lifetime of friendship, inspiration, and encouragement. His 'down there' basement was the incubation point for much of this book and the earliest days of The Dream Syndicate in particular. He was unbelievably tolerant and patient with the volume and noise we cranked out regularly from below the floorboards.

My mother, Marlena DuRon, gave me not only love and guidance but also the freedom to find my own way, each in equal measures. It was the perfect balance, and the right one needed to become a songwriter and test my independence from an early age. She raised me for most of my childhood as a single mother, and that's no easy or small thing. She continues to inspire me with her support, tenacity, and flair for the dramatic.

And finally, what can I say about my wonderful wife, Linda Pitmon Wynn? Plenty, as it turns out. Linda gave me boundless encouragement every step of the way from the first words to the last edit. She made this all seem and actually become possible, inspiring and motivating me in the moments when it would have been easy enough to walk away and leave the book unfinished. She is the steady beat of my heart, even when she's not rocking from behind the kit. I only wish she was in this story more often but, alas, it ends in 1988, so you'll all just have to stick around for Part Two. Because there will be a Part Two.

See you 'round the clubs . . .

STEVE WYNN

QUEENS, NY

MAY 2024

SELECT DISCOGRAPHY

THE DREAM SYNDICATE

The Dream Syndicate EP (Down There, 1982)
The Days Of Wine And Roses (Ruby/Slash, 1982)
Medicine Show (A&M, 1984)
Out Of The Grey (Chrysalis/Big Time, 1986)
Ghost Stories (Enigma, 1988)
Live At Raji's (Enigma, 1989)
How Did I Find Myself Here (Anti-, 2017)
These Times (Anti-, 2019)
The Universe Inside (Anti-, 2020)
Ultraviolet Battle Hymns And True Confessions (Fire, 2022)

SOLO

Kerosene Man (Rhino, 1990)
Dazzling Display (Rhino, 1992)
Fluorescent (Brake Out, 1994)
Melting In The Dark (Brake Out, 1996)
Sweetness And Light (Zero Hour, 1997)
My Midnight (Blue Rose, 1999)
The eMusic Singles Collection (Blue Rose, 2000)
Here Come The Miracles (Blue Rose, 2001)
Crossing Dragon Bridge (Blue Rose, 2008)
Make It Right (Fire, 2024)

DANNY & DUSTY

The Lost Weekend (Cowpunk, 1985)
Cast Iron Soul (Blue Rose, 2007)

GUTTERBALL

Gutterball (Mute/Brake Out, 1993)
Weasel (Brake Out, 1995)

THE BASEBALL PROJECT

Volume 1: Frozen Ropes And Dying Quails (Yep Roc, 2008)
Volume 2: High And Inside (Yep Roc, 2011)
3rd (Yep Roc, 2014)
Grand Salami Time (Omnivore Recordings, 2023)

WITH THE MIRACLE 3

Static Transmission (Blue Rose, 2002)
... Tick ... Tick ... Tick (Blue Rose, 2005)
Northern Aggression (Blue Rose, 2010)

WITH AUSTRALIAN BLONDE

Momento (Astro Discos, 2000)